Basic Child Psychiatry

Basic Child Psychiatry

Third edition

Philip Barker, MB, BS, FRCPEd, MRCPsych

CROSBY LOCKWOOD STAPLES
GRANADA PUBLISHING
London Toronto Sydney New York

First published in Great Britain 1971 by Crosby Lockwood Staples

Second edition published by Granada Publishing Limited
in Crosby Lockwood Staples 1976
Reprinted 1977

Third edition 1979

Granada Publishing Limited
Frogmore, St Albans, Herts AL2 2NF
and
3 Upper James Street, London WIR 4BP
1221 Avenue of the Americas, New York, NY 10020, USA
117 York Street, Sydney, NSW 2000, Australia
100 Skyway Avenue, Toronto, Ontario, Canada M9W 3A6
110 Northpark Centre, 2193 Johannesburg, South Africa
CML Centre, Queen & Wyndham, Auckland 1, New Zealand

Copyright © Philip Barker 1971 and 1979

ISBN 0 258 97158 4 HB
     0 258 97153 3 PB

Printed in Great Britain by
Richard Clay (The Chaucer Press) Ltd, Bungay, Suffolk

To Heather, Edmund, Elsa, Lorna, Brenda and Alice

Contents

Foreword

Like a good wine a book of promise matures, doing so in fits and starts
as each successive edition appears. This process tends to accelerate as
time passes. Thus, while about five years separated the appearance of
the first and second editions barely two have passed since the publication of the third. This, together with the very favourable reviews
awarded to its predecessors, are sure indicators of the book's future and
of the author's growing achievement.

In the interim Dr Barker has moved from England to Canada,
relinquishing his appointment as Consultant Children's Psychiatrist at
the Charles Burns Clinic in Birmingham. He is now Professor of
Psychiatry at the University of Toronto and also holds a position at
Thistletown Regional Centre for Children and Adolescents in Ontario.

In writing the new edition Dr Barker has tried to take in the best
aspects of the practice of children's psychiatry in both the United
Kingdom and North America. Although there is much common
ground, there are differences in practice on the two sides of the
Atlantic, in particular those of classification. Consequently two systems
of classification, one used mainly in England, one in North America, are
referred to throughout. Other differences are largely those of emphasis.
For example it is likely that family therapy and group psychotherapy
may be used with rather greater enthusiasm in children's psychiatry on
the West as against the East Coast of the Atlantic, although a movement
in this direction can be further predicted.

What else is new? The author's style has matured so that the text
flows more smoothly. It has indeed been almost completely rewritten.
The number of chapters has been increased from fifteen to seventeen

with some rearrangement in their order achieving perhaps a more logical sequence, as well as the inclusion of much new material. The section on child abuse has been expanded reflecting a growing interest in and understanding of what must surely be regarded as one of the most dismal of all disorders, affecting not only the physical but also the mental health of young children.

There are many other changes: too many to enumerate. These reflect what was said in the Foreword to the previous edition – that children's psychiatry is not a static discipline but a rapidly evolving one. The book is also greatly enhanced by a considerable increase in the number of references so that the original handful at the conclusion of each chapter has grown into a bibliography of very respectable size.

Introduction

This third edition of *Basic Child Psychiatry*, like the two previous ones, is intended to give the newcomer to the field the basic facts of the subject and guidance as to where to obtain further information. I hope it will be useful to undergraduate and postgraduate medical students, and also to students of social work, child care, psychology, education, nursing and related subjects. Medical and psychological jargon has been avoided as far as possible, and such terms as have proved necessary are explained either in the text or in the glossary.

The book has again been revised to incorporate advances in the field. Other changes include a new chapter on disorders of young children, a more extensive account of problems of child abuse and a brief section on disputes concerning the custody of and access to children by parents. Family therapy and systems theory receive more emphasis, a reflection of their increasing use in many centres.

A continuing problem is that of how to classify child psychiatric disorders. It is clear that disorders do fall into groups with common properties, and that some form of classification is essential to research and to the accumulation and teaching of new knowledge of the subject. Unfortunately no entirely satisfactory system of classification exists. Since the last edition of this book was prepared, however, the ninth edition of the *International Classification of Diseases* (ICD) has appeared; this has greatly improved coverage of child psychiatric disorders, compared to previous editions, and has also been adapted for use as a multi-axial scheme by Professor Michael Rutter and colleagues at the Institute of Psychiatry, London. These workers have also added an axis of their own, dealing with psychosocial problems. This new ICD system has been used as the basis for the description of disorders in this edition, but mention is also made of the classification of the Group for the Advancement of Psychiatry, since this is widely used in North America. Another promising scheme, also multi-axial, is the third *Diagnostic and Statistical Manual* of the American Psychiatric Association, but unfortunately it was still under development when this edition was being written, although its draft form is mentioned briefly. The use of yet another classification has meant some further rearrangement of material, compared with the second edition.

This edition contains many more references than the previous editions did. In addition references relevant to points being discussed are specified by numbers in the text, and in various places specific advice is given on where to look for further information. I hope these changes will help readers wanting to study topics in greater depth. Preference has again been given to review articles and to other papers and books which include reviews of earlier work; the interested reader should therefore find in the book pointers to much further information.

The case histories are all from my own practice, except for Quentin, the boy with snake phobia mentioned on page 228; he was treated by Mary Browning, psychologist at the Charles Burns Clinic, Birmingham. Names and other data which might identify the children or their families have been changed.

Once again many people have helped me with this edition. Among the staff of Thistletown Regional Centre who have made helpful comments on sections of the book are Barbara Dydyk, Nancy Fraser, Jack Perlov and Jeff Sherman. Gerry Wallach, formerly chief of speech and hearing, made many helpful suggestions concerning the sections on speech and language development and its disorders. Klaus Minde of the Department of Psychiatry, University of Toronto, kindly reviewed the text of the second edition and made some very helpful suggestions. Many other colleagues have helped in various ways, not least Priscilla Wagner and Arlene Iguchi, the librarians at Thistletown; they have worked long and hard to obtain reference material and to identify and check references. Without their help the book would be much less well annotated.

Grateful as I am to all these people, responsibility for the contents of the book and any errors there may be, remains mine.

In addition to all the above people, I am deeply grateful to Audrey Mullan who has typed, and often retyped, most of the material in the book in a cheerful, efficient and enthusiastic way, often under great pressure and sometimes from barely legible script. Her colleagues Mary DeLuca and Shirley Taylor also helped by sharing this and some of her other work.

Finally I must thank Richard Miles, from Crosby Lockwood Staples, Granada Publishing, for his help and for the efficient way he and his colleagues have dealt with the publication of this new edition.

Philip Barker

CHAPTER ONE

Normal Development

Psychiatric disorders in childhood and adolescence have to be looked at against the background of the normal process of development from helpless infant to independent adult. When emotional, social and intellectual functioning are assessed, the range of normal for the child's age and social setting must be taken into account. What is normal is best learnt by contact with developing children and their families. This chapter outlines the process for those whose contact has been limited. Many theories of child development also exist. The beginner should pay particular attention to those of Erik Erikson[1] and Jean Piaget. An excellent concise summary of Piaget's work has been written by Beard[2] and a fuller one by Flavell[3]. Bowlby has also studied and reviewed the literature on the making and breaking of emotional bonds which are important processes in child development[4].

The First Year of Life

Following birth, infants are totally dependent on those caring for them. They may respond in a variety of ways however. Their reponses in turn influence the behaviour of those looking after them. Thomas, Chess and Birch[5] have shown that newborn babies show different *behavioural styles*. They distinguished nine traits: activity level, rhythmicity of biological functions (sleeping, eating, etc.), approach or withdrawal in new situations, intensity of emotional reaction (to both pleasant and unpleasant situations), reaction threshold (the ease with which the child copes with changed circumstances), quality of mood, distractibility and 'attention span/persistence'. The course of events during infancy depends in part on the 'fit' between the child's behavioural style and the parents' temperaments and ways of reacting. X The first year of life is called the 'oral' stage by psychoanalysts because the baby's main satisfactions seem to arise from feeding and sucking things. Erikson[1] calls this period that of 'basic trust versus basic mistrust'. This is the first of his 'eight ages of man'. A healthy outcome occurs when the child experiences the world, during this period, as nurturing, reliable and trustworthy. The child who has this experience develops the capacity for intimate relationships. If, by contrast, he does not have this warm nurturing experience the capacity for intimacy will have been correspondingly impaired.

There is a rapid development of motor functions in the first year, culminating in walking at about one year, though the range of normal is wide. There are also big developments in social behaviour. By three weeks the child smiles at people's faces. At first this is a reflex response, but by six months children learn to distinguish people and will selectively smile at their mothers and other familiar people. This leads, at about eight months, to signs of fear and anxiety in the presence of strangers. Soon afterwards *separation anxiety* appears. This is anxiety upon separation from mother, especially if in an unfamiliar place or with unfamiliar people. It is a sign that the child has developed a close relationship with the mother. For this to occur it is necessary for the child to have been cared for constantly by the same person (mother or consistent mother-substitute), and for there to have been a reasonably good 'fit' between the child's behavioural style and the parent's temperament. The process is called *bonding*.

Bowlby[4] has described the development of *attachment behaviour* in early childhood. This behaviour is characterised by the subject attaining or keeping physical proximity to the object of attachment. In infancy this is commonly the mother. This is held to be a biological phenomenon, characteristic of many primate species. Attachment theory conceives of this behaviour as being a class of behaviour at least as important as feeding and sexual behaviour, but distinct and different. Features of it in the first year are crying, calling, stranger anxiety and separation anxiety, these all being behaviours which tend to bring about proximity to the mother-figure. The theory states that an infant's attachment results primarily from the availability of a familiar figure. The more social interaction there is with the figure, the more likely it is the subject will become attached to the person. The process does not depend on gratification of needs. Indeed in monkeys attachment can occur to a soft, cuddly dummy as well as to a live mother monkey[6].

By the end of the first year the child should have a close, warm, secure relationship with mother (or mother-substitute), and an ordered pattern of feeding and sleeping should have been established. Fixed, rigid feeding schedules are not nowadays usual in western countries, but by the end of the first year a pattern of feeding at intervals by day and sleeping, without feeds, by night has usually emerged.

Weaning is usually accomplished during the first year. Breast feeding is nowadays the exception rather than the rule in most western countries, and semi-solid foods tend to be introduced earlier, often at two or three months. These factors seem to make weaning less of a problem than it once was. Nevertheless giving up breast or bottle is one of the first demands made on the infant. Its successful accomplishment is a good augury for the many other changes required later.

Intellectual development proceeds rapidly in the first year. Piaget[2,3], calls the first two years of life the *sensori-motor period*. During this period children learn certain basic things about their relationship to the environment. They discover that objects exist apart from themselves, and continue to exist when they do not perceive them. They also learn simple cause-and-effect relationships. The come to understand spatial relationships, and acquire some idea of how one thing can symbolise another. All these processes, however, involve action by the child and depend on current sensory input and motor activity.

The Second Year

Rapid development continues in the second year. Children start to walk and so become able to actively explore their environment. They also start to talk. More demands are made of them, particularly over bowel and bladder training and limiting their exploratory behaviour.

Erikson[1] considers the main issue of the second year to be that of 'autonomy versus shame and doubt'. The child should develop a feeling of being in control of his or her self, combined with pleasant, self-confident feelings. These features contrast with feelings of shame and doubt about oneself and one's body. The acquisition of bowel and bladder control is an important process. During this period children should obtain pleasure from gradually gaining control of their sphincters, and indeed of their bodies generally. Erikson's views differ from classical psychoanalytic theory in that he does not relate anal activity and defaecation to sexual gratification, to which he gives a less central role.

The successful performance of the developmental tasks of the second year requires a warm, secure relationship between children and their parents. In such contexts children want to please their parents, and will be made anxious by their disapproval. They learn to inhibit or release their behaviour accordingly. This applies not only to bowel and bladder training (which may not be started until the end of the second year or even the third year), but also to motor behaviour generally.

Attachment behaviour should be well established by the second year[4]. It contrasts with exploratory behaviour, which becomes possible once the child can walk. From a secure base the child can move into the environment to explore it, returning to mother when frightened or tired. As the child grows, the time and distance he can be away from his mother or family base steadily increases.

Nevertheless, some exploratory behaviour has to be limited. Children must learn not to play with fire, run out on to the roadway, drop crockery on the floor and so on. There is usually some resistance to such learning, often expressed as temper tantrums. These commonly start in the second year and are a normal reaction when a child's wishes are not gratified. They can, nevertheless, cause great concern to an inexperienced mother, as when a previously well-behaved child suddenly starts throwing himself or herself on the floor, screaming, kicking and waving arms around. Normally, however, tantrums are a transient feature of the toddler period, which die away as children learn to accept the constraints placed on their behaviour by their parents and others. This process is of course greatly helped by a secure loving relationship between children and parents.

The development of speech and its comprehension considerably refines the process of communication between child and parents. These important features of the second and subsequent years are discussed more fully in Chapter 9, page 150.

The second year sees the end of Piaget's period of sensori-motor intelligence and the beginning of the period of *concrete operations of classes, relations and numbers*. The latter begins with the start of the acquisition of language, which occurs about mid-way through the second year, and extends up to about eleven or twelve years of age. It has a number of sub-stages. It will be discussed further in the following section.

During the second year, children continue to see themselves as the centre of their world and remain closely dependent on their parents.

The Pre-school Period (ages two to five)

During this period there is further development of intellectual functions, especially a rapid increase in the complexity of language used and understood (see Chapter 9). A big advance in socialisation is made: the child learns to live as a member of the family group.

Because of the importance of the development of sexual identity and feelings, psychoanalysts have called this the 'genital stage'. It is the period during which the child learns his or her sexual identity; Erikson considers this period to be that in which the issue of 'initiative versus guilt' must be resolved. A successful outcome is a child who feels able to do many exciting, even almost magical, things, as opposed to being frightened and guilty about taking the initiative. Erikson believes that failure at this stage results in a child who feels that others will be angry with, or even destroy, him if he does what he wants. Ideally the child should emerge confident in his abilities but with his impulses under adequate control.

Other features of this period are identification with the parents, and consequently development of motivation to do certain things, or be a certain kind of person; the beginning of conscience formation; the establishment of ways of dealing with anxiety and guilt; and the development of patterns of behaviour towards individuals outside the family. The child still feels at the centre of the world, and tends to consider inanimate objects as having feelings and opinions.

The establishment of the sex role starts with the acquisition of a general idea that people are divided into male and female categories. This is fostered by the different appearance, clothing and behaviour of the sexes. The child then comes to feel a member of one or other group. This is brought about partly through the attitudes and expectations of parents and others, partly through the child becoming aware of the anatomical differences between the sexes, and partly because of the operation of inborn biological factors. The parents are normally the child's main model of the male and female roles. Sex play, often with undressing or sexual exploration, is common at this time[7]. Interest in the genitals of siblings and playmates is common and normal. As sexual awareness develops, the boy or girl is faced with the problem of his or her position *vis-à-vis* the parents, and there is often for a time a feeling of rivalry with the parent of the same sex for the affection of the other parent, the 'oedipal' stage. Normally this problem is resolved by close identification with the parent of the same sex. Its persistence in severe form beyond about six years of age is abnormal.

While the appropriate sex role is being adopted most children go through a period of uncertainty and curiosity on the subject. Fear of loss of male characteristics ('castration fears') in the boy and concern about lack of male genitals in the girl, are frequent causes of transient anxiety at this stage. Masturbation is so common in this period as to be a normal phenomenon. If sensibly handled it usually lessens in frequency or ceases; if it continues the child normally learns to avoid it at socially unsuitable times.

The development of conscience is important. It arises through the adoption of parents' standards, which in turn results from identification with the parents. The child comes to feel that certain types of attitudes and actions are right and others wrong, and thus feels guilty about activities which are in the 'wrong' category. The child made anxious in this way will often be unaware, at the conscious level, of the cause of the anxiety. It is due of course to the standards of the parents which have been made the child's own (or 'internalised'). Obviously if the child lacks a stable relationship with parents or parent substitutes the process of conscience formation will be impaired. Conscience, and the capacity to feel guilty, are liable to be poorly developed in children brought up in large impersonal institutions, and in children who have been moved frequently from one home to another during their early years.

Defence mechanisms are means whereby the individual copes with feelings of anxiety which might otherwise not be tolerable. Anxiety is a normal, indeed an essential, experience. It may arise from an act or threat from outside (for example the 'stranger anxiety' mentioned above), from the lack of familiar or expected objects or experiences, or from the operation of conscience. It may also be communicated, as from an anxious parent with whom a child is closely identified.

At first anxiety is directly expressed, but then it comes to be expressed more often indirectly, through the operation of 'defences' (or defence mechanisms) appearing in the pre-school age period. Normal anxieties are dealt with this way as are the abnormal anxieties occurring in psychiatric disorders. The use of defence mechanisms (or mental mechanisms) is in itself a normal process. A basic one is *repression*, the consigning to the unconscious of ideas not acceptable (because too threatening, anxiety-producing or otherwise intolerable) at the conscious level. The ideas or feelings repressed may, however, continue to influence the individual's behaviour and emotional state. They may be expressed in dreams, during hypnosis or in the course of psychoanalysis.

The repressed ideas may be denied at the conscious level, and actions or attitudes arising from them may be *rationalised*, that is an alternative consciously acceptable explanation given. Thus the child asked to go to the shops may say he is too tired or is frightened of the shopkeeper, but his reluctance may arise from repressed (and so unconscious) anxiety about what will happen to his mother while he is away, or a fear that she may play with his brother towards whom he feels (again perhaps unconsciously) some jealousy. *Compensation* is an attempt to make up for unconsciously felt inferiority; *reaction-formation* is a more extreme form of compensation, the individual developing character traits or behaviour the exact opposite of the 'true', unconscious ones. For example, the individual who unconsciously wishes someone dead may consciously feel and show special solicitude and concern for that person.

Displacement and *projection* involve the transfer of feelings from one to another, more acceptable, object. Thus the child who hates his father may repress this and consciously express much of the hate towards, for example, his teacher. Projection is the attribution of one's own disclaimed characteristics on to another person. So the individual tempted by the desire to steal (about which he feels guilty) may unjustly attribute the propensity to steal to others.

Obsessional ideas are apparently irrational but nevertheless intrude into the consciousness. They have their origin in unconscious anxiety or guilt, and represent a sort of 'magical' way of dealing with guilt. *Compulsions* are actions arising from such thoughts. 'Normal' compulsions in children include avoiding the cracks in paving stones and touching lamp-posts as they are passed. Such actions are usually means of dealing with the normal anxieties of this period. Indeed, anxiety resulting from any cause in everyday life may be dealt with by means of these mechanisms. So may guilt feelings arising from the newly-developed conscience. All these mental processes are, in themselves, normal phenomena which can be found operating in all of us.

Fantasy is important to children. A rich and vivid fantasy life is normal in children in the two- to five-year-old range, and persists into later childhood. It is a means of temporarily substituting for the real world, one in which desires and wishes can be fulfilled regardless of reality. Young children especially have a complex fantasy life, often expressed in play with other children and with dolls and toys. Despite their apparent involvement in such play, they normally remain able to distinguish fantasy from reality. Persistent inability to do so is a sign of deviant development. Children lacking siblings or friends to play with may invent imaginary playmates with names and detailed descriptions. They may carry on long conversations with them. One boy, an only child, always insisted on a place at table being laid for his 'friend'. This ceased however soon after he started attending a nursery school at age four.

Fantasy ideas and play help young children to understand the world of which they are gradually becoming aware. Relationships such as mother–child, father–child, sibling–sibling, teacher–pupil and patient–nurse can be enacted and explored. The knowledge that it is all fantasy makes this safe and less anxiety-provoking than in real life. The child develops his own inner life, partly corresponding to reality, partly fantasy, and the world can be distorted to meet his current emotional needs. As development proceeds fantasy becomes less prominent, but most adults nevertheless resort to it sometimes.

The term *transitional object* has been given by Winnicott[8] to items which children in the pre-school age range use in a special way. The object may be a teddy bear, a piece of blanket or a toy of some sort. It is treated by the child as of special value. It may be cuddled or sucked and is often taken everywhere the child goes. The child may not be prepared to settle down to sleep at night without it. It may be used to provide comfort, protection, or reassurance, and also as an object for sexual or aggressive feelings. The use of a transitional object is considered to be a stage in the progression from a relationship with the mother to one with a much wider social circle and range of experience.

The pre-school period is one of rapidly increasing socialisation. By the end of it the business of learning to live in a group of three (the other two being the parents) should have been mastered. Progress should also have been made in coming to terms with any siblings though some degree of rivalry at this stage is normal.

Temper tantrums usually continue in the two- to five-year age range but lessen in intensity and should have largely died out by the time the child starts school.

In many countries children have an organised pre-school experience (nursery school, playgroup, or kindergarten) before starting primary school at age five or six. This is usually a useful and constructive experience, especially for children who lack siblings or neighbourhood friends of similar age. It is a first, gentle step into the world outside the family. The child can spend a few hours each day in a sheltered but warm and stimulating environment, in the company of other children of similar age and of understanding adults. This experience is likely to make it easier for the child to enter school.

The child's awareness and curiosity about his environment increase rapidly in the two- to five-year age period. This is a concomitant of intellectual development and advance in the use of language. Healthy children of this age are naturally curious about their environments. They want to know why things are as they are, how things work and what is their own relation to everything. This often results in the constant asking of questions about the what, how and why of a vast range of matters. Irrational fears are common.

Attachment behaviour continues to be readily activated until about the end of the third year. In the normally developing child it then becomes less readily elicited. Bowlby believes, however, that it remains a feature of the behaviour of a healthy person of any age[4].

The pre-school period comprises the first part of Piaget's period of concrete operations. This is subdivided, the first section (about 18 months to 7 years) being a *pre-operational period*. This is again sub-divided into a *pre-conceptual stage* (up to about four) and an *intuitive stage*. In the pre-conceptual stage children become increasingly able to represent one thing by another, so that they can use language symbols and can represent things by drawing them. But they cannot yet form true concepts or properly understand that an item belongs to a class of objects. Between ages 4 and 5 this sub-stage gives way to the intuitive sub-stage which is dealt with in the next section.

Middle Childhood (ages five or six to ten)

By the start of this period the child should have a clear conception of his position in the family group as well as a clearly-defined identity as boy or girl. Psychoanalysts refer to it as the *latency period*, because psychosexual development has been considered relatively quiescent. This view has been questioned by Rutter in a review of research[9]. In many non-western cultures sex play and lovemaking have been found to be common in this period, and recent research in the USA has yielded similar findings. In western society there may be greater concealment of sexual interests and activities but they are nevertheless present. Masturbation in boys gets common as middle childhood proceeds. It is less common in girls. Heterosexual play also increases and one study[10] showed that it occurred in one-third of boys at age 8 and two-thirds at age 13. Homosexual play also increases during this period. Broderick and Rowe[11] have developed a 'scale of pre-adolescent heterosexual development', derived from a study of 1029 boys and girls in the age range 10–12. They found definite evidence of a set of stages which most pre-adolescents go through on their way to 'social hetero-sexual maturation'.

Erikson[1] calls this period the stage of *industry versus inferiority*. A healthily developing child gains satisfaction from doing the things which are taught, in one way or another, to children in all cultures at this stage. Children learn the 'fundamentals of technology' and come to enjoy the personal satisfaction, recognition from others and chance to relate to other people which result. The main danger is that the child will develop instead a sense of inadequacy and inferiority. This may happen if he despairs of his skills and capabilities or of his status among his partners. The development of self-esteem is thus a central issue.

In western society the main formal vehicle for teaching skills to children is school, but instruction is also carried out in the home and in activities like Cub Scouts, Brownies, religious teaching groups and more informal associations with neighbourhood groups. Children's adjustment to school, and any other social groups they may enter, is a crucial matter. They must learn to cope with a more complex and less supportive social environment than the family group, as well as mastering reading, writing and numerical concepts. The teacher becomes an important person. Children's attitudes towards learning depend largely on their relationships with their teachers, though parents' attitudes are important too.

Gradually the children get an idea of their capacities and limitations, as well as working out patterns of social behaviour which may be in various degrees active or passive, leader or follower, outgoing or in-turning. Temperamental characteristics continue to be important determinants of the child's behaviour. Garside and his colleagues[12] studied 39 temperamental attitudes in a group of 209 school children aged 5 to 7. They found that among 30 of these attitudes there were four clusters representing four dimensions of temperamental style: (a) withdrawal, poor adaptation and dependence; (b) high activity, intensity and distractibility; (c) moodiness and sulkiness; and (d) irregularity. Each of these features may thus be present in any degree in a child at this age.

During this period there is further development of the use of defence mechanisms against anxiety and guilt. This parallels the continuing development of the conscience. Children come to have their own patterns of psychological defences, depending partly on constitutional and partly on environmental, especially family, factors. Standards of social behaviour are further refined and ideas of right and wrong elaborated. The personality attitudes which a child has acquired by the end of this period tend to persist into adult life.

Piaget describes the period from about 4½ to 7 years as the *intuitive sub-stage*. Children can give reasons for their actions and beliefs, but their thinking remains 'pre-operational'. Such thinking depends on immediate perceptions, rather than on mental representation of the relevant concepts. This imposes great limitations, including the attribution of causation to something which just happens to occur at the same time, frequent changes of opinion and a continuance of the young child's egocentric attitude. Life and feelings are still attributed to inanimate objects, and relationships between classes are not well under-stood. This stage is followed at about age 7 by the *sub-period of concrete operations*. This in turn continues until the onset of adolescence which marks the start of the period of *formal operations*.

The main changes in the concrete operational period are that children can internalise the properties of objects and their thinking becomes less egocentric. The capacity to internalise properties means that children can put objects in order, or classify them by size, shape or colour, without physically comparing them with each other. They can, as it were, arrange them in their minds and thus come up with answers much more rapidly. The other principal change affects play and activities with others. Previously children have mainly played on their own or in the company of others; now we see the start of co-operative play. Piaget considers this to be related to their increased capacity to perceive relationships.

Beard[2] warns that at this stage thinking is still largely intuitive, however, and that the development of individuals is often more piece-meal than Piaget suggested. Children's verbal fluency may conceal the fact that they have not yet grasped concepts such as weight or numerical relationships – as when they know their multiplication tables by rote, but do not understand what they signify.

Adolescence

Adolescence starts at puberty. While emotional and physical develop-ment do not always go hand in hand, the onset of menstruation in the girl and seminal emission in the boy are usually taken as marking puberty's onset. The age of onset is most often between eleven and thirteen in girls and between thirteen and seventeen in boys, but the range of normal is wider. The biological changes are spread over a longer period of time. The pattern of production of sex hormones starts to change, in both sexes, between the ages of eight and ten. The physical changes, including a marked growth spurt, the growth of the genitals and of hair in certain parts of the body and breast development in girls, are spread over several years. The period tends to be longer in boys (four to five years) than in girls (usually three to four years).

Erikson[1] considers that the main issue to be dealt with during the adolescent period is that of *identity versus role confusion*. With the end of childhood proper, the youth must now achieve a view of his own identity and individual characteristics. By the end of the adolescent period the young person should know who he or she is, and be confident in making this identity known to the world. This personal identity becomes the basis for the individual's relationships. Those who have failed to negotiate this period successfully do not know who they are or where they want to go in life. Identity formation has of course started much earlier in childhood, but the process intensifies during adolescence and should have been largely completed by the end of the person's teens.

The Group for the Advancement of Psychiatry, in a helpful little book on normal adolescence[13], has defined four main developmental tasks. These are changing from being nurtured and cared for to being able to nurture and care for others; learning to work and acquiring the skills to become materially self-supporting; accepting and becoming proficient in the adult sexual role and coping with heterosexual relationships; and finally moving out of the family of origin to form a new family of procreation.

Adolescence sees a marked increase in heterosexual interests and activity. The early adolescent usually first makes tentative and unself-confident approaches to the opposite sex. In time these approaches become more direct and self-assured. By late adolescence the individual should be able to enter into relationships involving tender affection as well as sexual feelings. In due course the person becomes able to enter into deeper and more lasting heterosexual relationships. These processes enable the third and fourth of the above development tasks to be accomplished.

The ways in which adolescents' developing sexual feelings are expressed depend greatly on sociocultural standards and on family rules and restrictions. Masturbation is almost universal in boys, though less common in girls. Heterosexual activities start earlier in girls than boys, but precise information is hard to obtain. A study of English teenagers in the early 1960s[14] showed the onset of dating and kissing to be usually between 13 and 16, but the range was much wider. By age 18 about one-third of the boys studied and one-sixth of the girls had had sexual intercourse, and there seemed to be evidence of a small group of very promiscuous girls. It is unlikely, however, that a similar survey in England today would yield the same results and behaviour in other sociocultural settings would certainly be different.

In the lives of most adolescents peer group relations are very important. Adolescents make friends easily and deep, sometimes lasting relationships commonly develop, especially among girls. As well as having individual friendships, adolescents often belong to groups. These appear to provide support for the members in the sometimes anxiety-provoking task of moving out of the family group to become autonomous adults. With group support adolescents can do things they could not manage on their own. Groups may be as small as two or three, but membership may run to ten, twenty or even more. An adolescent may belong to more than one group, and the membership of larger groups may change quite often. The influence of the group is often beneficial, but can be harmful as in the case of delinquent gangs.

Relationships with parents gradually change in the adolescent period. The nature of these changes has been reviewed by Rutter and his colleagues using especially the results of an epidemiological study in the Isle of Wight[15]. It is clear from this research, and other studies reviewed, that parent–child alienation is not common, certainly at age 14 (the age group studied in the Isle of Wight). It may be a little commoner in late adolescence, but most adolescents trust their parents, share many of their parents' values and accept the need for parents to set restrictions and controls on their behaviour. The process of moving out of the family group thus proceeds smoothly and gradually in most instances. Research in both Britain and North America suggests that alienation, breakdown in communication between adolescents and their parents and overt rebellion are more characteristic of that small segment of the teenage population that is referred for psychiatric care.

The same review[15] uses the Isle of Wight findings to discover whether 'inner turmoil' is characteristic of adolescence, as is sometimes alleged. There was some support for this notion in that more than one-fifth of these 14- and 15-year-olds reported feeling miserable and depressed, in response to a questionnaire, and a similar proportion reported sleep difficulties. In psychiatric interviews with a sample of adolescents from the general population studied, nearly one-half reported some misery or depression, though only one in eight actually looked sad to the psychiatrist. Self-depreciation was less common, occurring in about 20 per cent, than reported misery. Only about 7 per cent of either sex had entertained suicidal ideas. There is thus some evidence of what might be called emotional turmoil, but in some cases it was apparently quite mild and just over half the group showed none at all.

Piaget calls adolescence the period of *formal operations*. This is characterised by much more flexible thinking. The main features, as summarised by Beard[2], are the ability to accept assumptions for the sake of argument and to make hypotheses and set up propositions to test them; and the ability to look for general properties and laws in symbolic (especially verbal) material and so to invent imaginary systems and conceive things beyond what is tangible, finite and familiar. Adolescents also become aware of their own thinking, using it to justify the judgements they make and they become able to deal with such complex ideas as proportionality and correlation.

The Group for the Advancement of Psychiatry[13] has summarised the resolution of adolescence as being characterised by:

1. The attainment of separation and independence from parents.
2. The establishment of sexual identity.
3. The commitment to work.
4. The development of a personal moral system.

5. The capacity for lasting relationships and for both tender and genital sexual love in heterosexual relationships.
6. A return to the parents in a new relationship based on a relative equality.

The ease with which these developmental challenges are met depends largely on the adolescent's relationships with his or her parents. Developments earlier in childhood are thus crucial. The more secure relationships have been, the easier the handing over of responsibility to the young person will be. Despite widely differing sociocultural norms, it seems that the handover of responsibility by parents to adolescents usually goes quite smoothly. Serious emotional turmoil or disturbance are the exception, not the rule.

Family Development

Development does not stop when adolescence is superseded by adulthood. Erikson[1] describes three more 'ages of man'. The first is that of *intimacy versus isolation*. The young adult, having completed his search for identity, is now ready for intimacy with others, in close relationships including sexual union. Failure at this stage results in isolation. Instead of developing close relationships the individual may isolate, or even destroy, forces and people that appear threatening in some way. The next stage is that of *generativity versus stagnation*. The essence of generativity is the establishing and guiding of the next generation, not only nor even necessarily by parenthood, though for many this is central. Failure to achieve generativity leads to a sense of stagnation and personal impoverishment. The final stage is that of *ego integrity versus despair*. Ego integrity is the mature integration of one's life's experiences, people and things taken care of, triumphs and disappointments accepted. It is the feeling of things accomplished, and life lived satisfactorily. Failure to achieve ego integrity results in despair, a characteristic of which is fear of death due to the feeling that time is now too short to live another life.

The above three stages are of interest to those who work with children, since they describe the developmental stages through which parents and grandparents go. The adults in the child's world are the basis from which the family created, and it is important to look at the stage of development of the family as well as that of the child.

The first stage is the courtship of a man and a woman. Following successful courtship the young couple form a group whose task is to teach any children they have about how to live in a family and also about the customs and cultural values of society. Fleck[16] summarises the evolutionary tasks of the family as being 'effecting a marital coalition capable of forming a triad of parents and infant, nurturing and weaning the infant to enable it to exist as a body apart from the mother, and imparting language and intrafamilial modes epitomised by the resolution of the oedipal phase. The family must introduce the child into society in school and through peer relationships'. The family goes on to help the child through the developmental tasks of adolescence (see page 12) and finally to emancipation from the family group.

In other words the family is a developing system, and it must progress in the right way for the child's development to be healthy. A system is made up of a group of dynamically interrelated and interdependent parts (in the case of a family the family members). The behaviour of the parts cannot be understood in isolation from the whole, which itself is more than the sum of the parts. Family systems are 'open' in that there is interchange between them and the surrounding environment. Every system has a pattern of functioning with built-in feedback mechanisms and a set of rules which determine how it operates. Family members are not consciously aware of the rules that govern their system, but the professional studying a family and its level of development needs to discover what they are. Systems theory and the investigation and assessment of family systems will be discussed further in the following two chapters. In studying developing children, the important questions about the family are whether the family system has reached a state of development such as to help its children through the developmental tasks they are currently facing, and also to see how each child's temperament and other characteristics are themselves affecting the system.

Family development involves a progressive changing of the implicit rules that govern the family system. In most marriages the partners are at first greatly influenced by their families of origin[17]. Various compromises and adjustments are necessary to enable the two people to live together satisfactorily, and in some marriages these are not made and the relationship either breaks down or continues in a state of unhappiness or tension. Further changes in the rules are necessary with the birth of children, their enrolment in school, their entry into adolescence and their final departure from the home. The extended family situation may also dictate alteration of the family rules, as when a grandparent or other relative dies, moves away from the area or comes to live in the family. Changes in the parents' employment, periods of unemployment, moving to a different place of residence and many other factors have their effects, great or small, on the developing family system.

In short, the family is a changing, open system with the task of facilitating the development of its members. In turn the changing needs and behaviours of the members cause shifts in the family's rules and pattern of functioning. A complete assessment needs to look at the individuals concerned and also the family system as a whole.

References

1. Erikson, E. H. *Childhood and Society*. New York: W. W. Norton, 1968 and London: Penguin Books, 1965. (See especially Chapter 7 'The Eight Ages of Man').
2. Beard, R. M. *An Outline of Piaget's Developmental Psychology*. London: Routledge and Kegan Paul, 1969.
3. Flavell, J. H. *The Developmental Psychology of Jean Piaget*. Princeton: van Nostrand, 1963.
4. Bowlby, J. 'The making and breaking of emotional bonds'. *British Journal of Psychiatry*, **130**, 201–210, 1977.
5. Thomas, A., Chess, S. and Birch, H. G. *Temperament and Behaviour Disorders in Children*. New York: New York University Press, 1968.
6. Harlow, H. F. 'The nature of love'. *American Journal of Psychology*, **13**, 673–685, 1958.
7. Newson, J. and Newson, E. *Four Years Old in an Urban Community*. London: Allen and Unwin, 1968.
8. Winnicott, D. W. *The Family and Individual Development*. London: Tavistock, 1965.
9. Rutter, M. 'Normal psychosexual development'. *Journal of Child Psychology and Psychiatry*, **11**, 259–283, 1971.
10. Ramsey, C. V. 'The sexual development of boys'. *American Journal of Psychology*, **56**, 217–233, 1943.
11. Broderick, C. B. and Rowe, P. 'A scale of pre-adolescent heterosexual development'. *Journal of Marriage and the Family*, **30**, 97–101, 1968.
12. Garside, R. F., Birch, H., Scott, D. McI., Chambers, S., Kolvin, I., Tweddle, E. K. and Barker, L. M. 'Dimensions of temperament in infant school children'. *Journal of Child Psychology and Psychiatry*, **16**, 219–231, 1975.
13. Group for the Advancement of Psychiatry. *Normal Adolescence: Its Dynamics and Impact*. London: Crosby Lockwood Staples, 1974 and New York: GAP, 1968.
14. Schofield, M. *The Sexual Behaviour of Young People*. London: Longmans, 1965.
15. Rutter, M., Graham, P., Chadwick, O. F. D. and Yule, W. 'Adolescent turmoil: fact or fiction'. *Journal of Child Psychology and Psychiatry*, **17**, 35–56, 1976.
16. Fleck, S. 'A general systems approach to severe family pathology'. *American Journal of Psychiatry*, **133**, 669–673, 1976.
17. Minuchin, S. *Families and Family Therapy*, (Chapters 1–4). Cambridge, Mass.: Harvard University Press and London: Tavistock, 1974.

CHAPTER TWO

Causes, Classification and Prevalence of Child Psychiatric Disorders

Causes

It is unusual to find a single clear-cut cause for a childhood psychiatric disorder. For the most part, child psychiatric disorders are not 'disease entities' like appendicitis or measles, but complex reactions to a variety of factors in a developing personality. Four main groups of factors require to be considered in every case:

Constitutional factors
The effects of physical disease or injury
Temperamental factors
Environmental factors.

Constitutional Factors

Constitutional factors are those with which the child is born. These result from the child's genetic make-up and any damage or ill-effects which the foetus may have suffered during pregnancy or birth. It might be better to consider constitutional only factors of genetic origin, but it is often impossible to distinguish between these and the results of intrauterine damage or disease.

Few of the psychiatric disorders of childhood are known to be caused by *specific genetic factors*, though such factors are responsible for some forms of mental handicap[1]. In these cases the genetic effect is to cause low intelligence rather than bring about emotional disturbance, though emotional disorder may be present also. *Phenylpyruvic oligophrenia*, or *phenylketonuria*, is a form of mental handicap inherited as a recessive trait, and due to a specific inborn enzyme defect; and the commonest distinct form of handicap, *Down's syndrome* or *mongolism*, is associated with the presence of an additional chromosome. Many rarer forms of mental handicap are also genetically determined.

It is possible that specific genetic factors contribute to disturbed behaviour in other ways. Some boys have an extra Y chromosome, so that their sex chromosome pattern is XYY instead of the usual XY. As a group, men and boys with this abnormality are usually tall, though the height of some is within the normal range. There is also an association between aggressive and antisocial behaviour and the presence of an extra Y chromosome[2]. Yet the association is not marked and most boys with an extra Y chromosome do not show such behaviour, while most who do show it do not have an extra chromosome.

More important than specific genetic factors are *polygenic influences*. These are the outcome of the operation of a combination of genes which together affect the probability of some disorder or characteristic being manifest. Whether or not the disorder does occur depends on the unique combination of environmental and genetic factors in each individual. The best way of determining whether polygenic factors play a part in causing a disorder is by the study of twins. If they do, the disorder under consideration will be commoner in monozygotic (MZ) twins (who are genetically identical) than in dizygotic twins (who are genetically dissimilar) brought up in the same environment. Another approach is to study MZ twins who are separated early in life, as by adoption into different families, and see whether there is concordance for the feature under study as often as in MZ twins reared in the same family. This shows the effects of different environments on genetically similar children.

Shields[3] has reviewed the results of twin studies and has concluded that polygenic factors are marked in the case of intelligence (see page 195), where they may account for up to 80 per cent of the variance in a population. This explains why intelligence may vary widely in children brought up in the same family. In some cases, however, as with children brought up in very adverse circumstances, the contribution of the environment may be much greater. It appears that a person's maximum intellectual potential is limited by his genetic make-up, and that the right environmental factors are needed for this to be realised.

Personality variation is more difficult to measure than intelligence, but it seems that here again genetic factors are important, if rather less so than with intelligence[3]. Present knowledge suggests that some basic features of personality are genetically determined. These leave room for development to take various lines. They are rather like foundations which permit a variety of types of house to be built on them, but which, by their size, shape and strength nevertheless place definite limits on the final result.

Temperamental attributes as evident in early childhood also appear to be determined to an important degree by polygenic factors[4]. Genetic influences seem to have only minor effects upon conduct disorders (page 48) and delinquency (page 57), but are rather more important in the case of neurotic disorders (page 63)[3].

An *adverse intrauterine environment* can undoubtedly affect the foetus in ways which influence subsequent psychological development. A number of diseases (for example rubella, toxoplasmosis and syphilis) transferred from the mother may affect the nervous system of the developing foetus. So also may an insufficient supply of oxygen. It has been suggested that there is an increased incidence of a wide variety of behavioural disturbances in children born following pregnancies complicated by toxaemia and some other obstetric conditions. Pasamanick and his colleagues formulated a theory of a 'continuum of reproductive casualty'[5]. They postulated that just as some pregnancies end in abortion or stillbirth, or are followed by neonatal death, there are other cases where there is less severe damage to the foetus, and in particular to the brain. Pasamanick considered that this process contributes to reading disability, epilepsy, mental handicap and certain behaviour disorders.

Pasamanick's work has since been criticised on methodological grounds but there is evidence that injury at birth, and also premature birth, are associated with abnormal development or behaviour disturbance in later life. For example, a follow-up study of a group of 461 Edinburgh children born in the period 1953–1960 has shown that in children with lower birth weights there is a higher incidence of mental and of physical handicap, as well as of disturbed behaviour[6]. The effect is especially marked in children weighing 2000 grams or less at birth. Even when those having moderate or several mental, neurological and physical defects were excluded, children of low birth weight attending normal schools did less well than those of higher birth weight, as judged by the sort of secondary school course for which they were selected, and also on the basis of group intelligence tests. This could not be explained by socio-economic differences between the children of low birth weight and the others.

Similar findings have come from the British Child Development Study, which studied nearly 16,000 children from birth through into their teens[7]. When these children were assessed at age seven, significant associations were found between 'social adjustment' (as measured by the Bristol Social Adjustment Guide see page 200) and birth order (first-born children being better adjusted than those born later); smoking in pregnancy (the mothers who smoked heavily having children who were less well adjusted at seven); period of gestation (the most favourable being 38 to 42 weeks); and birth weight, those with very low birth weights being less well adjusted. While these associations do not prove that the factors mentioned are causal, they do suggest the possibility that the developing child may be affected adversely during pregnancy and birth in such ways, even though there is no gross, obvious evidence of damage.

Physical Disease and Injuries

Physical disease or injury may contribute to the development of a psychiatric disorder. Brain disease or damage may produce impairment of intelligence, loss of particular motor or sensory functions, epilepsy (see page 139) or (probably) specific forms of abnormal behaviour like motor overactivity. It can also have less specific effects; in the Isle of Wight epidemiological studies, children with definite evidence of brain damage were found to have psychiatric disorders five times as often as the general child population, and three times as commonly as children with chronic physical handicaps not involving the brain[8].

Shaffer, Chadwick and Rutter[9] reported a study of children who had suffered injuries known to have damaged some part of the brain. As in the Isle of Wight study, they found a high rate of psychiatric disorder, which could not be fully accounted for by the adverse socio-cultural factors which also afflicted the injured children as a group. These increased prevalence rates in brain-damaged children were due to an increase in psychiatric disorders generally, not to an increase in disorders of any particular type. There was no constant relation to the site of the brain damage or the age at which it occurred.

Brain damage may be caused by injury, infection, metabolic abnormality or tumour, and by some degenerative disorders of unknown cause. Development of the brain can also be adversely affected by severe malnutrition in early life[10]. Exactly what effect this has on behaviour and intelligence is uncertain and study of the matter is made difficult by the usual association of malnutrition with other adverse social circumstances. It is probable however that intelligence is impaired. 'Non-accidental injury', usually by parents, can cause physical damage to the brain, and may be combined with under-nutrition, psychological neglect, or both.

Infections which may cause injury to the brain include various virus and bacterial diseases causing infection of the brain as a whole (encephalitis) and localised infections, for example those spreading from the ear or elsewhere.

Metabolic abnormalities affecting the brain are being discovered in increasing numbers. Most have as their main effect the production of a degree of mental handicap. In these disorders there is an inborn, often hereditary, disorder of the production or functioning of a particular enzyme, or group of enzymes. This may lead to accumulation in the brain (and other tissues) of fatty substances (as in lipidoses), carbohydrates (the commonest being galactose in galactosaemia), or aminoacids (for example phenylalanine in *phenylketonuria*, methionine and homocysteine in *homocysteinuria*, and histidine in *histidinaemia*). Organic causes of mental and behavioural disorders of children are further discussed in Chapter 6 (pages 92 to 95).

Physical diseases not directly affecting the brain can also have psychological repercussions. They may act through the physical handicap they impose or the anxiety, or guilt, they cause in child, parents or both. The possible effects on a child of a severe physical handicap such as may occur in cerebral palsy, or of blindness, are obvious. Much can be done to enable such children to lead a full life and to prevent them developing emotional problems as complications of their physical ones. It often requires skill and patience, however, and a standard of care greater than that needed by physically healthy children. Many other chronic conditions, for instance diabetes, asthma, congenital heart disease and the various forms of dwarfism may cause emotional problems, through their physically handicapping effects, their possible restricting effects on the child's social life, the anxiety and fears of death they may cause, and their effects on the attitudes of family and perhaps friends and teachers.

Temperamental Factors

There is evidence that adverse temperamental characteristics contribute to the genesis of psychiatric disorders in children. Thomas and his colleagues[11], in their New York longitudinal study, identified a subgroup of 'difficult children'. These showed irregularity of biological function, a tendency to respond to new stimuli by withdrawal, slow adaptation to changes in the environment, unhappy and unpleasant mood states and 'intense reaction', that is a relatively large behavioural response to an environmental stimulus. These features were identifiable

before the age of two and the children with this cluster of characteristics more often later developed behaviour disorders. By contrast a
group of 'easy children' showed a happy, contented mood, high
regularity of biological functions, rapid adaptability, reactions to
stimuli that were of low or mild intensity and a positive approach to
new situations. These children developed behaviour disorders less often.

Graham and colleagues[12] studied a group of mainly working class
children in London and found a significant association of three
temperamental characteristics – low regularity, low malleability and
low fastidiousness – with later behaviour problems in school, as rated
independently by the teacher. They concluded that temperamental
characteristics probably act by making the child more vulnerable to
family stress or other adversity. Thus what might be a passing problem
in one family could, as a result of the parental reaction it evokes, lead
to a big problem in another.

Although temperament seems to be partly genetically determined,
environment apparently affects it as well. Indeed it is probable that
the temperamental attributes of all family members are gradually
modified over time as they interact with each other. Cameron[13], in
another study using data from the New York longitudinal study, has
found that there are associations between temperamental changes over
time in children, and parental characteristics. Seventy items on which
parents were rated using interviews given them when the children were
aged 3 were subject to cluster analysis. One cluster of parental characteristics was described as 'parental disapproval, intolerance and
rejection'. These parental features were associated, by the second year,
with daughters who were less persistent and less active in their reactions
than the majority, and also with a change in their daughter's temperaments over a 2–3 year period towards less adaptability and less
positive mood. While such associations as these are not proof of causal
effects, they suggest that the child's developing temperament is related
to factors in the family environment, as well as to genetic factors;
research on temperamental factors in children is, however, as yet at an
early stage.

Environmental Factors

Whether or not parental characteristics affect children's temperaments,
the family environment is very important. The family should provide
a sheltered training ground in which the individual learns to live as
a member of a society. Families are miniature societies in which

children make their first attempts at adapting to others and in which they learn patterns of social behaviour which tend to persist throughout life. The child's family should facilitate development from a state of complete dependence in infancy to one of independence of the family in adult life. Poor early adjustment in family life is likely to be followed by poor adjustment in society at large. Attitudes towards parents may later become generalised and applied to a much wider circle of people. At any particular age too much must not be asked of children in the way of self-control and responsibility for their actions, but at the same time too much must not be done for them. If too much *is* done the process of growing up and becoming independent may be retarded. If too little, a child's level of anxiety may become intolerably great and psychiatric disorder may appear.

Childhood should thus be a process of gradual transfer of responsibility from parents to child. This process requires, for a background, a secure and stable family setting, with reasonably consistent and constant parent figures. This does not mean there must never be disagreements or arguments, or that members of the family will not sometimes become angry with one another or with the child. On the contrary, it is essential that children be exposed to a range of emotions and situations as they will be in adult life. The repression by parents of all their emotions would in itself be harmful to their children.

So the whole family must be considered when a psychiatric assessment is made of a child. Children who are deprived of a normal family group in which to grow up suffer a serious handicap. How well they develop depends partly upon their own personality resources, but largely upon the substitute environment in which they live.

In looking at environmental, especially family factors, use is being increasingly made of *general systems theory*. This was originally conceived by von Bertalanffy[14] and has been found useful as a theoretical basis by many family therapists[15,16]. General systems theory deals with interactions and the rules which govern them, rather than with individual phenomena. As applied to families it involves 'viewing the family unit as a biosocial sub-system within a larger cultural-social system'[17]. The family is conceived of as a system made up of parts (its members) which are dynamically interrelated and interdependent. The behaviour of the parts cannot be understood in isolation from the whole, which is itself more than the sum of the parts. The system is 'open' in that it is in constant interaction with forces outside itself, namely the wider socio-cultural setting. It is thus a part of, usually several 'supra-systems', such as the extended family, the neighbourhood network, the village, the tribe and so on. Families usually also contain sub-systems, such as parental, marital and child sub-systems. Individuals can, and usually do, belong to more than one system, for example at school or at work as well as in the family.

Every system has a *boundary*. Certain materials, feelings and communications can pass through the boundary and others cannot. It is thus selectively permeable in both directions. Some system boundaries are rigid and well defined, others are flimsy and blurred. The more rigid the boundary, the harder communication across it is; the more flimsy, the easier communication becomes. Minuchin uses the term 'disengagement' for situations in which there is a very rigid boundary and 'enmeshment' for those where there is a weak boundary[18].

All systems are governed by rules. In family systems the members are not aware of the rules, which, nevertheless, operate powerfully to maintain the system. This process is often called 'homeostasis'. French has defined two processes, one of which is concerned with maintaining homeostasis, the other with changing the rules when necessary[19]. Type I process involves all the mechanisms which maintain the steady state of the system, with its fixed reference points. Type II process involves a change in the reference points leading to a new and different homeostatic balance. The former is much easier to achieve than the latter and is always the preferred method that is tried in the face of stress. The latter is however sometimes essential, as when family circumstances change, and failure to achieve the necessary adjustments may precipitate symptoms in one or more family members.

Disturbed behaviour in a family member or members is often found to be associated with a 'dysfunctional' family system. That is to say the rules and way of functioning of the system depend on one or more members being symptomatic or disabled in some way. The family system is then not operating, as it should, to realise each member's potential for healthy development and constructive activities.

Haley has pointed out, that central to many of the problems is a malfunctioning hierarchy[20]. To take a simple example, consider a three-member family in which there is over-involvement of one parent and child, let us say mother and son, to the exclusion of the other parent. This can lead to various problems for the son who may become over-dependent on the mother and in time get to be so immature and anxious that he develops school refusal (see page 75). Instead of the parental couple helping the boy to grow up, one of them is keeping him a baby while the other is uninvolved in the family. That parent may instead have an intense involvement in his work or in some other relationship outside the family. Another possible outcome is obesity in the son, the focus of the close, involved relationship leading to the mother over-feeding the child whose weight problem then becomes another of her concerns: fruitless attempts at treatment and dieting can then perpetuate the dysfunctional over-involvement. In such cases a therapist's task would be to lessen the involvement of mother and son, and increase that of mother and father. The aim would be to change the sub-system pattern as follows:

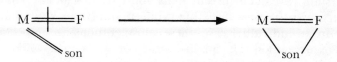

Methods whereby this may be done will be discussed in Chapter 16.

Many other and more complex dysfunctional family patterns are possible. They may involve three generations, or even four; and extended family members, or even non-members of the family, may be important too. Dysfunctional systems can, and indeed often do, occur elsewhere, for example in schools, places of work and neighbourhood groups. The therapist wishing to understand a person's disturbed behaviour may have to look at systems such as these as well as at the family system, in order to do so.

The study of family systems has led to the identification of certain roles into which family members may be cast. A commonly used term is 'scapegoat', although it is not strictly accurate. The term has biblical origins, and the use of a scapegoat was one of the procedures laid down by Moses for use by the people of Israel[21]. The priest was to lay his hands on the head of the goat and 'confess over it all the iniquities of the Israelites and all their acts of rebellion, that is all their sins'. Having laid the sins on the goat's head, the goat was to be sent into the wilderness to 'carry all their iniquities upon itself into some barren waste'. It is true that the 'scapegoated' family member (often a symptomatic child) appears to be the person upon whom all the family's problems and difficulties are projected, but he is usually maintained in the family system to serve a particular function, rather than being sent out into a barren waste. Some families depend on having a 'bad' child for their, often precarious, stability. The 'acting-out', difficult child may be the only thing that keeps the parents, or the whole of the rest of the family, together. The symptomatic member may then be the only subject the parents can be united about.

Another abnormal role is that of the 'parental' child. Some parental functions in relation to younger siblings may be appropriate for an older child, but if too much responsibility is given to the child – and especially if the delegation of authority is not explicit – the child may be unable to function as required and become symptomatic; or it may be that some other member presents as the identified parent. In extreme cases there is reversal of roles, the child taking care of the parent, while at the same time the inversion of roles is camouflaged (see Skynner[16], page 417).

While it can be helpful to regard the family as a system when trying to understand a child's current behaviour, it is clear also that past experiences can be very relevant. While nothing can be done about the past in an individual case, these considerations are important in the field of prevention. The quality of the parental care a child receives undoubtedly affects that child's development, and sometimes severe problems are seen in children who have been seriously deprived[22]. Loss of a parent can also have serious effects[23], although it is not clear whether children are especially vulnerable to loss at any particular age. The effects vary and it is not only the actual loss, but also the circumstances preceding and following it that are important. The matter is discussed more fully in the book *Maternal Deprivation Reassessed*[22].

In summary children bring with them into their families, and later their schools and neighbourhood groups, certain genetic characteristics and temperamental styles. These are modified as a result of any organic brain damage or disease they may suffer, and also powerfully by their environments. Ideally, children's family, school and neighbourhood environments should be adaptively functioning systems into which they can fit to the mutual benefit of themselves and the other members of the systems. In that case the needs and assets of family members are mutually complementary. Sometimes they are not, however, and this is often due to a poor 'fit' between the temperaments and personalities of different family members, as well as to specific problems in individual members. But many severe individual handicaps are compatible with the absence of psychiatric disorder. Thus a boy with a severe learning disorder may do well if he is in a special class for learning-disordered children and belongs to a warm, accepting family which takes a constructive and helpful attitude towards his disability. If either or both of these conditions are not met, emotional disorder may result. Indeed all the people in a child's environment – parents, siblings, other relatives, teachers, fellow-students at school, neighbourhood folk – contribute to that child's development as models for identification, people loved or feared and so on. At the same time each child has an effect, great or small, on the various systems of which he or she is a part.

It will be clear from the above that it is seldom possible to assign a single cause to a child psychiatric disorder. These problems are usually multifactorial in origin.

The Classification of Emotional Disorders in Children and Adolescents

No entirely satisfactory classification of child psychiatric disorders exists, but recent years have seen the development of *multi-axial systems* which have already proved valuable[24,25]. These systems provide a series of parameters, or axes, upon which every disorder must be classified. They avoid the problems inherent in multi-category systems which consist simply of lists of categories, usually covering widely different concepts such as presenting clinical syndrome, aetiology, intelligence level, developmental deviation and environmental stress. By contrast, multi-axial schemes lay down the axes to be used, and of course each must have 'no abnormality' and 'information unavailable' codings. They can then separate out the clinical syndrome present from the aetiological factors and from level of intellectual functioning. This is important in dealing with disorders of multifactorial origin, as child psychiatric disorders usually are.

The work on multi-axial systems referred to above has led to the development of a 5-axis scheme. This scheme, devised at the Institute of Psychiatry, University of London[26], has the additional merit of being based, in four out of its five axes, on the ninth (1975) edition of the *International Classification of Diseases*[27]. The items in this classification have been subdivided so that those which cover clinical psychiatric syndromes form the first axis, those which cover 'specific delays in development' constitute the second, those dealing with intellectual level form the third and all the remaining codes in the ICD – that is all non-psychiatric disorders – make up the fourth axis. In addition, a fifth axis has been devised which deals with 'abnormal psychosocial situations'. This does not form part of the ninth edition of the ICD. Operational definitions are provided for all axes except the fourth. The main categories on the five axes are shown below.

CLASSIFICATION OF THE MAIN CATEGORIES

AXIS One (Clinical Psychiatric Syndrome)
  Psychoses (290–299)
  Code 290   Senile and Presenile Organic Psychotic Conditions
  291   Alcoholic Psychoses
  292   Drug Induced Psychoses
  293   Transient Organic Psychotic Conditions
  294   Other Organic Psychotic Conditions (Chronic)
  295   Schizophrenic Psychoses
  296   Affective Psychoses
  297   Paranoid States

298   Other Non-organic Psychoses
299   **Psychoses Specific to Childhood**

Neurotic Disorders, Personality Disorders and Other Non-Psychotic Mental Disorders (300–316)
Code 300   **Neurotic Disorders**
301   Personality or Character Disorders
302   Sexual Deviations and Disorders
303   Alcohol Dependence
304   Drug Dependence
305   Non-Dependent Abuse of Drugs
306   Physical Conditions arising from Mental Factors
307   **Special Symptoms or Syndromes not Elsewhere Classified**
308   Acute Reaction to Stress
309   **Adjustment Reaction**
310   Specific Non-Psychotic Disorders following Brain Damage
311   Depressive Disorders not Elsewhere Classified
312   **Disturbances of Conduct not Elsewhere Classified**
313   **Disturbances of Emotions Specific to Childhood and Adolescence**
314   **Hyperkinetic Syndrome of Childhood**
316   Psychic Factors Associated with Diseases Classified Elsewhere

Axis Two (Specific Delays in Development)
No Specific Delay
Specific Reading Retardation
Specific Arithmetical Retardation
Other Specific Learning Difficulties
Developmental Speech/Language Disorder
Specific Motor Retardation
Mixed Developmental Disorder
Other Specified
Unspecified

Axis Three (Intellectual Level)
Normal Variation
Mild Mental Retardation
Moderate Mental Retardation
Severe Mental Retardation
Profound Mental Retardation
Unspecified Mental Retardation
Intellectual Level Unknown

Axis Four (Medical Conditions) Includes all remaining codes in ICD.

Axis Five (Abnormal Psychosocial Situations)
No significant distortion or inadequacy of psychosocial environment
Mental disturbance in other family members
Discordant intra-familial relationships
Lack of warmth in intra-familial relationships
Familial over-involvement
Inadequate or inconsistent parental control
Inadequate social, linguistic or perceptual stimulation
Inadequate living conditions

Inadequate or distorted intra-familial communication
Anomalous family situation
Stresses or disturbance in school or work environment
Migration or social transplantation
Natural disaster
Other intra-familial psychosocial stress
Other extra-familial psychosocial stress
Persecution or adverse discrimination
Other psychosocial disturbance in society in general
Other (Specified)
Not known

In axis 1, the items likely to be most used in childhood and adolescence are printed in heavy type, though any may be used. The first and second axes are the basis for the classification used in this book, but the system as a whole is a clinically useful one and is recommended as the best available at the time of writing.

Many other classifications of child psychiatric disorders exist, and one widely used in North America is that proposed by the Group for the Advancement of Psychiatry in 1966[28]. This has the following categories:

1. Healthy Responses
2. Reactive Disorders (see Adjustment Reactions in Chapter 8)
3. Developmental Deviations (see Chapter 9)
   (a) Deviations in Maturational Patterns
   (b) Deviations in Specific Dimensions of Development, i.e. motor, sensory, speech, cognitive, social, psychosocial, affective and integrative functions
   (c) Other Developmental Deviations
4. Psychoneurotic Disorders
   This category is divided into 7 sub-categories.
5. Personality Disorders
   This category is divided into 13 sub-categories which are listed in Chapter 8
6. Psychotic Disorders (see Chapter 6)
   (a) Psychoses of infancy and early childhood
   (b) Psychoses of later childhood
   (c) Psychoses of adolescence
7. Psychophysiologic Disorders (see Chapter 10)
8. Brain Syndromes
   (a) Acute
   (b) Chronic
   These are considered in this chapter (pages 20 to 21) and in Chapter 6

9. Mental Retardation (see Chapter 12)
10. Other Disorders

Yet another system, currently under trial in North America, is the third edition of the Diagnostic and Statistical Manual ('DSM III') of the American Psychiatric Association[29]. Not specifically designed for use in children's disorders, but rather for all age groups, it is multi-axial and has the following five axes.

1. Clinical Psychiatric Syndrome(s) and Other Conditions
2. Personality Disorders (adults) and Specific Developmental Disorders (children and adolescents)
3. Non-mental Medical Disorders
4. Severity of Psychosocial Stressors
5. Highest Level of Adaptive Functioning, Past Year

This system has a number of features in common with the scheme developed at the Institute of Psychiatry, and it also makes some use of the ninth edition of the *International Classification of Diseases*. At the time of writing, however, it is still under development.

Prevalence of Child Psychiatric Disorders

Several studies of the prevalence of psychiatric disorders in children have been carried out in Britain. The Isle of Wight study[30], was designed to cover all the 10- and 11-year-old children in the island in 1965. The researchers concluded that the prevalence of psychiatric disorders, as they defined them, in this island of small towns and rural areas was 6·8 per cent. Psychiatric disorder was considered to be present if 'abnormalities of behaviour, emotions or relationships were sufficiently marked and sufficiently prolonged to be causing persistent suffering or handicap in the child himself, or distress or disturbance in the family or community'. There were nearly twice as many boys with psychiatric disorder as there were girls.

A subsequent survey, by some of the same workers, in an inner London borough showed a rate of disturbance about double that in the Isle of Wight[31]. Prevalence rates thus vary considerably, and they probably vary also in different age groups. Leslie[32] studied 13- to 14-year-olds in Blackburn, a northern industrial town. Prevalence rates are given separately for each sex. The relevant percentages were:

	Boys	Girls
Moderate disorder	6·2	2·6
Severe disorder	14·6	11·0
Total	20·8	13·6

A study in an Australian town of about 2000 inhabitants suggested prevalence rates of 10 per cent in children and 16 per cent in adolescents[33,34].

Psychiatric disorders in children and adolescents are thus a major problem affecting large numbers of individuals. The prevalence of particular types of disorder will be considered when the different syndromes are described.

References

1. Penrose, L. S. *The Biology of Mental Defect*. London: Sidgwick and Jackson, 1972.
2. Nielson, J. and Christenson, A. L. 'Thirty-five males with double Y chromosome'. *Psychological Medicine*, **4**, 28–37, 1974.
3. Shields, J. 'Polygenic influences'. In *Child Psychiatry: Modern Approaches*, ed. M. Rutter and L. Hersov. Oxford: Blackwell, 1976.
4. Torgersen, A. M. and Kringlen, E. Quoted in Rutter, M. and Madge, N. *Cycles of Disadvantage*. London: Heinemann, 1976.
5. Pasamanick, B., Rogers, M. E. and Lillienfield, A. M. 'Pregnancy experience and development of behaviour disorders in children'. *American Journal of Psychiatry*, **112**, 613–618, 1956.
6. Drillien, C. M. 'School disposal and performance for children of different birth weight, 1953–1960'. *Archives of Disease in Childhood*, **44**, 562–570, 1969.
7. Davie, R., Butler, N. and Goldstein, H. *From Birth to Seven*. London: Longman, 1972.
8. Rutter, M., Graham, P. and Yule, W. A. *A Neuropsychiatric Study in Childhood*. Philadelphia: Lippincott, 1970.
9. Shaffer, D., Chadwick, O. and Rutter, M. 'Psychiatric outcome of localised head injury in children'. In *Outcome of Severe Damage to the Central Nervous System*, ed. R. Porter and D. W. Fitzsimons. Amsterdam: Elsevier–Excerpta Medica-North Holland, 1975.
10. Scott, P. D. 'Non-accidental injury in children'. *British Journal of Psychiatry*, **131**, 366–380, 1977.
11. Thomas, A. Chess, S. and Birch, H. G. *Temperament and Behaviour Disorders in Children*. New York University Press, 1968.
12. Graham, P. Rutter, M, and George, S. 'Temperamental characteristics as predictors of behaviour disorders in children' *American Journal of Orthopsychiatry*, **43**, 328–339, 1973.
13. Cameron, J. R. 'Parental treatment, children's temperament and the risk of childhood behavioural problems'. *American Journal of Orthopsychiatry*, **47**, 568–576, 1977.
14. von Bertalanffy, L. *General Systems Theory*. New York: Braziller, 1948.
15. Walrond-Skinner, S. *Family Therapy: The Treatment of Natural Systems*. London: Routledge and Kegan Paul, 1976.

16. Skynner, A. C. R. *One Flesh: Separate Persons*. London: Constable, 1976 (Published in USA as *Systems of Family and Marital Psychotherapy*. New York: Brunner/Mazel.)

17. Brown, S. L. 'Family group therapy'. In *Manual of Child Psychopathology*, ed. B. B. Wolman, New York: McGraw-Hill, 1972.

18. Minuchin, J. *Families and Family Therapy*. Cambridge, Mass.: Harvard University Press. 1974.

19. French, A. *Disturbed Children and Their Families*, New York: Human Sciences Press, 1977.

20. Haley, J. *Problem Solving Therapy*. San Francisco: Jossey-Bass, 1976.

21. The Bible, Leviticus, Chapter 16, verses 20–22 (Quotations from the New English Bible translation).

22. Rutter, M. *Maternal Deprivation Reassessed*. Harmondsworth: Penguin, 1972.

23. Bowlby, J. 'Childhood mourning and its implications for psychiatry' *American Journal of Psychiatry*, **118**, 481–498, 1961.

24. Rutter, M. *et al.* 'A tri-axial classification of mental disorders in childhood'. *Journal of Child Psychology and Psychiatry*, **10**, 41–61, 1969.

25. Rutter, M., Shaffer, D. and Shepherd, M. *A Multi-Axial Classification of Child Psychiatric Disorders*. Geneva: WHO, 1975.

26. Rutter, M., Shaffer, D. and Sturge, C. *A Guide to a Multi-Axial Classification Scheme for Psychiatric Disorders in Childhood and Adolescence*. Dept. of Child and Adolescent Psychiatry, Institute of Psychiatry, London, SE8 8AF.

27. World Health Organisation. *International Classification of Diseases*, 1975 Revision, Geneva, 1977.

28. Group for the Advancement of Psychiatry. *Psychopathological Disorders in Childhood: Report No. 62*, New York, 1962.

29. American Psychiatric Association. Diagnostic and Statistical Manual III (draft). APA: New York: 1977.

30. Rutter, M., Tizard, J. and Whitmore, K. *Education, Health and Behaviour*. London: Longman, 1970.

31. Rutter, M. 'Why are London children so disturbed?' *Proceedings of the Royal Society of Medicine*, **66**, 1221–1225, 1973.

32. Leslie, S. A. 'Psychiatric disorders in the young adolescents of an industrial town'. *British Journal of Psychiatry*, **125**, 113–124, 1974.

33. Krupinski, J. *et al.* 'A community mental health survey of Heyfield, Victoria'. *Medical Journal of Australia*, **1**, 1204–1211, 1967.

34. Henderson, A. S., Krupinski, J. and Stoller, A. 'Epidemiological aspects of adolescent psychiatry'. In *Modern Perspectives in Adolescent Psychiatry*, ed. J. G. Howells. Edinburgh: Oliver and Boyd, 1971.

CHAPTER THREE
Assessing Children and their Families

A flexible approach is needed when assessing children and their families. Many psychiatrists prefer to interview child and parents separately, but some start by seeing the family as a whole. When child and parents are separated for interview, the parents may be seen first. A disadvantage of this, however, is that the child may feel, often rightly, that the parents have been reporting unfavourably on him. This can make it harder to gain the child's confidence. On the other hand, if the parents have been seen first the interviewer is better aware of the nature of the problem and so can try to steer the course of the interview accordingly. With children the relative advantages of the two approaches are often evenly balanced. Adolescents, however, are usually best seen first and on their own.

Seeing the whole family together avoids the pitfalls inherent in seeing sections of it separately, though it can make it more difficult to obtain a comprehensive, factual history. Some psychiatrists believe that observing the family group together, and seeing how the members interact with each other, is more important than obtaining facts about the history and symptoms. Moreover, facts can if necessary be ascertained by means of later interviews with family members. Increasing use is being made nowadays of family group methods and allied to this is the increasing acceptance of the family, rather than the individual child, as the unit for treatment. Family interviews will be considered later (pages 41–45) after guidelines for assessing children and their parents in the more traditional way have been given.

Taking the History

If possible both parents should be seen, but often only one, usually the mother, attends with the child. It is a good plan to state, when the appointment is made, that both parents should attend if possible. If only one can come on the first occasion, attempts should be made to see the other later. It is important that if at all possible both parents should be concerned with the study and treatment of the child from the start.

It is best to let the parents start by talking as freely as they wish about the problems which have led them to the consultation. They should be allowed to explain the situation as they see it, in their own way and with a minimum of prompting. When they have finished speaking of one problem they can be asked if there are any others and, if so, again allowed to explain in their own words. There is thus obtained not only information about the child's symptoms but also, quite often, an indication of the nature of the relationship between the parents.

When the parents have finished their account of the symptoms and problems they have noticed, supplementary questions should be put to them as necessary. These aim to identify the duration, frequency and severity of the symptoms, preferably illustrated by specific examples; also whether the symptoms are getting better, or worse, or staying much the same.

Enquiry should next be made about areas which have not been covered so far in the interview. The following scheme indicates these areas, but does not cover all possible symptoms.

1. *Digestive system:* eating habits, pica, nausea, vomiting, abdominal pains, constipation, diarrhoea, faecal soiling.
2. *Urinary system:* bedwetting, wetting by day, over-frequent micturition.
3. *Sleep:* problems of going to bed and of sleeping, nightmares, night terrors.
4. *Circulatory and respiratory systems:* breathlessness, cough, palpitations.
5. *Motor system:* restlessness, overactivity, underactivity, clumsiness, abnormal gait, motor weakness, whether right- or left-handed.
6. *Habitual manipulation of the body:* nailbiting, thumbsucking, nose picking, head banging, rocking and similar habits.
7. *Speech:* over talkativeness, mutism, faulty speech of any type, including late development of speech and stuttering, comprehension of what is said.

8. *Thought processes:* poor concentration, distractibility, disordered thought, day dreaming.
9. *Vision and hearing:* any defects, evidence suggesting hallucinations.
10. *Temperamental traits:* rhythmicity, approach/withdrawal, adaptability, intensity of reaction, quality of mood, persistence/attention span, distractibility, reaction threshold (see pages 1 and 21).
11. *Behaviour:* follower or leader, relationship with siblings, parents, teachers, friends. Fearfulness, sensitiveness, tearfulness, sulking, irritability, temper tantrums. Obedience/disobedience, co-operativeness/negativism, constructiveness/destructiveness, truth-fulness/untruthfulness, stealing, wandering from home, staying out late or not, fighting, group or gang membership, smoking, drinking, drug-taking. History of court appearance, probation or placement away from home.
12. *Mood:* whether mood is appropriate or child is depressed, elated, angry, fearful or showing evidence of other mood disturbance. Does the mood vary a lot? If so is this related to environmental circumstances or not?
13. *Fantasy life:* the sort of games the child plays. Does he/she have a lot of imagination? Dreams? Fantasy friends, transitional objects. Content of fantasy expressed through the foregoing, or in drawing, painting, conversation.
14. *Sex:* sex instruction given, sexual attitudes, masturbation, heterosexual or homosexual experiences, onset of menstruation, dysmenorrhoea.
15. *Attack disorders:* epilepsy, fainting, other alterations of consciousness, breath-holding attacks.
16. *School:* attitude to school, behaviour at school, progress in school work, social adjustment at school.

Do not look only for problems, but also note areas of strength and healthy function. When symptoms are reported ask for examples, and note duration, frequency and severity. Observe also how parents describe symptoms: do they try to make light of the child's abnormal behaviour, or describe it in over-dramatic or rejecting terms, and so on? Interviews conducted in this way have been shown to be generally reliable, the main exception being in the area of relationship problems[1].

The next step is to enquire about the child's *developmental history*. This should cover the child's development from the time of conception up to the date of the interview. Information should be obtained about pregnancy; about the child's birth and neonatal condition; about subsequent progress; and about any illnesses and injuries. It is useful to have a description of the child's behaviour as a baby, as a toddler, over the period of starting school and so on, up to the present date. Particular points are the acquisition of motor skills and of speech; toilet training methods and the child's response to them; past family and peer group relationships; and adjustment to school experiences.

Examining the Child

There is no set routine for the psychiatric examination of children. Much depends on the child's age, capacity and willingness to talk, and personality. In children below the age of about five, contact usually has to be largely through the medium of play, though even pre-school age children can sometimes reveal a lot about themselves in conversation. Older children, and especially adolescents, can often be examined rather as adult patients are. In the intermediate age range a mixture of play and conversation is used.

It is seldom the child who is complaining of symptoms, but an adult, usually a parent or teacher, who is either complaining on the child's behalf or more probably is objecting to some feature of the child's behaviour. So it is usually unwise to start the interview by discussing the presenting complaints. Indeed this may be a great mistake; it can cause the child to identify the person carrying out the assessment with other disapproving adults, and so develop a guarded or even suspicious attitude. A trusting relationship will be more difficult to establish.

The first step is to gain the child's confidence rather than to ascertain facts. The child must come to feel respected and valued, with a point of view and opinions that are important to the interviewer. The atmosphere in the consulting room should be relaxed and friendly, but not condescending. Toys, play materials and painting and drawing materials, appropriate to the child's age, should be available and in view. Younger children are best seen in a playroom. It is preferable not to have a desk between child and interviewer. To do so puts the child at a distance and makes *rapport* more difficult to establish.

It should be made plain to younger children that the materials and toys are there for them to play with and use as they choose. Some children do not at first wish to engage in conversation. This must be accepted and they should be allowed to play for a while. A conversation can then often be started while the child plays.

It is best to start talking with children on topics well away from symptom areas, such as how they got to the clinic, their interests and hobbies, games they like to play, any recent birthday, school, friends, siblings and ambitions for the future. If Christmas, Easter, Thanksgiving, a holiday or other such events have occurred recently, this can be discussed. Direct questioning about the symptoms is usually best avoided. The subject may well come up as the interview proceeds; if not, it often does not matter. This is especially so with children who have been engaging in 'antisocial' acts, such as stealing. There is little point in asking, 'Did you steal such-and-such?' The child, if he answers at all, must say yes or no. If yes, the interviewer is none wiser; if no, the child has been forced into the position of withholding information. His relationship with the interviewer will thus have been tarnished, and a barrier to communication erected. Still less should one say 'Why did you steal?' Such a question is futile and it also puts the interviewer, in the child's mind, in the same category as other figures of authority who may have been questioning, lecturing and perhaps punishing him for whatever the problem may have been. While one wishes to discover why the child has been stealing it is naïve to suppose that this can be done simply by asking. Often the child does at some point speak about the particular acts which have led to the referral, but this is a different matter.

The early part of the interview, sometimes the whole of the first session, is thus spent gaining the child's confidence. Once this has been achieved, at least in some measure, it is justifiable to ask, in a general way, what has brought the child to the clinic. An accurate reply is often given, but if not the subject should not be pressed.

Once *rapport* has been established with the child, particular areas may be explored. This should be done gently, using words and in a manner appropriate to the child's age and personality. It is not a matter of asking a series of questions; such an approach seldom gives the desired result. It is more a matter of saying, 'Lots of people have dreams when they are asleep at night ... I wonder if you do?' If the child says he does he can be invited to recount one, and then perhaps asked whether they are mostly nice dreams, or mostly nasty ones. If he says he does not have dreams, or cannot remember them, one could say, 'Often when people who don't have dreams come to see us, they like to make up a dream ... to pretend they've had one ... perhaps you'd like to do that?' This is one way of exploring children's fantasy lives. Another method is to ask them to imagine that they have three magic wishes. One can then go on and say something like, 'Now I'd like you to pretend you were all alone on a desert island (or in a boat) and you could choose one person to be with you ... anyone you like but just one person ... I wonder who you would have?' It is then possible to get the child to choose a second, then a third person.

The interviewer should enquire for fears, worries, and somatic and other symptoms, in a similar way. Conversation about family, friends (whom the child can be asked to name and describe) and school is also encouraged. Throughout this process the interviewer must respond appropriately to what the child is saying, trying to share the child's sorrow at the loss of a pet and pleasure at being a member of a winning football team. Above all it is important to convey interest in the child's point of view. This does not necessarily imply approving of what the child does or thinks.

All children who have not reached adolescence should be invited to draw, paint and/or play with some of the toys. This enables their concentration, attention-span, distractibility and motor dexterity to be assessed. The content of their play may also give helpful information. Adolescents may or may not wish to paint, draw or play but it can usually be judged whether or not it is appropriate to suggest such activities.

By means of an interview such as has been described it should be possible to make an assessment of the following points about the child.

GENERAL APPEARANCE

Is the child's size normal for his age or is he or she larger or smaller than normal? Are there any abnormalities of facial appearance, head, body build or limbs? State of nutrition? Is there any sign of bruises, cuts or grazes? Mode of dress and appropriateness for the climate and time of year? Does child look happy or unhappy, tearful or worried? Attitude to the examiner and the consultation?

MOTOR FUNCTION

Is the child overactive, normal or underactive? Motor activities carried out? Are they done normally or clumsily, quickly or slowly? Are there any abnormal movements such as tics (see page 135)? Right-handed or left-handed? Can child distinguish right from left? Is the gait normal, and if not, in what way is it abnormal? Can child write, draw or paint? (If possible any productions should be preserved for further reference).

SPEECH

Articulation, vocabulary and use of language should be noted. Does the child speak freely, little or not at all (as in mutism)? Is there any stuttering (see page 136)? Receptive and expressive language should be assessed, as well as the child's capacity to read and write.

CONTENT OF TALK AND THOUGHT

What does the child talk about? How easy is it to steer the conversation towards particular topics? Are any subjects avoided? Does the child's stream of thought flow logically from one thing to another? Is there any abnormal use of words or expressions? Any delusions or hallucinations?

INTELLECTUAL FUNCTION

A rough estimate of intelligence should be made, based on the child's general knowledge, conversation and level of play. (This may later be supplemented by administration of intelligence tests – see page 194.) Knowledge of time, day, date, year, place and people's identity, compared with what is normally expected of a child of the age concerned.

MOOD AND EMOTIONAL STATE

Happy, elated, unhappy, frankly depressed, anxious, hostile, resentful, suspicious, upset by separation from parents and so on? Level of *rapport* which can be established with the child. Has the child ever wanted to run away, or to hide, wished to be dead or contemplated suicide? Does he or she ever cry? If so what about? Specific fears and if present how are they dealt with? Appropriateness of emotional state relative to subject being discussed.

ATTITUDES TO FAMILY

Indications during conversation about family members or during play.

ATTITUDES TO SCHOOL

Does the child like school? Attitudes towards school work, play, staff, other pupils? Child's estimate of own abilities and progress in school.

ENQUIRY INTO FANTASY LIFE

What would the child's three magic wishes be? Who would be his most desired companions on a desert island? What sort of dreams are recounted or made up? What is the worst thing – and the best thing – that could happen to the child? Ambitions in life? ... and so on.

SLEEP

Does the child have any difficulty in getting to sleep, with waking during the night or with disturbed sleep of any sort? This can often be enquired about when dreams or nightmares are being discussed.

ATTITUDE TO REFERRAL

How does the child see the referral, and the reasons for it? Is he or she aware of a problem and if so what?

INDICATIONS OF SOCIAL ADJUSTMENT

Number of friends, hobbies, interests, games played, youth organisations belonged to and so on. Does the child feel that he or she is a follower or a leader, or bullied, teased or picked upon? If so, by whom?

OTHER SYMPTOMS

Do any other points come up in conversation, for example, worries, pains, headaches, other somatic symptoms, school problems, relationship difficulties and so on?

PLAY

A general description of the child's mode of play. What is played with and how? To what extent is play symbolic? Content of play. Concentration and constructiveness?

It is often not possible to obtain all this information at the first interview and more is usually obtained in subsequent sessions. Clearly many of the points do not apply in non-speaking children.

Unless the child's physical state has already been assessed or is being investigated by a colleague other than the interviewer, a physical examination should next be carried out. A convenient time to do this is at the end of the first diagnostic interview. With younger children it is helpful to ask the mother to come into the room during the examination and if necessary help undress and dress the child. This has the additional advantage of providing an opportunity to observe interaction between child and parent.

Useful books on interviewing and examining children have been written by Simmons[3], Rich[4] and Goodman and Sours[5], and Rutter and Graham[2] have investigated the reliability and validity of a procedure for interviewing children.

The Family

While the history is being taken, the background of each parent should be explored and at least a brief account obtained of the parents' origins and childhood experiences. The latter largely determine the way parents bring up their own children. An assessment should be made of each parent's personality. It can be useful to ask each of them to make a self-assessment and also to describe their spouse's personality. Enquiry should also be made about any psychiatric or physical illness in the family.

If the parents are interviewed together the way they interact should be noted. Is one of them dominant? If so, to what extent? Are they united about their children or are the children the subject of disagreement between them? What is the nature of the marital relationship?

Parental attitudes are very important. An estimate must be made of how far they are accepting or rejecting, anxious or relaxed, consistent or variable, protective or disinterested, tolerant or intolerant and, above all, loving, towards their children.

FAMILY INTERVIEWS

Increasing use is being made of interviews in which all family members are seen together, usually by one therapist but sometimes by two 'co-therapists'. This approach is the one normally used by family therapists although it need not necessarily be followed by family therapy (see page 222). There are various schools of family therapy, and many techniques and styles of assessment. That which is described here is based on the view that the family is a system (see page 23) and owes much to Minuchin[6] and Haley[7]. Haley gives a particularly clear account of how to conduct a first interview with a family.

The systems-oriented therapist is primarily concerned with the functioning of the family in the here and now. There is less concern with how the present family situation developed or what precipitated the problem. The key to solving the problem is to discover how the present situation is being *maintained*, and to understand what it is about the functioning of the family system that makes it necessary for one or more family members to have symptoms. Thus the focus is away from the historical development of the disturbed individual and away also from intra-psychic processes; instead it is on the individual's current social situation. In this connection it is also relevant to point out that most of the symptoms with which children present are *interpersonal*, that is they are concerned with how they relate to others.

In order to assess how a family system functions it is necessary to join it and participate in its transactions. A family cannot describe its system. The system can only be experienced by the interviewer who at the same time must not lose a sense of objectivity, nor become emotionally involved with the family, which might lead to a situation in which he becomes an ally or sympathiser to one or more members, or a critic or antagonist towards others. It is helpful to approach the process in stages.

1. *The greeting stage.* This consists of a period during which the family are greeted, and made to feel at home in a courteous, friendly and relaxed fashion. Haley[7] recommends, however, that the therapist should note carefully the behaviour of the family, its seating arrangements and mood, who tells whom to do what, who speaks and so on, while at the same time keeping conclusions tentative.

2. *Getting the interview in context.* The interviewer shares with the family his understanding of the purpose of the interview, mentioning any contact there has been with the referral source, as well as explaining about anyone (supervisor or student) who may be watching through a one-way screen. If the interview is being recorded on audiotape or videotape, this also will be mentioned.

3. *The problem stage.* The first two stages will have taken a few minutes at most. This next stage is longer and involves asking the family what the problem is; other ways of putting the question are, 'What has brought you here?' or 'What are the changes you want to achieve?' It is usually best to ask the parents first, then the children. By the end of this stage the therapist should have sought everyone's opinion on each problem that has been voiced and enquired how they have tried to solve the problems. As well as noting the problems mentioned by the family, the therapist should observe how people talk, who takes the lead and non-verbal as well as verbal behaviour.

4. *The interaction stage.* The therapist now drops out of the conversation and allows the family to interact among themselves. It is sometimes necessary to encourage the family actively to do this, and it is better if they can act out their problems as well as talk among themselves. The family's 'structure' and way of functioning will usually become clearer during this period.

5. *Defining the changes that are wanted.* The therapist now reviews with the family the changes desired, and sets up a contract to work towards achieving these changes. It is helpful if all family members assent to the plan, including the identified patient.

6. *Bringing the interview to an end.* The interview ends with the setting of the time for the next appointment, if there are to be more, or discussion of any further investigations or measures that are suggested. The family should leave knowing what is to happen next, including who is to attend any therapy session and at what intervals of time. In addition many therapists give the family a task to do;

this keeps them involved with the therapist and enables therapy to continue between sessions.

It is often possible to complete all the above stages in a single interview of an hour or so, but occasionally a second session will be necessary. Various schemes exist for the assessment of families. Minuchin[6] lists six aspects which should be considered.

1. The family 'structure'. This consists of the arrangements which govern the transactions between members. It is discussed further in Chapter 16.
2. The flexibility of the family's patterns of functioning, and its capacity for change.
3. The family's 'resonance'. This is its sensitivity to the actions of individual members. At one extreme is 'enmeshment', that is, very high sensitivity, where the whole family at once reacts to counter any behaviour that deviates from the family pattern; at the other extreme is 'disengagement', where the sensitivity of the family system is low and there is little or no family reaction to behaviour in one member which deviates from the family pattern
4. The family's life context. This consists of the sources of support and stress in its environment – the extended family, neighbours, housing, work and school environments of family members and so on.
5. The family's developmental stage (see page 14).
6. The ways in which the identified patient's symptoms are used to maintain the family's preferred way of functioning (its 'transactional patterns').

Another method of describing family functioning has been proposed by Santa-Barbara and colleagues[8]. This covers six aspects of family functioning.

1. *Task accomplishment.* It is assumed that the family's main goals are to provide for the social, psychological and biological development and sustenance of family members. Under this heading a rating is made of how well the family does this. Tasks are divided into 'basic', 'developmental' and 'crisis' tasks. Basic tasks are the provision of food, shelter and protection. Developmental ones are associated with the growth of individuals or changes in the family's composition or situation. Crisis tasks are those presented by stresses or traumatic events which threaten the social, psychological or biological functioning of the family or of one or more members.

2. *Communication.* This is the process by which family members exchange information. Communication is assessed according to its sufficiency, clarity and directness. Is enough information communicated? Is the communication clear or masked? Are messages sent directly to those for whom they are intended, or are they sent indirectly, via other members?

3. *Role performance.* This refers to the repetitive sets of behaviours and responsibilities assigned to each family member. Roles may be traditional or idiosyncratic, but should meet the particular needs of each family member, while at the same time enabling the family as a whole to function effectively and without symptoms.

4. *Affective involvement.* This concerns the degree and quality of the emotional involvement which family members have in each other's needs, interests and activities. At one extreme is total absence of involvement, at the other total symbiotic enmeshment of two or more members. In between are interest devoid of feelings, self-centred involvement designed to meet the subject's own needs and empathic involvement of a sincere, consistent and concerned type.

5. *Control.* This is the way in which rules concerning the functioning of the family are maintained. They may be explicit, but many are implicit. They govern how members behave and relate to each other and to the outside community. They may be flexible or rigid and the family may or may not be well organised in a predictable way. It may have 'functional' rules which serve it well, or 'dysfunctional' ones which are ill-adapted to the family's situation. If there is a general lack of organisational control, a chaotic family situation may result.

THE CHOICE OF ASSESSMENT PROCEDURE

A fully comprehensive assessment should include both individual and family interviews. In some cases, however, one or other approach may be all that is necessary. Children being assessed away from their families, as in residential institutions or schools, or for Courts, may be best approached through individual assessments. When a child living at home is referred, especially if the presenting problems are being manifested in the home, a family approach may be more appropriate. In such cases individual interviews with child or parents may be needed later. This will certainly be true if there is evidence of severe psychopathology in one or more of the family members. Conversely when individual interviews are done first, it may often become evident that an assessment of the whole family will be needed later. A comprehensively trained clinician should be able to consider problems from both points of view and to carry out both individual and family interviews.

The Formulation

When the assessment of a child and family is complete, a formulation should be made. This is even more important than putting the child's disorder into a particular diagnostic category. In clinics and treatment centres where staff function as a team, the formulation is usually worked out at a conference attended by all members of the team; the same process should also be carried out by a practitioner working alone.

The formulation is a concise summary of the case in the light of all the information available. It should start with a brief statement of the current problem. This is followed by a description of how the clinician understands the case. It is helpful to look at:

(a) Predisposing factors: what factors in child or family predisposed to the development of the disorder? These can be considered under the headings constitutional (including genetic) factors, physical disease or injury, temperamental factors and environmental factors.
(b) Precipitating factors: did anything precipitate the onset of the problem, if so what? Here again constitutional, physical, temperamental and environmental factors should be considered.
(c) Perpetuating factors: what is maintaining the condition? Again the four headings above need to be considered.
(d) Protective factors: what are the child's and the family's strengths? What factors are limiting the severity of the disorder and assisting in healthy functioning?

The formulation is not just a listing of factors, but a description of their interplay and relative importance. It should be a clearly written, logical, dynamic explanation of the case, leading to a plan of treatment, management or further assessment. It should also give an indication of the expected outcome. It is important that strengths are mentioned as well as weaknesses. Where a 'problem-oriented' or 'goal-oriented' system of clinical recording is used, the formulation should be the basis of the problem and strength lists. It is a good idea to update the formulation from time to time during treatment. A therapist's view of a case usually changes as treatment proceeds. The following is an example of a formulation.

Angela is a reserved, anxious twelve-year-old girl with a three-year history of failure to attend school despite three changes of school arranged by her mother at Angela's insistence. She is a physically fit, pubertal girl who apparently has from birth been a quiet child, slow to adapt to change and overdependent on her mother. The latter has long been unable to resist Angela's demands, and behaves similarly towards Angela's nine-year-old sister who seems, however, to have a more self-assertive personality than Angela, and is developing more independence than her sister. Before the onset of school refusal Angela did well at school and she appears to be of above average intelligence. Non-attendance was precipitated by a change to a stricter, male teacher and a period of illness in mother. Now attempts to get Angela to school result in panic and an acute exacerbation of anxiety symptoms. She has, however, a keen interest in horses and attends riding school on her own.

Mother and the two daughters have a close enmeshed relationship with each other; there is a clear boundary between their family subsystem and father, who makes little contribution to the bringing up of the children and said little during a family interview. He spent much of his childhood in a children's home. The whole family needs support over sending Angela to school. At the same time the relationship between the parents requires to be strengthened, and boundaries must be delineated between the parents on the one hand and the two daughters on the other.

Although the problem is a longstanding one, the parents are strongly motivated to receive help and are concerned about Angela's prolonged lack of education. In addition Angela is a physically healthy girl of above average intelligence whose progress when in school is good. She also has some other interests outside the home, notably horse-riding. With treatment, which will have to deal with the family as a whole as well as with Angela's school attendance problem, substantial improvement seems possible. Angela may require some individual therapy and it is possible that a period of inpatient treatment will be of help.

Using the multi-axial classification described in Chapter 2 the diagnosis would have been as follows:

1st Axis: Neurotic disorder: anxiety state
2nd Axis: No specific delay in development
3rd Axis: Normal intelligence
4th Axis: No associated medical condition
5th Axis: Familial over-involvement (referring to the over-involvement of mother and Angela)
          Inadequate or distorted intra-familial communications (referring to lack of communication between parents)

It will be seen that the formulation gives considerably more information than even the 5-axis diagnostic scheme. On the other hand, being a free-flowing literary vignette, it is not suitable for statistical analysis nor for grouping disorders together for research or clinical purposes.

References

1. Graham, P. and Rutter, M. 'The reliability and validity of the psychiatric assessment of the child: 2. Interview with the parent'. *British Journal of Psychiatry*, **114**, 581–592, 1968.
2. Rutter, M. and Graham, P. 'The reliability and validity of the psychiatric assessment of the child: 1. Interview with the child'. *British Journal of Psychiatry*, **114**, 563–579, 1968.
3. Simmons, J. E. *Psychiatric Examination of Children*, 2nd edition. Philadelphia: Lea and Febiger, 1974.
4. Rich, J. *Interviewing Children and Adolescents*. Toronto: Macmillan, 1968.
5. Goodman, J. D. and Sours, J. A. *The Child Mental Status Examination*. New York: Basic Books, 1967.
6. Minuchin, S. *Families and Family Therapy*. Cambridge, Mass.: Harvard University Press, 1974.
7. Haley, J. *Problem Solving Therapy*. San Francisco: Jossey-Bass, 1977.
8. Santa-Barbara, J., Steinhauer, P. and Skinner, H. 'A process model of family functioning'. In press.

CHAPTER FOUR

Conduct Disorders

Conduct disorders are characterised by antisocial behaviour. The ninth edition of the *International Classification of Diseases*[1] defined 'disturbances of conduct not elsewhere classified' (code 312) as being disorders 'involving aggressive and destructive behaviour and involving delinquency'. The behaviour should not be part of some other psychiatric disorder such as a neurotic disorder (see Chapter 5) or a psychosis (Chapter 6), but 'minor emotional disturbance' may be present.

A useful definition of conduct disorder is that of Wardle[2], who uses the term for disorders in which:

(a) The behaviour is socially disapproved.
(b) The behaviour includes 'acting-out' against people or property.
(c) The behaviour is persistent and fails to respond to normal sanctions.

In the classification proposed by the Group for the Advancement of Psychiatry (GAP) (see page 29), disturbances of conduct are not given a separate category. Most fall either in the 'reactive disorder' group or among the 'personality disorder' categories, though in a few cases where brain damage is prominent the 'brain syndrome' category might apply. This situation arises largely because the GAP scheme does not have axes dealing separately with clinical syndromes and with aetiological factors.

Prevalence

Conduct disorders are the largest single group of psychiatric disorders in older children and adolescents. Satisfactory epidemiological data are lacking for younger children. In the Isle of Wight Survey[3] nearly two-thirds of the 10- and 11-year-olds with psychiatric disorder had conduct disorders. When the children with mixed neurotic and conduct disorders were included, the prevalence of conduct problems was 4 per cent. In the London borough studied later it was 12 per cent[4]. Leslie's survey of adolescents in Blackburn showed prevalence rates of 13 per cent for boys and 6 per cent for girls, on the basis of the sample seen by the psychiatrist[5].

As the prevalence figures indicate, conduct disorders are commoner in boys than in girls, and this is reflected in referrals to psychiatric clinics, appearances in juvenile courts and numbers in residential treatment and correctional settings.

Causes

Conduct disorder may represent a failure of the child to reach a normal adjustment within the family, or the family may be one that has itself failed to make a satisfactory adjustment in the wider community of which it is part. Children who lack a permanent family group, or its equivalent, are also particularly at risk. For example, those who have been moved repeatedly from one home to another, or who lived in large impersonal orphanages, are likely to have special difficulty in acquiring socially desired standards of behaviour. This is partly because they lack consistent, permanent and stable parent figures with whom to identify. It has been shown that children who have been 'in care' earlier in childhood show significantly more deviant behaviour later in childhood, and that this most often takes the form of antisocial behaviour[6].   unstable family life | institutionalised.

It has been suggested that failure of early 'bonding' between mother and child may be a factor in causing the later development of antisocial behaviour. Since the development of socially acceptable behaviour is thought to be dependent on the development of secure, loving relationships between children and their parents (or parent-substitutes), the possible role of early bonding failure has been much discussed. Bowlby's theories concerning attachment (see pages 2 to 4), and the work of Winnicott, Dockar-Drysdale and Balbernie (see pages 133 to 134) are relevant here. Rutter has also discussed helpfully the formation of bonds and the ways in which failure to form them may cause disorders in children[7].

Factors in the child are important too. Some children are easier to bring up than others. An extreme example of a child difficult to bring up to behave in an entirely socially acceptable way would be one who was seriously brain-damaged and mentally retarded. Such a child would not have the neurological capacities needed to become a normally socially adapted individual. The vast majority of children with conduct disorders do not, however, show evidence of either brain damage or mental retardation. But, as mentioned in Chapters 1 and 2, there are constitutional and temperamental differences between children, which affect how easy they are to raise[8]. The compatibility of a child's temperament and the temperaments of the parents is probably also important.

Antisocial behaviour *is* commoner in children with brain damage and with epilepsy, though in epileptic children the reaction of others to the fits, and the effects of medication (especially phenobarbitone – see page 229), seem sometimes to be the main factors. Thus when one child develops a conduct disorder and another does not, the reason may not lie entirely, mainly or even at all in different upbringing or parental attitudes. Too great an effort to explain the differences in terms of the children's respective environments may lead to an incorrect diagnosis.

Environment is none the less very important. The more stable, secure, accepting and consistent the family, the greater the chance of the child identifying with the parents and behaving as they wish – and as they do. Within the family, desired behaviour is normally encouraged verbally or in other ways, while undesired behaviour is discouraged or punished. Very often it is a matter of a smile or word of approval from mother, or a frown or an expression of disapproval. Sometimes more forceful methods, including corporal punishment are used. The important points are that there should be consistent responses from people with whom the child has a good relationship; a prompt response is helpful too. The younger the child, the more important promptness seems to be.

The type of reward also matters. Normally the parents' attention or approval are effective ways of reinforcing behaviour, while the withholding of attention and approval have the reverse effect. This seems to be because the parents' attention and smiles have become associated early on with more basic – or primary – reinforcers such as food. In children who have had unusual backgrounds, for example those who have lacked a constant mother-figure, social training may be more difficult. Nevertheless their behaviour is governed largely by the responses their actions stimulate. It may be that they only get consistent, approving attention from members of a delinquent gang when they indulge in antisocial behaviour. This influence may be stronger than that of an unstable, disorganised family.

Rejecting attitudes are often found in the parents of children with conduct disorders. These children have also been found to come from broken families significantly more often than neurotic children. Indeed broken homes have been found more often in the grandparents' generation too[9], and parents tend to bring their children up in the same way they themselves were brought up as children. Their own childhood experiences provide their internal model of parenthood. Rejection, lack of love and instability all militate against effective social training and against conscience formation in the child. The process can be self-perpetuating, the child's antisocial behaviour causing the adverse parental attitudes to be intensified.

Other factors can contribute to the development of aggressive and antisocial behaviour. Fatherless households in which are to be found one-tenth of the children in the USA, tend to be associated with aggressive and antisocial behaviour in boys[10]. This may be due to the mechanism of reaction formation (see page 6) in boys who are concerned about their masculinity. Even in institutionalised boys, it seems that lack of contact with the father makes antisocial behaviour more likely, whereas in girls a more important factor seems to be prolonged early experience of residential care[11]. Large family size is also associated with an increased probability of antisocial behaviour in the children[3]. There is an association with social class, and even at age seven, lower class children have been shown to be more aggressive and destructive than middle class children[12]. This may be due in part to different child rearing patterns. Neighbourhood and school also play their part. The existence of 'delinquent neighbourhoods' where antisocial behaviour is the cultural norm is well established[13]. It is also clear that, even allowing for differences in intake, some schools have a much higher prevalence of antisocial behaviour in their pupils than others[13,14]. This seems to be a function of their qualities as social institutions.

Another way of looking at the causes of conduct disorders in children is to use the approach of systems theory (see page 23). This seeks to explain the behaviour of individual family members in terms of this functioning of the family system, that is, its boundaries, rules, sub-system patterns and other features. An example of a severely dysfunctional family is the following.

Robin, aged eleven, had had long periods of treatment in two child psychiatric units because of his aggressive, disobedient, restless and generally difficult behaviour. When he, his two brothers, his sister and his parents were seen as a group, chaos was evident. Everyone spoke, or more usually shouted, at once and nobody seemed to be listening to what anybody else was saying. Instructions by the parents were ignored by the children: the mother was more active in issuing orders than father, who seemed to be in semi-retirement from the fray, but neither parent appeared to expect to be obeyed. All family members competed on apparently equal terms. There was no differentiated parental system, and no clear boundary between parents and children. Robin had become the identified patient perhaps because, as a big, strong, active and outgoing boy for his age, his antisocial behaviour was more threatening than that of the others. But the behaviour of the other children was little different. Only if the family changed could Robin or the others, change – unless they were removed to live long-term elsewhere, that is, in a different system.

When the family is investigated as a system, antisocial behaviour in one member may emerge as an important factor in keeping the family, or the parents, together. It may be found that the identified patient's misdeeds are the main topic of conversation and the principal focus of mutual concern. The symptoms are needed to maintain the family's precarious stability. There may however be severe problems in such areas as communication, role behaviour, organizational control or affective involvement (see page 44); if these can be cleared up the identified patient's symptoms often disappear.

A 'systems' diagnosis and the types of causes listed earlier are not mutually exclusive. For example, a boy with certain temperamental characteristics may be better suited to the role of 'scapegoat' than the other children, or a dysfunctional family system may be more likely if father is absent. Similarly where the family, or a part of it, is also part of a dysfunctional school or neighbourhood system, disorder in one of the children may be more likely.

The value of a systems approach is that it offers a rational and practical method of treatment. A therapist can often, by joining the system and then using himself to change its way of functioning, bring about some improvement (see pages 222 to 226). On the other hand the elucidation of some other causes, while no less valid, may be less useful as a basis for therapy.

Description

The symptoms of a conduct disorder most often start within the family group. Early symptoms may be stealing, lying, disobedience and verbally or physically aggressive behaviour towards other family members. As the condition worsens these symptoms may spread and be manifest outside the family, notably at school but also in the neighbourhood. The child may play truant from school, stay out late, engage in frank delinquency (housebreaking, stealing from shops and cars and so on), run away from home and commit acts of vandalism. Failure in schoolwork often accompanies conduct disorders, the child's hostile attitude to the adult world manifesting itself in refusal to take part in the activities of the school.

Conduct disorder symptoms do not always appear first within the family group. In adolescence especially they may appear when the child becomes involved in the activities of an adolescent gang. But even when symptoms are mainly, or entirely, manifest in such a setting there are often relationship difficulties within the family.

The ninth edition of the *International Classification of Diseases* distinguishes 'unsocialised' and 'socialised' disturbances of conduct. Symptoms of the former include disobedience, quarrelsomeness, aggression, destructive behaviour, tantrums, solitary stealing, lying, teasing, bullying, disturbed relationships with others and sexual misconduct. Related to this behaviour is the 'runaway reaction'[15]. In these families parental rejection of the child and severe and inconsistent behaviour are typical. By contrast, socialised disorders of conduct also called the 'group delinquent reaction' by Jenkins[15], occur in individuals who have adopted 'the values or behaviour of a delinquent peer group to whom they are loyal'. In company with this group they may steal, play truant, stay out late, or engage in group delinquency or sexually promiscuous behaviour.

A study in a Japanese population of problem children[16] confirmed the presence of a group in which there were 'association with undesirable company, co-operative stealing and gang activities' (the 'socialised delinquent') and another group with aggressive characteristics, such as quarrelsomeness, bravado, rudeness towards those in authority, fights and malicious mischief (the 'unsocialised aggressive type'). Also distinguished were an 'over-inhibited type', and an 'unstable type', which seemed to have some characteristics of the hyperkinetic syndrome (page 120).

Truancy often accompanies other antisocial behaviour. It is different from school refusal in which neurotic anxiety prevents the child getting to school. The truant is not prevented by anxiety, but by a stronger desire to do something else – for example, play in the park or just sit at home playing or watching television. In one common form the child leaves home, and returns there, at the appropriate times but without having attended school. The parents think he is at school, and the school staff often conclude he is sick. It is surprising how long this can sometimes continue. If both parents work during the day the child may sit at home unknown to them, ignoring anyone from the school who comes to the house, and even destroying notes from the school. Some parents show little interest in ensuring that the child attends school, and do not regard school and its benefits as important. Sometimes the parents actively encourage the truancy, perhaps to have help with housework or shopping, or with feeding the baby. Most truants are poor pupils at school (unlike school refusers who usually have good academic records), and their consequent failure to get satisfaction from school work is an additional factor in discouraging attendance. They tend to come from materially and culturally impoverished homes, a further contrast to school refusers.

Stealing is another common symptom. Like other features of conduct disorders, it only becomes abnormal when severe and persistent, and particularly when it is resistant to parental attempts to stop it. Certainly the vast majority of children take other people's property at one time or another. Persistent failure to respect the possessions of others is, however, a sign that psychological development is not proceeding smoothly. It is often associated with rejecting, inconsistent or indifferent parental attitudes.

As well as looking at child and family in these cases, it is also of interest to look at the stealing itself. Rich[17] classified the stealing of a group of boys in the following way.

(a) *Proving offences* tend to be attempts at self-reassurance rather than at obtaining the approval or admiration of the offender's group. The individual is trying to prove to himself his toughness or manhood. The offences are carried out alone and the stolen goods are exhibited; or a symbol of dominance such as a gun or racing bicycle is stolen; or the boy may be obviously showing off as in the common offence of taking and driving away a motor vehicle.

(b) *Marauding offences* are unplanned or semi-planned acts carried out by the three or more boys. In such a group it would be understood that an opportunity for theft would be taken. There is often considerable risk of detection.

(c) *Comforting offences* represent, in varying proportion, a substitute for affection in a deprived child and an expression of resentment against those depriving him. They include stealing from parents and impulsive stealing alone or with one other boy.

(d) *Secondary offences* are planned thefts, alone or with others, with definite objectives and reasonable precautions against detection.

In addition to the foregoing types, Rich distinguished a small group of 'other' offences, for example, stealing under parents' instructions, stealing food after having run away from home and stealing things needed by a sick parent.

This classification is only one of many that have been applied to delinquent activities of various sorts. Its main value is in underlining that the nature and type of a delinquent act (and indeed of any conduct disorder symptom) are themselves important in diagnosis.

Aggressive behaviour is a common cause of referral to child psychiatric clinics. It often occurs along with other conduct disorder symptoms. It can complicate the hyperkinetic syndrome, of which poor impulse control may be a feature (see page 120). Aggression often presents as temper tantrums.

Disapproved sexual behaviour may be one symptom, or even the main one, of a conduct disorder. Masturbation is so common as to be normal, as is sexual curiosity and an interest in the anatomy of the other sex. These may both be present in exaggerated form, or they may be manifested in a socially unacceptable, and perhaps unduly public, way. Sexual intercourse at an early age is another manifestation of failure to accept the pattern of behaviour laid down by the adult world. In most countries it is a criminal offence to have sexual intercourse with a girl who is below a certain age (in Britain sixteen). While there may be no abnormality of psychosexual development, when boys or girls below sixteen are discovered to have had intercourse it is often regarded as indicating the need for special care or treatment.

There is a marked association between retardation in reading and antisocial behaviour in children[3]. This applies to reading retardation generally but also to specific reading retardation, that is retardation greater than would be expected taking into account the child's age and intelligence quotient (see page 194). In the Isle of Wight study[3] one quarter of the children with specific reading retardation showed antisocial behaviour, a very significantly larger percentage than in the general child population. The reasons for the association are not certainly established, but it is probable that many of the factors leading to antisocial behaviour also predispose to failure to learn to read – that is large family size, depriving and disturbed families and adverse temperamental factors in the child. In addition failure in as basic a subject as reading may adversely affect a child's school adjustment; and conversely disturbed and antisocial behaviour in school may impair the learning process.

The following is an example of a severe conduct disorder, which had led on to frank delinquency by the time of first referral for psychiatric assessment.

Paul was referred at the age of ten. He was reported to be one of a group of boys who had been staying out late, damaging public telephones, stealing from cars and breaking into shops and a school. He had also been truanting from school. His school attendance had been poor for two years, his school progress was well below average, he was usually badly dressed and dirty and he was considered a hostile and unco-operative pupil. A few weeks earlier he had been placed in the care of the local authority by the juvenile court as beyond his parents' control.

At interview Paul answered questions guardedly and made no spontaneous conversation. He spoke in a matter-of-fact way and showed little emotion. He said he did not like either of the schools he had attended, and referred quite freely to his truancy and to having stayed out for periods of up to two days and nights, during which he said he and his friends slept rough. He showed little evidence of any affection for his parents, though he looked perhaps a little unhappy when speaking of how they argued. He said that on a desert island he would have three of his friends. His 'three wishes' were to go to London, to have a bicycle and go to Blackpool. His only ambition seemed to be membership of a pop group. Testing him showed him to be of low average intelligence, with marked retardation in both reading and arithmetic.

The parents' marriage had been far from happy. The parents had been separated for several short periods following rows. Father had also served a short prison sentence a few years previously. During this period mother had lived with another man and become pregnant by him, though this boy (aged four when Paul was referred) was accepted into the parents' household. An older brother had been educated in a residential school for disturbed children since the age of eight; he had been placed there because of repeated stealing and truancy.

Throughout Paul's childhood the parents' marriage had been precarious, he had had no secure and consistent background for his emotional development and the parents had failed to set for him, or to demonstrate, any clear example of socially acceptable behaviour. Little interest was taken in his schooling, and indeed the parents were so preoccupied with their own problems that they had little time at all for Paul, who grew up insecure and without any strong relationship with anyone. He came to get most satisfaction from relationships with a delinquent gang, but mainly he lived for the moment. After full investigation, a recommendation was made that he should be placed in a residential school, to return to live at home during school holidays. Simultaneously a social worker undertook to try to give some help and support to the family, though the difficulty of doing so was recognised.

COMMENT

Paul had throughout his childhood been deprived of a stable, dependable background. He had lacked the relationships needed for normal psychological development. Apart from his rather dull intelligence (perhaps in part a consequence of his deprived background) there was no evidence of constitutional abnormality to account for his deviant development. In a more stable family he would probably have developed more normally, and indeed response to the treatment outlined above was good. His was a case of unsocialised conduct disorder. Paul has now left school and, at follow-up, was well settled working in a factory.

Juvenile delinquency has already been referred to as a more severe form of conduct disorder. The point of progression to delinquency is arbitrary. Delinquency is usually taken to mean the commission of acts which are against the law and which could thus lead to police action. Alternatively, it has been defined as behaviour actually leading to appearance in court; but with the tendency to revise upwards the age of 'criminal responsibility', and the increasing use of other methods of dealing with children who break the law, this definition is of diminishing usefulness. Moreover, only a small proportion of individuals committing offences are brought to the attention of courts[18].

Most boys who will later be convicted of delinquent acts can be distinguished by their trouble-making behaviour when aged between 8 and 10[19]. Those that do fall foul of the law seem to be a special group distinguished, among other things, by the persistence of their delinquent behaviour.

Vandalism, the wanton damage to or destruction of property, is a form of delinquency that seems to be on the increase. It is often a group activity of adolescents. Whether done by a group or by an individual, it is usually a means of expressing hostile, aggressive feelings towards the adult world. These feelings often stem from a similarly disturbed relationship with the parents. In the child whose emotional development is following a healthy course, aggressive instincts are channelled into constructive activities (or 'sublimated'). Failure of such sublimation tends to be due to faulty relationships and identifications. Social factors may operate also; in many areas, especially urban ones, there are too few outlets available for the energies of young people. The influence of antisocially inclined groups can be important, the pressure to conform with other members causing some of their number to commit destructive acts in which they would not otherwise engage. Closely related to vandalism is the raising of false alarms, for example sending for the fire brigade to attend a nonexistent fire. All these behaviours are common in socialised disorders of conduct but may occur also in the unsocialised variety.

Fire-setting and *fire-raising* are less common but serious symptoms. Many children go through a phase of playing with matches and lighting fires but this responds to parental training and precept. Children who instead progress to starting fires at home, at school or elsewhere, are often expressing severe, deep-seated feelings of aggression arising from disturbed relationships with their parents.

One study of 860 child psychiatric outpatients showed that fire-setting occurred in 2–3 per cent[20]. Most of the children were referred because of impulsive behaviour such as stealing and disruptive behaviour at school. Their peer relationships were poor, the families tended to be severely disturbed and father absence was common; indeed in no case was a stable, effective father present in the home. Fire-setting appears to be an overwhelmingly male symptom, 19 out of the 20 children in this study of prepubertal children being boys.

The ninth edition of the ICD also includes a sub-category of conduct problems, described as 'mixed disturbance of conduct and emotions'. Children with this group of disorders show conduct disorder symptoms, combined with considerable neurotic anxiety, expressed either overtly or through any of the other symptoms described in Chapter 5. In the Isle of Wight study[3] it was shown that these 'mixed' cases had more in common with the antisocial group (most of whom had some neurotic symptoms) than with the neurotic group (who mostly did not have antisocial symptoms). This applied to sex ratio, family size and association with reading retardation. It probably applies also to treatment needs and results. Nevertheless, these children may be especially handicapped in that they have, very often, neurotically anxious families as well as unstable, disorganised or rejecting ones.

Treatment

As far as they are reactions to unfavourable and unhappy social, especially family circumstances, conduct disorders should ideally be treated by alteration of such circumstances. The problem is thus more one of work with the family, than of treatment of the child. This is well illustrated by the case of Paul (page 55), where the limitations of an approach confined mainly or wholly to treatment of the child are obvious. Paul's was a family problem, and if he was to change the family needed to change also.

Because of the complex causation of many conduct disorders, careful diagnosis is necessary to identify the important social, educational, medical and psychiatric factors in child and family.

In deciding upon the treatment needed, the structure and functioning of the family, the parental attitudes towards the child, the prospects of altering the family, the presence of psychiatric disorder in the parents (depression is often present), the role of temperamental and educational factors in the child and the duration and severity of the problems are important points. The less disturbed and better functioning the family, the greater the need to look for factors in the child, including possible associated problems like depression, neurotic disorder, epilepsy or brain damage. Another crucial matter is the degree of active co-operation which can be obtained from the family. Finally, the child's personality development to date, and the quality of his relationships and identifications, are important.

Having made such an assessment the treatment needs are usually fairly clear. Many milder problems can be dealt with a minor intervention. Indeed some conduct disorders subside without treatment. They may be little more than a testing-out of the limits of behaviour which are allowed. Commonsense advice to the parents about consistent and firm, but accepting, treatment may be all that is needed. On the other hand the repairing of family relationships in severe cases may be a difficult and/or even an impossible task. The parents may be emotionally immature, unhappily married and of limited intelligence, making effective help difficult to give. Many families are also burdened with other problems like poor housing and an inadequate income. There is a continuum from the family with only minor problems requiring brief counselling, through to those that are most severely socially and emotionally handicapped.

Where family problems are prominent, an approach by family therapy may be the best way of helping the child. This is especially so when assessment of the family suggests that the child's antisocial behaviour can be understood as a symptom of a dysfunctional family system. This is very often the case. Family therapy is discussed further in Chapter 16. Sometimes a more traditional social casework approach is better; this also is discussed further in Chapter 16.

Individual psychotherapy for children with conduct disorders has generally poor results, though in some individual cases, where there is evident psychopathology in the child, it appears to help.

Behaviour therapy, also described in Chapter 16, does seem to have a useful role in treatment. The persistent positive reinforcement of acceptable behaviour, combined with no response, or in some programmes a negative response, to undesired behaviour can be effective in school classrooms, day treatment programmes and residential settings. Sometimes parents can support the professionals treating the child by employing the same techniques at home.

Group therapy (see page 226) may be of help, and in socialised disorders of conduct treatment programmes which use peer pressure are often beneficial. The concept of a therapeutic community, which can be used in day and residential treatment programmes, aims to bring group pressure to bear on individuals displaying deviant behaviour.

Related to this are programmes using positive peer culture (see page 236).

When a conduct disorder is severe and persistent, the child's development is going seriously awry, and treatment of the family is impossible or ineffective, residential placement away from home may be best. This should never be decided on lightly or without careful assessment, but sometimes a period in a residential treatment centre[2] or school, group home or foster home, or special therapeutic family placement (see page 237) offers the best prospect for the child.

In the treatment of truancy similar considerations apply. If the wider family problem can be solved the child will return to school; but if it cannot, or if it can only be expected to improve slowly, specific efforts must be made to get the child back to school. Indeed a direct, energetic attempt to overcome the truancy is usually advisable. Increased pressure to attend should be brought to bear directly on the child, and through the parents. Close liaison between school and parents is vital so that further absence is discovered at once and prompt and vigorous action taken. The threat of court proceedings, or their actual institution, may be justified and helpful. In some cases, however, the truancy is unconsciously or consciously motivated by the child's desire to get away from an unhappy situation. Antisocial behaviour which is so motivated may continue until this is achieved. If there is an associated educational problem, as there often is, this too should be tackled. If special help over seriously retarded reading or arithmetic is being given, the child's interest in attending may be much increased.

The treatment of severely deprived children presents special problems. Some children who have suffered severe emotional deprivation in early childhood, or through a long period of their childhood, lack the capacity to form deep and satisfying emotional relationships. Neither psychotherapy nor a simple change of environment is likely to be effective. The best hope of cure sometimes lies in a long period of treatment in a specialised residential setting (see page 234). Theoretically a good foster home might be better still, but few foster parents have the resources to cope with such children, from whom they may get little response over a long period. Moreover, failure and rejection from the foster home would be a further adverse experience for the child. Some recent schemes have, however, been specially devised to select suitable alternative families, who are given continuing professional and group support[21,22,23]. These schemes seem to offer a prospect of helping some children.

Drug treatment has little part in the treatment of conduct disorders, unless there is an associated condition such as epilepsy, depression, severe anxiety or hyperkinetic behaviour. Occasionally the use of tranquillisers may be needed to control acutely disturbed or violent behaviour in these children, on a short-term basis (see page 231).

Outcome

Most minor, and some major, conduct disorders clear up without psychiatric or other treatment. Much depends on the stability of the family, parental attitudes, the willingness of the family to participate in treatment, the child's personality and capacity to form relationships and identifications, and any physical, intellectual or educational handicaps affecting the child. Children with severe conduct disorders, if not successfully treated, tend as adults to have a high incidence of psychiatric illness and often show antisocial and criminal behaviour[24]. Such individuals often have difficulty in making stable marriages, and thus put the next generation at risk also.

References

1. World Health Organisation. *International Classification of Diseases.* 1975 Revision. Geneva: WHO, 1977.
2. Wardle, C. J. 'Residential care of children with conduct disorders' (page 50). In *The Residential Psychiatric Treatment of Children*, ed. P. Barker. London: Crosby Lockwood Staples, 1974.
3. Rutter, M., Tizard, J. and Whitmore, K. *Education, Health and Behaviour.* London: Longman, 1970.
4. Rutter, M. 'Why are London children so disturbed?' *Proceedings of the Royal Society of Medicine*, **66**, 1221–1225, 1973.
5. Leslie, S. A. 'Psychiatric disorders in the young adolescent of an industrial town'. *British Journal of Psychiatry*, **125**, 113–124, 1974.
6. Wolkind, S. and Rutter, M. 'Children who have been "in care" – an epidemiological study'. *Journal of Child Psychology and Psychiatry*, **14**, 97–105, 1973.
7. Rutter, M. *Maternal Deprivation Reassessed.* Hardmonsworth: Penguin, 1972.
8. Thomas, A., Chess, S. and Birch, H. G. *Temperament and Behaviour Disorders in Children.* New York University Press, 1968.
9. Wardle, C. J. 'Two generations of broken homes in the genesis of conduct and behaviour disorders in children'. *British Medical Journal*, **2**, 349–354, 1961.
10. Biller, H. B. 'Father absence and the personality development of the male child'. *Developmental Psychology*, **2**, 181–201, 1970.
11. Wolkind, S. N. 'Sex differences in the aetiology of antisocial disorder in children'. *British Journal of Psychiatry*, **125**, 125–130, 1974.
12. Newson, J. and Newson, E. *Seven Years Old in the Home Environment*, London: Allen and Unwin, 1976.
13. Power, M. J., Benn, R. T. and Morris, J. N., 'Neighbourhood, school and juveniles before the courts'. *British Journal of Criminology*, **12**, 111–132, 1972.
14. Rutter, M. 'Invulnerability or why some children are not damaged by stress'.

In *New Directions in Children's Mental Health*, ed. S. J. Shamsie. New York: Spectrum, 1979.

15. Jenkins, R. L., 'Classification of behaviour problems of children'. *American Journal of Psychiatry*, **125**, 1032–1039, 1969.
16. Kobayashi, S., Mizushima, K. and Shinopara, M. 'Clinical groupings of problem children based on symptoms and behaviour'. *International Journal of Social Psychiatry*, **13**, 206–215, 1967.
17. Rich, J. 'Types of Stealing'. *Lancet*, **1**, 496–498, 1956.
18. Hood, R. and Sparks, R. *Key Issues in Criminology*. London: Weidenfeld and Nicolson, 1970.
19. West, D. J. and Farrington, D. P. *Who Becomes Delinquent?* London: Heinemann, 1973.
20. Vandersall, J. A. and Wiener, J. M. 'Children who set fires'. *Archives of General Psychiatry*, **22**, 63–71, 1970.
21. Rubinstein, J. S. 'Institutions without walls for emotionally disturbed children'. *Hospital and Community Psychiatry*, **28**, 849–851, 1977.
22. Hazel, N. 'How family placements can combat delinquency'. *Social Work Today*, **8**, 6–7, 1977.
23. Barker, P., Buffe, C. and Zaretsky, R. 'Providing a family alternative for the disturbed child'. *Child Welfare*, **57**, 373–379, 1978.
24. Robins, L. N. *Deviant Children Grown Up*. Baltimore: Williams and Watkins, 1966.

CHAPTER FIVE

Neurotic Disorders

Neurotic disorders are morbidly anxious reactions to stress, though sometimes the stress is slight. They are not associated with disordered perception of, or relation to, the environment as in psychosis. The concept of neurosis derived originally from the study of disorders occurring in adult patients, and some authors, for example Hersov[1], prefer the term 'emotional disorder'. This is because many of these disorders in childhood are relatively undifferentiated, and milder, compared with the neuroses commonly seen in adults.

The ninth edition of the *International Classification of Diseases* (ICD)[2], attempts to overcome this problem by having a category for 'neurotic disorders' and another for disturbance of emotions specific to childhood and adolescence, so that the clinician can make a choice. The latter are defined as 'less well differentiated emotional disorders characteristic of the childhood period', and there are the following sub-categories:

(a) With anxiety and fearfulness.
(b) With misery and unhappiness.
(c) With sensitivity, shyness and social withdrawal.
(d) Relationship problems.
(e) Other or mixed.

While the distinction between 'neurotic' and 'emotional' disorders may be helpful, it can be difficult to make and in this chapter the two will be discussed as a single group.

The Group for the Advancement of Psychiatry's classification[3] has a category for 'psychoneurotic disorders'. This covers 'those disorders based on unconscious conflicts over the handling of sexual and aggressive impulses which, though removed from awareness by the mechanism of repression, remain active and unresolved'. This definition thus implies a specific psychopathological cause for the disorder. While it is often hard to prove that these disorders are due to unconscious conflicts of the sort mentioned, it is clear that the disorders referred to in this category approximate closely to the 'neurotic disorders' of the ninth edition of the ICD.

All of us are anxious from time to time, and it is natural for a child to be anxious, for example, when going to a new school or meeting an unfamiliar adult. The normal child in such circumstances shows anxiety no greater than the situation merits, and is not overwhelmed by the anxiety. The neurotic or emotionally disordered child, by contrast, shows excessive anxiety in a variety of circumstances. To justify a diagnosis of neurotic or emotional disorder, the anxiety should be severe and persistent and interfere in some way with the individual's adjustment in society. It is not necessarily directly expressed, but may instead be dealt with in part by the various mental mechanisms or defences mentioned in Chapter 1 (pages 6 to 8).

Prevalence

Epidemiological studies show that neurotic disorders are the second commonest group of psychiatric disorders of childhood. In the Isle of Wight study (page 30) a prevalence rate of 2·5 per cent was found in the 10- and 11-year-olds studied, about half the rate for conduct disorders. In the Inner London Borough (page 30) later studied, a prevalence rate twice that in the Isle of Wight was found. In Leslie's study of teenagers in Blackburn (page 30) conduct disorders occurred twice as commonly as neurotic disorders among boys, though a slightly larger number of the girls were diagnosed as neurotic.

Causes

The threshold for the development of neurotic anxiety varies from individual to individual. Some people develop neurotic symptoms only under great stress. Others develop them in response to everyday living. This variation in vulnerability is due in part to constitutional factors; previous experience is also important in determining a child's level of emotional development and tolerance of emotional stress. Examples of questions which are relevant are: How much has the child been allowed to mix with other children or to make decisions for himself or herself? Has too much been done and decided for the child? How secure is the child's relationship with the rest of the family? These, and other related factors, all affect children's capacity to cope with particular situations. So does the degree to which they have been brought up by anxious, worrying parents, perhaps themselves suffering from neurosis. If children are identified with parents who themselves see the world as an anxious place in which they do not feel secure, they will tend to see it the same way.

The concept of emotional maturity is helpful. At any particular age, the normal child has learnt to cope with a range of emotionally stressful situations, and the extent to which the child can deal with stress without becoming excessively anxious is one measure of his emotional maturity. Childhood should be a process of progressively decreasing dependence on parents, as the child learns to cope with more and more challenges without outside support. When this process has been slowed up, halted or even reversed, a neurotic disorder is likely to appear. Children who are faced with more anxiety and stress than they can cope with may regress to an earlier stage of development. The symptoms often express the child's conflicts in a symbolic way. 'Fixation points', a concept discussed more fully by Anna Freud in *Normality and Pathology in Childhood*[4], are points at which psychosexual development is held up. This may result from excessive frustration, excessive gratification or a traumatic experience. The point at which fixation occurs depends on development to date: fixation will normally occur where a developmental phase has not been successfully negotiated and the relevant conflicts resolved.

According to psychodynamic theory, consciously felt anxiety is always due in part, and often almost entirely, to causes of which the child is unaware at the conscious level. The repressed conflicts are considered by psychoanalysts to be concerned with difficulties over the handling of sexual and aggressive impulses[4]. Such difficulties are likely to have arisen in children who have experienced unsatisfactory and insecure relationships with their parents, especially during their first five years. The normal processes of development outlined in Chapter 1 have been distorted. The anxiety and guilt aroused by the Oedipal conflict, for example, are more easily, quickly and satisfactorily overcome in the context of secure relationships with the parents. If these relationships are tainted by anxiety and unpredictable gross changes of parental mood, the child will not overcome anxiety arising from the Oedipal situation and the various other demands of growing up. Not being able to depend on and trust his parents, the child may come to see the world as a threatening and hostile place. Parental factors are thus important in the genesis of neurotic disorders in children, but the reaction of children to them varies greatly. Some children seem able to cope with much more anxiety and instability in their families than others – probably because of constitutional and temperamental factors.

There are other views of the causes of neurotic symptoms. The 'behaviourists', among whom Eysenck[5] is prominent, believe that neurotic symptoms constitute learned behaviour and are themselves 'the neurosis'. There are no underlying causes. Indeed the behaviourist of extreme views believes that all behaviour, 'normal' or 'abnormal', has been brought about by the effects on individuals of environmental contingencies. This view is not as much at variance with dynamic views as it might at first seem to be. Psychodynamic theories see neurotic (and other psychiatric) symptoms as having been learned as a result of the quality and nature of the intimate relationship of the child with his parents during infancy. An examination of the environmental contingencies operating then might show that they explained the development of the neurotic symptoms; and an examination of the contingencies operating during psychoanalysis (see page 218) might explain how this process can remove neurotic symptoms. From a practical point of view, therapy based on learning theory appears to be of value in monosymptomatic or relatively uncomplicated neurotic states, such as specific phobias, but it is less helpful in neurotic disorders in which there is more widespread symptomatology.

The importance of the family in the causation of neurotic disorders has been mentioned, and some psychiatrists believe that often the whole family group is the basic unit suffering from the neurosis, and therefore the unit to be treated. For example Skynner[6], in discussing school refusal, has emphasised the advantages of a family-centred approach over more traditional methods. Thus where the individual psycho-therapist will look hard at the child and his intrapsychic processes to find a cause for his neurotic symptoms, so the behaviour therapist will look at his learning experiences in terms of environmental contingencies, and the family therapist will look at the functioning and structure of the family as a whole. All have something to contribute to the understanding of these complex disorders. The family group approach is discussed further in Chapter 16.

Description

The capacity to cope with stress without developing a neurotic reaction varies with age. While infants can develop anxiety (as indicated in

Chapter 1) in various circumstances, the term neurosis is not usually applied at this stage of development. It is probably best not employed until the use of mental defence mechanisms (see page 6) is established. It has been pointed out that children aged four to five often show many irrational fears (of flies, birds, dogs, earthworms, wind, the dark, and so on). These are usually transient phenomena, and are normal in this age range. In older children or adults, however, they would not be normal and might be symptoms of neurosis, so that in diagnosis the patient's age, and the normal stress tolerance for his age, must be taken into account.

Neuroses in children tend to be less fixed and chronic than in adults so that the prognosis and response to treatment are on the whole better. They usually disturb the family and people in the patient's environment as much as the child himself; in this respect neurotic children differ from many neurotic adults, who live their lives without causing distress to others.

Neurotic disorders may be subdivided into the following subgroups:

(a) Anxiety neuroses.
(b) Phobic states.
(c) Obsessive–compulsive neuroses.
(d) Hysteria.
(e) Neurotic–depressive conditions.

Clear-cut examples of these categories are less common in children than in adults. In childhood, neurotic disorders tend not to have fixed symptom patterns. Instead hysterical symptoms, obsessions and compulsions, phobias and depression may replace each other, or alternate one with another, or successively dominate the clinical picture – all against a background of anxiety.

Anxiety Neuroses (or Anxiety States)

In anxiety neurosis the anxiety is directly expressed. The child is often shy, timid and clinging, emotionally immature, overdependent upon the parents, and mixes poorly with other children. He may be afraid of losing his family, or of dying or being subject to some other disaster. He may have difficulty in getting to sleep, and sleep may be disturbed by dreams, nightmares or frequent waking. There may be free-floating anxiety. This is anxiety which comes to be associated with any situation in which the child finds himself: the child often perceives it as being due not primarily to the environment but to something within himself. Common somatic manifestations of anxiety are loss of appetite, nausea, abdominal pain, diarrhoea, vomiting, headaches, sleep disturbance, poor concentration, tension, restlessness, increased frequency of micturition and palpitations. Anxiety states are often accompanied by phobias.

The distinction between anxiety neurosis and 'emotional disorder' (the 'disturbance of emotions specific to childhood and adolescence' mentioned in the ninth edition of the ICD) is not clear cut. Many disorders which could, and in the past would, have been regarded as mild anxiety states would probably now be classifiable under the new ICD code, particularly the sub-category 'with anxiety and fearfulness'.

Phobic States

In phobic states, apparently irrational fears of particular objects or situations may dominate the picture[7]. The fear may be due to the defence mechanism of displacement. This means that it is transferred from its true (unconscious) source to the phobic object. Thus the individual who is afraid of going out of the house (agoraphobia, the fear of open spaces) is effectively preventing himself, or herself, from coping with a great many stressful situations which might be met with away from the security of home. The phobic object or objects may change during the course of an illness. While they may dominate the clinical picture, phobias are often but one feature, even a minor and transient one, of an anxiety state. There is an almost infinite variety of phobic objects. They include buses, dogs, cats, doctors, heights, enclosed spaces, open spaces, shops, crowds, insects and so on.

Monosymptomatic phobias are occasionally encountered in children. In these conditions the child has a severe and often seriously handicapping fear of one particular thing, for example water, dogs or snakes. The isolated phobias may differ in their causation from other neurotic disorders. They are not usually accompanied by general emotional immaturity. Their development is more easily understood on the basis of learning theory than are other neurotic disorders. Moreover they respond better to behaviour therapy. The treatment of a case of snake phobia is described later (page 228).

'School phobia' is probably not, in most cases, a true phobic condition but a variety of anxiety neurosis. It is better called 'school refusal' and is described below.

A fuller discussion of phobias in childhood is provided by Miller and colleagues[8].

Obsessive–compulsive Neuroses

Obessive–compulsive neuroses are less common than anxiety neuroses. Obsessions are intrusive thoughts and ideas of which the individual cannot be rid despite conscious awareness of their unreasonableness, and resistance to them. Compulsions are actions resulting from such thoughts. Obsessions and compulsions are unwelcome, unpleasant and disturbing to the individual. Psychodynamic theory regards them as manifestations of a mental defence mechanism against unconscious anxiety; they are a sort of 'magical' means of coping with the underlying problem.

Just as mild degrees of anxiety are a normal feature of childhood, so also are obsessional ideas and actions arising from normal anxiety. Examples are avoiding cracks in pavements, touching lamp-posts as they are passed and many feeding, dressing and bedtime rituals. In an obsessive–compulsive neurosis the symptoms are more severe and persistent, and interfere with the child's life. Complex rituals are sometimes observed. One child had to shut the dining-room door three times, and then touch each corner of the table before he could start his meal. Obsessional symptoms are sometimes found in children who also show some degree of overt and free-floating anxiety. It will be noted that Tracie, whose case history is outlined below (page 76) showed compulsive washing before admission. This continued also for a few days after admission, but disappeared as her anxiety lessened. Severe, chronic neuroses involving compulsive washing, such as may occur in adult patients, are not often seen in childhood, and present difficult treatment problems when they are. It may be, however, that children who appear abnormally clean and tidy have mild degrees of this condition. An emotionally healthy child is as a rule a none too clean one!

Barry was referred at age nine. He was said always to have been fussy about cleaning his hands, which he washed unduly frequently. For six months he had been avoiding 'imaginary' lumps in the carpet. He would take a long time saying his prayers at night in case something went wrong or because he thought he might have made a mistake and so had to start again; and there were other obsessive–compulsive symptoms. Barry acknowledged that these ideas and actions were irrational and tried to resist them, but without success.

After outpatient treatment had failed, and because Barry was becoming increasingly depressed and withdrawn, as well as expressing fear of dying, he was admitted for inpatient care. On admission he was tearful and communicated little with other children. He was always clean and well-dressed, but quiet and unassertive. It soon became clear that his whole life was ruled by certain rituals. For example he had to get his clothes out of the locker without touching the locker; he had to cut his food into very small pieces before he could eat it; when getting his books out of his 'tidy box' in school he had to bring them backwards and forwards four times across the side of the box; and he could only walk across the dining-room by a particular route. He also had complicated rituals for getting up and going to bed.

Eventually Barry told us that the reason for most of his habits was that he was afraid something would happen to his parents if he did not carry them out. He was an intellectually bright boy, but reluctant to say much about his feelings or to talk about family relationships.

Barry proved a difficult boy to treat by psychotherapy because of his passive, uncommunicative behaviour at interview. A behaviour modification approach (see page 227), to be applied both in the clinic and at home during weekends, was instead worked out. This had considerable success, over a period of months, in reducing his symptoms almost to none. His parents were co-operative, middle class people and the family seemed stable, though mother was unduly anxious about Barry and had probably tended to 'infantilise' him long after he had ceased to be an infant.

COMMENT

This is an example of a severe and quite chronic obsessive–compulsive neurosis in a prepubertal child. Treatment was difficult and extended, with outpatient treatment following Barry's stay in hospital, over more than two years.

While severe obsessive–compulsive neuroses are not common in children, transient obsessional symptoms occur quite frequently in the course of neuroses with other symptomatology. Obsessive–compulsive symptoms, being less severe and chronic, are thus more easily treated, and have a better prognosis, than similar conditions occurring in adults. Adams[9], in an important review and study, reported that obsessive children made up about 1 per cent of referrals to a child psychiatry clinic. Reporting on 49 such children (29 boys, 20 girls), he found that symptoms usually started about age 6, with referral coming on average about 4 years later, and more than half the children also had phobias. He considers the outcome is usually good for a first attack of mild obsessional symptoms. It appears though that chronic, long-established cases can be among the most difficult neuroses to treat.

Obsessive–compulsive symptoms should be distinguished from 'impulsions', which were originally given this label by Bender and Schilder[10]. Impulsions include behaviour such as constantly looking at or handling an object, drawing the object, being preoccupied with an object in fantasy or in thought, hoarding things, counting repeatedly and being preoccupied with numbers. The behaviour is similar to compulsive behaviour but there is little or no conscious resistance to it. Impulsions are commoner in younger children (aged four to ten) while obsessive–compulsive phenomena are more often found in pre-pubertal children, adolescents and adults. Some older children and adolescents who present with severe obsessive–compulsive neurosis have shown impulsions when younger. Impulsions and compulsions are sometimes present together at the beginning of puberty.

Hysteria

In the various forms of hysteria it is considered that the individual is unconsciously using a physical symptom or symptoms for a particular purpose. Hysterical symptoms may represent the 'conversion' of anxiety into a physical symptom, or they may be a means of avoiding anxiety-provoking situations. The symptoms may be motor (paralysis, or weakness or inability to speak except in a whisper) or sensory (lack of sensation to pain or touch in some part of the body, or the presence of pain, discomfort or other sensations). Mild, often transient, hysterical symptoms occur fairly often in the course of other neuroses, but severe, established hysteria is uncommon in childhood. In a survey of Maudsley Hospital case material Caplan[11] found an incidence of only 0·3 per cent of diagnosed 'hysteria' in pubertal children. In pubertal and pubescent children the incidence was 1·8 per cent. Another interesting finding was that 46 per cent of these cases were found to have an organic illness related to the presenting symptoms, either at the time or at follow-up four to eleven years later. The symptom most likely to be wrongly diagnosed as hysterical was deterioration of eyesight.

Joan, aged 13, was anxious about leaving home to go to school. Despite superior intelligence and a place at the top of the form, her relationships with other children in the school were poor. One Monday morning she complained of pain and weakness in her legs. The doctor was called and advised aspirin and a few days rest in bed. The symptoms subsided. They recurred on the first day of school after the half-term break. This time Joan was sent to a paediatrician who could find no evidence of physical illness. After two weeks off, Joan again appeared well and she returned to school and completed the term.

On the first day of the next term Joan was again unable to go to school because she could not walk and had painful legs. A psychiatric cause was now considered by the parents, and the family doctor. Joan had to be carried into the psychiatric consultation, but despite her inability to walk she showed a bland indifference to her symptoms. Her social difficulties at school, and her fear of leaving mother, soon emerged in discussion, and after three sessions she understood her physical symptoms as a means of avoiding school. It appeared that she had unconsciously seen them as the only way of avoiding school acceptable to her very ambitious parents. Her problems were tackled by a series of psychotherapeutic interviews, while a social worker saw the parents and helped them recognise their part in the situation.

The hysterical symptoms did not recur but Joan remained anxious about school, and it was about ten weeks before she was able to return. She then did so, without recurrence of pain or paralysis.

It will be seen that in this case the hysterical symptoms were partly a way of expressing anxiety, but also a means of preventing Joan from getting into a situation which was anxiety-provoking for her. She had some conscious appreciation of her desire to remain at home rather than cope with the other children at school. Initially, however, she did not recognise that her physical symptoms were unconsciously motivated in the way they turned out to be. Her 'choice' of symptoms was probably related to her father's longstanding limp and pain, the result of a war wound.

While the abdominal pain, sickness and other physical symptoms occurring in many neurotic conditions (such as school refusal) arise in a similar way, in practice the term 'hysteria' is usually confined to conditions where anxiety has been largely repressed and replaced by hysterical symptoms. Because the symptoms serve the purpose of reducing anxiety, the patient often shows little or no concern about them, despite what may appear to be a crippling disability. This so-called *belle indifférence* was well displayed by Joan who, when first seen, expressed little or no concern about her inability to walk unaided, and smiled when describing the severity of her pain.

A rare hysterical symptom in children is *hysterical aphonia*, in which the voice is largely lost so that the subject can speak only in a whisper.

Caution should always be exercised in diagnosing hysteria as there is a real danger of misdiagnosing organic disease as hysterical. In one study[12] of neurological disease presenting as child psychiatric disorder it was found that falling-off of school performance, loss of vision, disturbance of balance and variability of symptoms were common features.

Neurotic–depressive Conditions

The ninth edition of the ICD (see page 27) includes a category, 'neurotic depression' under 'neurotic disorders' and under 'disturbance of emotions' specific to childhood and adolescence, a category 'with misery and unhappiness'. There are also codes for depression associated with acute reaction to major stress, adjustment reaction and manic–depressive psychosis, together with one for 'depressive disorder, not elsewhere classified'. This variety of diagnostic categories reflects the confusion and varied opinions about the diagnosis of depression, especially in childhood and adolescence[1,13]. Nevertheless it *is* clear that children may experience depressive symptoms of varying severity, and that a smaller number show what many psychiatrists regard as depressive disorders. In these, depression is frequently accompanied by anxiety, with anxiety often coming first.

The predominant clinical feature in these cases may be depression, the child having attacks of weeping, lacking normal interest in things and being unable to concentrate and despondent about the future. There is often disturbance of sleep and appetite. The child may express the desire to be dead, or to run away from the family, a wish which is sometimes acted out. The depression is not of psychotic intensity in that there is no disordered contact with reality. Indeed many children with neurotic–depressive conditions are found to be facing considerable environmental stress, most often due to tensions or disturbance in the family. The details are almost infinitely varied. The loss of a loved family member through death or other circumstances is a possible cause, but much more often the stress does not involve break-up of the family. Serious depression or other psychotic illness in one or other parent may be a factor; so may neurotic illness in a parent. Or the child may be unable to meet the parent's desires and expectations, for example academically at school. Physical illness in any member of the family (including parent) is particularly likely to cause anxiety or depression in the child. Disharmony between the parents has a similar effect. These circumstances, and others like them, do not necessarily cause depression. Other forms of neurotic reaction may occur, or the child may not react by neurotic breakdown at all. However, depression is particularly likely to occur when there has been chronic, long-standing stress of the varieties mentioned above.

George, an only child born to a single mother, was referred for psychiatric assessment at the age of eleven, after he had run away from home and been picked up by the police in a town about sixty miles away. His chronically depressed mother had had three periods in a psychiatric hospital during the previous two years, each for treatment of an exacerbation of her depression. George, his mother and a large dog lived an isolated existence. Mother did not mix with the neighbours and said they looked down on her because she was an unmarried mother. She lived on social security payments but from time to time bought George surprisingly expensive presents (a tape recorder and an electric organ were examples). She and George doted on the dog, for whose affections there was some rivalry between them. George was discouraged from mixing with other children and was frequently warned by his mother against friendships with neighbourhood families. On each of the three occasions when his mother had been in hospital he was placed in a foster home. At school he was considered a bright pupil but his work was patchy and unreliable. He ran away after leaving a note 'bequeathing' all his possessions, except the few things he chose to take with him, to his mother.

When first seen George was found to be very depressed. He spoke of his long-standing anxiety about his mother, who would from time to time threaten suicide, and the restrictions placed by her on his contacts outside the family. He said he ran away with the intention of going to stay with an aunt he knew slightly who lived in another part of the country. Intelligence testing showed him to be of superior intelligence, but in tests of attainment in basic school subjects he was performing at a level about average for a child of his age – not up to the standard appropriate to his intelligence. In later interviews he spoke of his desire to meet and know more of his father, of whom mother had never spoken to him.

George was at once admitted to hospital where his depression rapidly lifted without any drug or physical treatment. It was eventually decided he would be best discharged to a residential school, a suggestion which he accepted readily. He did well there, returning home to his mother for school holidays. Meanwhile mother was supported by visits from a social worker, and seemed to benefit greatly from this.

COMMENT

George had been chronically anxious for many years, but had maintained a precarious adjustment until the approach of adolescence. Following three separations from mother he became increasingly worried and then depressed. He perhaps ran away more to draw attention to his plight than for any other reason. (In children, running away from home may be motivated in a way similar to some adult suicidal attempts.) The depression was almost severe enough to be called psychotic, but a diagnosis of psychosis was not made in this case as the symptoms could be understood in terms of the difficulties George was facing. They were, moreover, effective in causing an improvement in his life situation through his placement in a residential school. The diagnosis was therefore one of a neurotic–depressive state.

Hersov[1] quotes one survey by Pearce[14] of 547 children aged 1 to 17 seen at the Maudsley Hospital, London. Children with severe mental retardation, organic psychosis, autism and schizophrenia were excluded. One quarter of the children had the symptom of depression, defined as 'morbid depression, sadness, unhappiness, tearfulness'. These 126 depressed children differed significantly from the remaining non-depressed children in being 'older, more emotionally disturbed and more likely to have experienced emotional stresses'. They were also more often admitted for treatment. Depressed mood did not inevitably mean that the syndrome of depression was present; also 11 per cent of the children who did not have the symptom of depression had a cluster of symptoms (suicidal feelings, morbid anxiety, sleep disturbance, school refusal) typical of the 'depressed' group. These tended to be younger children, and it seems that at this age especially depression can occur in atypical forms. (Depression is discussed further in Chapter 6, pages 99 to 103.)

School Refusal

School refusal is a reluctance to attend school associated with anxiety and, often, depressive mood[15]. It is sometimes called school phobia, because the child appears frightened to go to school. Such a fear can certainly be a feature of the condition, but it is not often the primary one, though at first it may seem to be. For example, fear of leaving home may be much more important. School refusual is distinct from truancy (page 53), which is the wilful avoidance of school. If attempts are made to force the child with school refusal to go to school, increased distress usually results – though sometimes this is the best treatment, the child learning to overcome his distress. Physical symptoms, such as poor appetite, sickness, pains and diarrhoea, may occur, especially at breakfast time. These often disappear once the time for going to school has passed. This may lead parents or school staff to believe, wrongly, that the child is malingering. In the more severe cases symptoms persist at other times, but are exacerbated when the child is faced with pressure to attend school.

These children cannot cope with life at school. They often find relationships with other children difficult and become acutely anxious away from what they feel is the safety and protection of home and family. School attendance may finally cease in response to a minor additional stress, like a change of teacher, bullying by other children or transfer from primary to secondary school. The emotional immaturity of these children is often manifest in their covert aggressiveness. Having grown up in an anxious and probably indulgent atmosphere, they have not learnt to channel their aggressive drives into socially useful and constructive paths. (That is, there has been a failure of sublimation of these drives.) Their anger may seldom have been consciously aroused as they have always been given their way. When this situation is challenged they may become not only panic-stricken but also very angry. So they are anxious away from, but also angry with, their parents. The anger may be expressed verbally, or physically through tantrums or even physical violence towards the parent, or silently by refusal to speak or co-operate (sometimes with the psychotherapist as well as with the parent). Either anxiety or anger may dominate the clinical picture. Anger and hostility are often particularly marked in adolescents, being exacerbated by the normal rebelliousness of this age period, and also by the individual's feeling of inability to fulfil the role appropriate to his, or her age.

In the following case anxiety dominated the picture, and there was an element of depression:

Tracie, aged 10, was referred because of school refusal. Her symptoms dated back two months, to the start of a new school term. At first Tracie became very anxious about her school books, worrying disproportionately about small mistakes in her work. Then after being coaxed by other children to eat a horse chestnut in the playground, she became acutely fearful that she was being poisoned. Afterwards she would eat only if her mother ate the same food with her. She was also washing herself unduly frequently, despite acknowledging that it was unnecessary when mother spoke to her about it.

During the month before she was first seen, Tracie became very over-dependent on her mother, to whom she confided frightening fantasies and dreams. Her mother responded to this by reassuring and comforting her. Tracie frequently wept for her father and any attempt to get her to go to school caused an acute state of panic. At night she would not go to sleep until she knew her mother was in bed. She sucked two of her fingers almost all day.

Four years previously Tracie's father had died of a subarachnoid haemorrhage, after a short illness. Tracie, the sixth of eight siblings, was said always to have been her father's favourite child. After father's death she cried bitterly for days, and she continued over the ensuing four years to cry for him whenever upset. Mother also was depressed after father's death, but did her best to comfort Tracie. This led to a mutually over-dependent relationship between them. Tracie seemed to have made little progress in becoming independent of mother during the ensuing four years.

Tracie was admitted to an inpatient unit for treatment. On separation from her mother she was very upset, crying constantly and insistently demanding that she must go home. For a few days she required constant attention, but it was not difficult to get her to go the unit school where she worked well and made steady progress. At first she was reluctant to mix with the other children but her relations with them became gradually more normal. After eight weeks in the unit she was able to spend weekends at home and return without upset. Towards the end of her three-month stay in the unit she was able to go out each day to an outside school.

During the early part of her stay in hospital Tracie declined to see her own doctor as she was invited to do daily. Instead she hung around the building sucking her fingers. This was accepted, but later she agreed to be seen on her own. She then began to talk about the obsessive thoughts which previously had distressed her so much, but she seemed to feel guilty about them and would give few details of their content. She spoke also of her relationships with her mother, her siblings and various friends, including another girl in the unit with whom she developed a rather ambivalent relationship. She also played out scenes in the doll's house, the figure of father being always left out.

While Tracie was in hospital her mother was seen weekly by a social worker. She responded well to discussion of Tracie's difficulties and her own part in them. She was able to become less protective towards Tracie, and to handle her firmly, despite her own strongly felt desire to 'baby' her.

Tracie was discharged after three months' inpatient care and was seen as an outpatient. At follow-up $3\frac{1}{2}$ years after admission she was attending school regularly, and making good progress, without showing signs of anxiety or any other symptoms. The whole family seemed to be functioning at a much better level.

COMMENT

This case is unusual in that father was dead, and the anxious over-protection of Tracie by mother was due to the reaction both showed to father's death. Nevertheless the combination of an anxious and over-protective mother with a weak, passive, ineffectual or absent father, is common[6]. The child becomes increasingly emotionally immature and sooner or later develops overt neurotic symptoms; in Tracie's case these consisted of school refusal coming on following a minor stress, namely the start of a new school term with a new teacher. Very little fantasy material emerged during interviews with Tracie, and this is often the case in children with school refusal. A period of skilled treatment in hospital nevertheless enabled her to overcome her problems.

Other Neurotic Syndromes

Sometimes particular symptoms such as poor appetite with weight loss may dominate the picture, and many cases of *anorexia nervosa* (see page 164) are neurotic disorders. *Elective mutism* (see page 138), in which there is refusal to speak to people outside the family circle, is often essentially a neurotic condition.

Treatment

This is usually psychotherapeutic, and in most cases parents and child should be involved in the treatment. The anxious child will usually benefit from the development of a relationship with a therapist. In many of the milder cases, this can be quite short-term and the interviews infrequent. The contact with the child may or may not involve the working through of unconscious conflicts. (Psychotherapy with children is discussed further in Chapter 16.) If the parents have been over-anxious about the child or have been over-protective, they will need help and perhaps even a period of psychotherapy. Family group therapy is often of value in such cases, and in adolescents with school refusal (where the family psychopathology is often more complex and chronic) it can be particularly valuable (see page 222). Skynner believes that non-involvement of the father is important aetiologically, and reports good results from family-centred treatment[6]. Where anxiety-producing environmental circumstances are important, at home, in school or in the course of peer-group relationships, it is some-times desirable to try and remove or reduce the stress in the early stages of treatment and then gradually reintroduce it. This process bears a relation to behaviour therapy which also is of value in the treatment of specific phobias. (See the case of Quentin, page 228.)

Other types of treatment are possible. A temporary reduction of anxiety may be secured by means of sedation with small doses of phenothiazine tranquillisers such as fluphenazine, chlorpromazine or perphenazine; or with benzodiazepine drugs such as diazepam or chlordiazepoxide (for doses, see Chapter 16). Children living in particularly insecure or anxiety-provoking home environments may benefit from daypatient or inpatient treatment in a children's psychiatric unit, combined with help for the family.

While children with severe and long-standing neuroses need specialist help, many milder cases can often be treated in the community. Unhurried interviews with child and parents, or with the whole family, are usually necessary, perhaps supplemented by drug therapy and/or by adjustments of the child's environment. The latter may be achieved as a result of discussion with the family or through change in the child's school environment.

In the treatment of neurotic school refusal it is necessary to consider carefully the stage at which efforts should be made to get the child to return to school. If the child is still attending school, even with great difficulty, efforts to make the school environment temporarily less stressful and to provide support for the child while attending, are well worth while. In mild and early cases an early return to school is advisable, and usually leads to good results[16]. This should be firmly presented to the child after the agreement and co-operation of school staff and parents, and anyone else who may be involved, has been obtained. Sometimes it can be agreed at a family interview at which a member of the school staff is also present. If the situation is handled firmly and calmly most children return to school. Any necessary treatment can then be offered to the family. The parents and/or the child may ask for a change of school and, while this can be helpful, it is seldom in itself adequate; it often represents an attempt by both child and family to deal with their anxiety, and perhaps guilt too, by attributing the difficulties simply to events at school. Attempts to force severely anxious or depressed children, and children who have been having serious attacks of anxiety ('panic attacks'), to school tend to aggravate the symptoms. In such cases, psychotherapy must usually be started first and it may be some months before the child can return to school. In severe cases, however, admission to a child psychiatric inpatient unit may be helpful and education can be continued in this setting[17].

Outcome

The outcome in childhood neurotic conditions is generally favourable. Neurotic symptoms, even severe ones, frequently clear up without any psychiatric treatment and without being followed by any observable psychiatric disability. Such an outcome is more probable in children whose emotional development has been satisfactory and also where the neurotic symptoms occur in response to marked environmental stress. In other instances neurotic symptoms persist, especially in the absence of suitable treatment. Emotionally immature children, who are often overdependent on their parents, tend to do less well. Constitutional predisposition, which may be shown by a positive family history and by the appearance of symptoms with little apparent environmental cause, may also be associated with a poorer response to treatment.

If psychiatric disorder persists, the type of disorder diagnosed in adult life is likely to be a neurosis or an affective psychosis[18]. This contrasts with conduct disorders (Chapter 4) which, if disturbed behaviour persists into adult life, are more likely to be followed by antisocial or criminal behaviour.

References

1. Hersov, L. 'Emotional disorders'. In *Child Psychiatry: Modern Approaches*, ed. M. Rutter and L. Hersov. London: Blackwell, 1976.
2. World Health Organization. *International Classification of Diseases*, 1975 Revision. Geneva 1977.
3. Group for the Advancement of Psychiatry. *Psychopathological Disorders in Childhood* (Report No. 62). New York, 1966.
4. Freud, A. *Normality and Pathology in Childhood*. New York: International Universities Press, 1966.
5. Eysenck, H. J. 'Learning theory and behaviour therapy'. *Journal of Mental Science*, **105**, 61–95, 1959.
6. Skynner, A. C. R. *One Flesh, Separate Persons* (Chapter 16), London: Constable, 1976 (Published in USA as *Systems of Marital and Family Psychotherapy*. New York: Brunner/Mazel, 1976).
7. Berecz, J. M. 'Phobias in childhood: aetiology and treatment'. *Psychological Bulletin*, **70**, 694–720, 1968.
8. Miller, L. C., Barrett, C. C. and Hampe, E. 'Phobias of childhood in a pre-scientific era'. In *Child Personality and Psychopathology: Current Topics*, ed. A. Davids. New York: Wiley, 1974.
9. Adams, P. L. *Obsessive Children*. London: Butterworth; New York; Brunner/Mazel, 1973.
10. Bender, L. and Schilder, P. 'Impulsions: a specific disorder of the behaviour of children'. *Archives of Neurology and Psychiatry*, **44**, 990–1008, 1940.
11. Caplan, H. L. M.Phil. dissertation, University of London, 1970. Findings summarized by Hersov, L. in *The Residential Psychiatric Treatment of Children* (pages 118–119), ed. P. Barker, London: Crosby Lockwood Staples, 1974.
12. Rivinus, T. M., Jamison, D. L. and Graham, P. J. 'Childhood organic neurological disease presenting as psychiatric disorder'. *Archives of Disease in Childhood*, **50**, 115–119, 1975.
13. Graham, P. 'Depression in pre-pubertal children'. *Developmental Medicine and Child Neurology*, **16**, 340–389, 1974.
14. Pearce, J. B. *Childhood Depression*. M.Phil. thesis, University of London, 1974.
15. Hersov, L. 'School refusal'. In *Child Psychiatry: Modern Approaches*, ed. M. Rutter and L. Hersov. Oxford: Blackwell, 1976.
16. Kennedy, W. A. 'School phobia: rapid treatment of fifty cases'. *Journal of Abnormal Psychology*, **70**, 285–289, 1965.
17. Barker, P. 'The inpatient treatment of school refusal'. *British Journal of Medical Psychology*, **41**, 381–387, 1968.
18. Robins, L. M. *Deviant Children Grown Up*. Baltimore, Williams and Wilkins, 1966.

CHAPTER SIX

Psychotic Disorders

Psychotic disorders are characterised by altered contact with reality. The psychotic child is attempting to adapt to a subjectively distorted concept of the world. This contrasts with neurosis in which the child is adapting in a morbid fashion to his real life situation.

In infants and young children it can be hard to be sure whether psychosis is present, because the child's concept of the world can only be inferred from observed behaviour. An important point is the presence of withdrawal from, or failure to make, normal emotional contact with people.

Another difficulty is that the onset of psychosis in early childhood, and especially in the first year or two, seriously distorts personality development and intellectual functions. Since intelligence is manifested mainly through learned behaviour (such as speech and motor skills) a child who has failed to learn such behaviour because of withdrawal and failure to make social contacts, cannot give evidence of his intelligence in the normal way. Thus it can be difficult or impossible to decide what a child's potential level of intelligence might have been had he not become psychotic. This makes the distinction between psychosis and mental handicap difficult. A further complication is that mental handicap and psychosis may co-exist.

The classification of childhood psychoses is hampered by the difficulty in assessing the state of mind of young children and by uncertainty about the causes of these conditions.

The ninth edition of the *International Classification of Diseases* (ICD) – see page 27) divides psychoses with origin specific to childhood into the following categories:

(a) Infantile autism.
(b) Disintegrative psychosis.
(c) 'Other': atypical forms of infantile psychosis which may show some of the features of infantile autism.
(d) 'Unspecified': includes 'schizophrenia, childhood type' and 'schizophrenic syndrome of childhood'.

In addition altered contact with reality occurs in *acute* and *subacute confusional states* (which the ICD classifies under 'transient organic psychotic conditions'), in certain forms of *dementia* which, rarely, occur in childhood and in *affective psychoses*.

The GAP classification (page 29) divides psychotic disorders into three groups, according to age of onset:

(i)   Psychoses of infancy and early childhood: this group corresponds roughly to groups 1 and 2 of the ICD.
(ii) Psychoses of later childhood; these include 'schizophreniform' psychoses, defined as a schizophrenic picture (see page 96) starting between ages 6 and 12, and other rare conditions such as affective psychoses (page 99).
(iii) Psychoses of adolescence, which include adult-type schizophrenia.

Infantile Autism and Other Infantile Psychoses

The disorders falling in categories (a) and (c) above will be considered together. In these conditions deviant development becomes manifest during the first two-and-a-half or three years (the ICD says two-and-a-half). The problems which most often cause the parents to seek help for their child include delayed or abnormal speech development, withdrawal and emotional coldness, and abnormal motor behaviour. The child may be thought to be backward or deaf.

In 1943 and 1944 Kanner[1,2] described a group of severely disturbed children and named the syndrome they presented *early infantile autism*. This term, often shortened to infantile autism, has continued in use, sometimes being applied to children with disorders conforming precisely to Kanner's description, and sometimes being used more loosely. Many other terms have also been applied to psychotic disorders of early childhood, for example *infantile psychosis, childhood autism, childhood schizophrenia, schizophrenic syndrome of childhood* and *symbiotic psychosis*. There is much evidence [3,4] that psychotic disorders of infancy and early childhood are quite distinct from schizophrenia as it occurs in adulthood or later childhood. Terms which imply that these disorders have a relation to schizophrenia are therefore best avoided. The best general term is probably *infantile psychosis*, implying a severe disorder starting in the first 2 or 3 years of life with evidence of altered reality contact. Infantile autism then becomes a form of infantile psychosis, and indeed the one with the most clear-cut clinical description.

Prevalence

About four children per 10,000 show clinical picture of infantile autism. A survey of the eight-, nine- and ten-year-old population in Middlesex, England, showed the following prevalence rates[5]:

Nuclear group (syndrome of 'infantile autism')	2·1 per 10,000
Non-nuclear group (not showing the classicial picture)	2·4 per 10,000
Total	4·5 per 10,000

The boy:girl ratio was over 2:1. There was an excess of families in the higher socio-economic groups compared with the general population.

Causes and Associated Factors

The causes of infantile psychoses are uncertain. Genetic, environmental, constitutional and organic cerebral causes have all been suggested. It is, however, established that there are associations between infantile psychosis and both mental handicap and language disorder.

Good evidence on the role of genetic factors is lacking. The rate of 'autism' in the siblings of autistic children is less than 2 per cent but much higher than in the general population (0·4 per cent). Rutter[4] reports a twin study which revealed that 4 out of 11 monozygotic twins were concordant for autism, while none of 10 pairs of dizygotic twins was. Genetic factors probably play a fairly small role but may combine with non-genetic factors to produce the condition, at least in certain cases.

Environmental, especially family, factors have been blamed. Some workers, including Kanner[1,2], have suggested a psychogenic cause and have asserted that the parents lack emotional warmth and are detached and of obsessional personality. There is no firm evidence of this, though parental personality attributes could conceivably contribute, given certain biological factors in the child. Alternatively, reported parental attitudes could be reactions to the children's conditions.

Brain damage is certainly present in some psychotic children, and occasionally a child with the clinical picture of infantile psychosis turns out to have a neurological disorder such as a cerebral lipidosis (see page 94). But most brain-damaged children are not psychotic, and many psychotic children show no evidence of brain damage. Nevertheless a surprising number (29 per cent in one study[6]) of non-epileptic psychotic children later develop epilepsy. This is much greater than the incidence of epilepsy in the general population.

Even if brain damage contributes to causation in some cases, it is not clear what part of the brain is involved. Various suggestions have been made but a recent review[4] concludes that there are no good grounds for locating the problem in any particular area of the brain.

The association of infantile psychosis with mental handicap is strong. A majority of a group of 'autistic' children studied by Rutter and Lockyer[7] obtained IQ scores in the 'mentally handicapped' range, though about a quarter fell in the 'normal' range. In most cases the low IQ did not appear to be due to the psychotic process, and it tended to remain at about the same level even following recovery from the psychosis.

The association with language disorder is important. Speech and language retardation are almost invariable in infantile psychosis. There is usually a severe receptive language problem and also a profound defect of inner language. This affects not only verbal language but language function generally, so that there is a failure to use gesture, which most children with developmental language disorders (see page 150) use extensively.

There is little evidence for the view that infantile psychosis is a form of schizophrenia coming on early in life. Studies by Kolvin and colleagues[3] of psychoses starting in infancy, and those commencing later in childhood, showed that the two groups of conditions differ in sex incidence, social background, family history of schizophrenia, intellectual level, cognitive function, presence of delusions and hallucinations, and course.

Description

Kanner[1,2] in his original account of autistic children, described four main features: autistic aloneness, delayed or abnormal speech development, an obsessive desire for sameness and onset in the first two years of life. These are still regarded as the basis for the diagnosis of infantile autism, though other infantile psychoses are recognised in which the clinical picture does not conform precisely to Kanner's description.

Autistic aloneness refers to failure to form normal social relationships with people. Attachment behaviour (see page 2) is lacking and instead of relating to individuals as people, psychotic children tend to treat them as inanimate objects. They are seen by their parents as unresponsive, they do not appear to want to be kissed or cuddled and may resist parents' attempts to give them physical affection, and they often fail to assume the posture appropriate for being picked up or nursed. They do not distinguish between parents and strangers, approaching either indiscriminately. A related behaviour is gaze avoidance, the failure to make eye-to-eye contact with people. While autistic children may at times look at people, they usually fail to do it when appropriate, for example during conversation. Also they may appear more fascinated by a person's spectacles, or facial contours, than with facial expression as a normal child would be.

Delayed, absent or *abnormal speech* is an invariable feature of infantile psychosis. Speech may not be acquired at all, or it may develop very late. Less frequently it develops normally for up to 2 or $2\frac{1}{2}$ years but is then partially or completely lost. The failure to speak is but one manifestation of a severe, and often profound, defect of language function[8]. This is shown in non-verbal as well as verbal behaviour. Thus there is an absence of symbolic or imaginative play, toys not being used as the objects they represent: a psychotic child may use a toy telephone to bang on the floor or to swing to and fro but will probably not imitate adults' use of a telephone as a normal child of similar age might do. There is a general failure to imitate and use gestures, or indeed to imitate the behaviour of others at all. In younger autistic children play tends to be repetitive, stereotyped and at a basic sensori-motor level.

As these children grow up some language skills usually develop, and about half of them acquire some useful speech. Language usually remains seriously impaired however. Pronominal reversal is common: asked, 'Do you want lunch?', the child will reply 'You want lunch', or may even repeat the whole question. Use of 'I' and 'me' is often absent or comes very late. Echolalia, the repeating of words and phrases spoken by others (of which the repeating of questions is an example), is common. Sometimes the echolalia is delayed, the words or phrases being repeated after a lapse of minutes, hours or days. This leads to the use of words and phrases, often highly stereotyped ones, totally out of context. Later still the child may be able to talk quite well about concrete, factual matters but have great difficulty with abstract ideas, producing no creative or imaginative ideas. Some of these children are greatly preoccupied with mechanical things like train or bus timetables, highway routes and their numbers and the like. Speech may be stilted or monotonous, without the usual intonations and inflexions. Associated with these problems there are usually some continuing difficulties in understanding speech, abstract ideas, or in following the plot of a story.

The *obsessive desire for sameness* tends to show itself through a 'fierce resistance to change', manifested 'either by severe distress if any article of furniture is moved from its accustomed place in the home, or if a different car route is followed to a familiar place. The child may restrict his food intake to a few similar articles (and the similarity may even be in shape ... such as sausages, fishsticks or chips only)'[9]. Some psychotic children show strong attachments to particular objects which seem to have special importance to them[10]; these seem to be special examples of transitional objects (see page 8). Others have rituals for dressing or undressing and may insist on wearing certain clothes.

In many cases the child's behaviour and development appear to have been abnormal from birth. In a minority of cases, however, there is a clear history of normal development for anything up to about 2 to $2\frac{1}{2}$ years, followed by development of psychotic behaviour; Elaine, described below, is an example.

Other symptoms frequently present are poor concentration, distractibility, overactivity (sometimes also periods of under-activity), sudden and apparently unprovoked anger or fearfulness, and outbursts of aggressiveness. These children tend to show a lack of fear about realistic dangers (fire, heights and so on) and resist learning new behaviour or skills. They often choose to examine objects, and people, by touching, tasting or smelling them, rather than by visual inspection. In infancy, feeding and toilet training problems are common. In place of normal play these children often engage in activities such as rocking, head-banging, flapping the hands up and down or whirling round and round.

Children with infantile psychosis often look healthy and intelligent and may also show limited areas of normal or even precocious intellectual function, while functioning at a retarded level in other respects. Their memory is sometimes remarkable. It may be combined with great musical skill, so that the child can reproduce accurately long and complicated pieces of music. Some children show special facility in mathematics, and are found to perform at a standard well ahead of their age. Patchy performance in intelligence tests is common.

Not all children with infantile psychosis present clinical features which conform precisely to Kanner's description of infantile autism, and the severity of the condition varies. The feature most often missing, or not well marked, is the preoccupation with sameness. This applied in the following case.

Elaine was born at full term following a normal pregnancy. Her birth weight was 2·5 kg. She appeared a healthy baby but feeding was difficult. Breast feeding was abandoned after two weeks, but even on the bottle she was difficult and fractious. She was an active baby and slept only for relatively short periods. Her parents considered her a quick and active baby and her motor development during the first year was if anything ahead of normal. She said her first words at ten months, and was reciting nursery rhymes by eighteen months. She was very musical and by this age could sing several songs. At just over twelve months Elaine had frequent breath-holding attacks and one of these was followed by a major convulsion. She was put on to phenobarbitone, but as it made her worse she was taken off it after a few weeks. She had no more fits.

When aged about twenty-one months, towards the end of her mother's second pregnancy, Elaine's behaviour began to cause the parents concern. She repeatedly and often inappropriately made remarks like 'I don't like Mummy poorly' and expressed her dislike of various other people.

Her condition deteriorated following the birth of her sister. Elaine was then twenty-three months old. Her speech regressed further and she started repeating people's questions instead of giving replies. She no longer talked to people. She spent long periods rocking and took little notice of people. Episodes of severe temper and screaming developed, but she retained her musical skill. At two years and six months a neurologist diagnosed her as 'autistic'.

At age three she was taken to a child guidance clinic but twelve weeks of weekly attendance brought no benefit. She had by this time lost most of her speech. She remained hyperactive and difficult to manage at home.

Elaine was seen at age four years and six months. Her parents described her as being hyperactive, impossible to communicate with, obsessed with food and unpredictable in mood, quiet periods being succeeded by severe tempers. She would not go on her own to the lavatory, as she had done, and often wet, and occasionally soiled, herself. But she was considered intelligent, had a good memory and knew where everything was. She now had no speech. Her hearing had been tested and pronounced normal. She was considered agile and good with her hands.

At this time Elaine appeared an attractive, well-dressed, overactive child. She ignored the examiner and engaged in a manneristic dance from time to time. At other times she moved restlessly and apparently aimlessly round the room. She put all the toys she touched into her mouth, but did not play with any of them in a conventional way. She made no response to speech. She vocalised a few sounds, but produced no recognisable words. She laughed once or twice but for no obvious reason. Otherwise she showed little emotional reaction. The presence in the room of three unfamiliar adults did not seem to affect her behaviour at all.

Elaine's parents were both university graduates, father a university lecturer, mother a secondary school teacher. Both were deeply concerned about Elaine and were prepared to go to great trouble to help her and obtain treatment for her. The family appeared a stable one and there was no family history of psychiatric illness.

COMMENT

This is a case of psychotic illness coming on in the second year, not conforming precisely to the classical picture of infantile autism in that there was no marked preoccupation with 'sameness'. Response to treatment was poor.

Differentiation from Other Conditions

The conditions with which psychosis of early childhood is most likely to be confused are deafness, mental handicap and developmental language disorders. The question of whether or not there is brain disease, for example cerebral lipidosis, can be very hard to decide and depends upon careful neurological examination and investigation.

In most cases there is good evidence, from the history and as a result of clinical examination, that the child can hear and is failing to respond to people rather than failing to hear. It is wise in all cases however to have expert audiometric investigation carried out. Electro-encephalographic measurement of evoked responses to auditory stimuli is sometimes of value in deciding whether the stimuli are reaching the cerebral cortex.

It has been mentioned that mental handicap may co-exist with psychosis, but retarded children usually relate freely with people, are not preoccupied with sameness and are more generally retarded, in contrast with psychotic children whose retardation is sometimes patchy. The psychotic child also has a specially severe form of impaired understanding of speech, in the use of gesture and in the understanding of grammatical structure, disabilities which have been shown to be relatively more severe than in normal or mentally handicapped children of the same mental age[11].

Developmental language disorders are described in Chapter 9. The main point is that there is no withdrawal, and language disordered children are usually normally responsive and communicate freely by non-verbal means. Echolalia and pronoun reversal are commoner in psychotic children. Preoccupation with sameness is not a feature of the behaviour of language disordered children. Severe receptive and central language difficulties are of course themselves features of infantile psychosis.

Treatment of Children with Infantile Psychoses

After infantile autism was first described it was thought by many to be psychogenic and in many centres psychotherapy was the main treatment offered. The results of psychotherapy have however been disappointing, and there is no evidence that it is generally effective in these children, though it may be helpful to certain children at particular points in the development of the disorder. The psychotherapeutic approach is discussed fully by Szurek and colleagues[12].

Rutter[4] has pointed out that changing views of the nature of autism have led to different treatment approaches. Autism, and other infantile psychoses, are no longer seen as due to the withdrawal into psychosis of basically normal children. There is now more emphasis on the severe language deficit which is usually a central feature of the condition, and a recognition that these are essentially disorders of development. This suggests that treatment should be directed primarily towards helping bring about more normal development, and in particular assisting the child in the development of language. The presence of a psychotic child can be very stressful for a family and help for the families is often required also.

Behaviour modification techniques are increasingly being used for children with infantile psychosis. It is clear that the behaviour of children can be changed by operant conditioning techniques[13,14], and these can be used to teach speech. While conditioning techniques cannot overcome a severe biological defect in the capacity to use language, they can ensure that whatever language potential the child has is realised, and as neurological maturation proceeds the child's potential may improve. Yet sometimes conditioning techniques do no more than teach the child simple receptive language (like obeying commands or responding to simple questions) and perhaps simple statement or requests. Whatever the level of function of the child, however, these techniques appear the most hopeful of those currently available. It also seems that changes brought about by treatment in an institution away from home may not always be accompanied by similar changes when the child goes home or to a school in the community[14]. Treatment located in the home and school seems to be of more benefit, and parents and teachers should be actively involved in it. Behaviour therapy is discussed further in Chapter 16 (page 227).

When these children grow up most require special schooling, usually in the form of skilled, small-group teaching. Special day units for autistic children and those with similar disorders are increasingly being provided. A few residential schools also exist, but it is probably better, in most cases, not to remove these children from their homes; sometimes however geographical conditions leave no choice but residential schooling.

Residential treatment may be required if the severity of the behavioural disturbance is greater than can be coped with at home, or if there are severe problems in the family. It should always be kept as brief as possible, with the family being involved in the treatment as much as possible. These children are particularly susceptible to institutionalisation because of their tendency to withdraw and their failure to communicate normally. For this reason long-term residential care is to be avoided whenever possible.

Drug treatment (see Chapter 16) may be of benefit in controlling overtly disturbed or hyperkinetic behaviour, and in dealing with the sleep disturbance which is sometimes present, especially on a short-term basis. But, like psychotherapy, drug treatment has not been shown to have any effect on the underlying disorder.

Casework with the families (see page 221) is often needed, since the stresses caused by having a psychotic child in the family can be great. Modern treatment methods, in which the parents work closely with the professional treatment personnel helping the child, seem to be helpful to the parents. It is also helpful, as well as true, to make it clear to the parents that they are not the cause of the disorder. Any guilt they may feel can be further helped by the process of making them 'co-therapists', as is the practice in many behaviour modification programmes.

OUTCOME

Many of these children show a measure of improvement, starting most commonly about age four to six, though it may be later. Much probably depends on whether, at this stage, they are in an environment in which their slowly improving language skills and increasing capacity to form relationships are exploited to the full. Some ten to twenty per cent of children with psychoses of early childhood recover or show marked improvement, sufficient to enable them to attend an ordinary school or to work. A further, probably similar, percentage can live at home under sheltered conditions and can attend a special school or training centre. Fifty to sixty per cent do not make any substantial improvement and ultimately require long-term institutional care.[15]

Children who do improve often show residual signs of the psychotic process. They may be emotionally cold and aloof, and unaware of, and so insensitive to, the feelings of others. They may be preoccupied with train timetables, spotting the makes of cars and other things. There is often continuing evidence of the underlying language disorder, with poor comprehension of speech and of abstract ideas. Speech may be stilted, mechanical, repetitive or echolalic, or any combination of these, or it may be absent, despite relatively good adjustment in other spheres. Hyperactivity and aggressiveness tend to lessen and have often disappeared by puberty, but epilepsy develops in up to 29 per cent of cases. It is commoner in individuals with low intelligence quotients.

The outlook is related to whether any useful speech has developed by the age of five. If not, later development of speech is less likely and the outcome generally poorer. The results of intelligence testing carried out early in the illness also tend to correlate with speech development. The lower the intelligence quotient obtained, the worse the outlook.

Disintegrative Psychoses

The ninth edition of the ICD (see page 27) defines disintegrative psychoses as those in which 'normal or near-normal development for the first few years is followed by loss of social skills and of speech, together with a severe disorder of emotions, behaviour and relationships'. The loss of speech and social skills usually occurs over a period of a few months. Overactivity and repetitive, stereotyped behaviour are common, and intellectual impairment is a frequent, but not invariable, part of the clinical picture.

CAUSES

Disintegrative psychoses are often due to organic brain disease, though cases occur in which no evidence can be found of organic disorder. Sometimes evidence of underlying brain disease emerges much later, even at post-mortem examination[15]. Cases due to brain disease can be divided into two groups according to whether or not they are associated with progressive cerebral disorders[16]. Non-progressive causes include various forms of encephalitis (in which there is either cerebral infection or a reaction in the brain to a generalised infection) which results in damage which does not progress once the infection has cleared up. Infantile myoclonic epilepsy, and lead poisoning (once exposure to lead is terminated) are other possible non-progressive causes.

Progressive causes include tuberous sclerosis, hepato-lenticular degeneration, Huntington's chorea, lipidoses, diffuse cerebral sclerosis and subacute sclerosing panencephalitis. Each of these is described briefly below. Fuller accounts are given by Norouha[17] and Wilson[18].

Description

The clinical picture of disintegrative psychosis is quite varied. The essential features are a severe, prolonged disorder, with loss of reality contact, occurring in the absence of any other family disturbance or, if there is family or other psychosocial stress, of a severity out of proportion to the stress[16]. Other features include relationship difficulties, usually withdrawal, ritualistic and manneristic behaviour, delusions, hallucinations and a deterioration of educational or social behaviour, or both. In progressive cases the intelligence quotient may drop, the performance score being first affected, and neurological signs indicating focal lesions in the nervous system may appear. The electroencephalogram (EEG) often becomes abnormal, and serial examinations may reveal deterioration. When psychotherapy or behaviour therapy are tried in progressive cases they are either unsuccessful or only have short-lived effects.

The history and clinical picture vary according to the cause, and the following are brief summaries of conditions which may underlie disintegrative psychosis.

(a) NON-PROGRESSIVE CAUSES

Encephalitis following measles, mumps, influenza or other infectious diseases may be followed by psychotic symptoms such as those described above. There is usually a history of an attack of the infectious disease, followed by such indications of encephalitis as loss of consciousness, fits and specific neurological signs. Examination of the cerebrospinal fluid in the acute stage usually provides evidence of cerebral involvement. Sometimes the evidence of encephalitis is less clear-cut, and when a psychotic child presents for assessment, it may be hard to be sure whether there was any brain damage at the time of an earlier infectious disease. The worldwide epidemic encephalitis which occurred after the 1914–1918 war led to many cases of severe post-encephalitic psychotic disorders and most of the earliest inpatient psychiatric units for children in the USA were opened primarily to deal with children suffering from post-encephalitic conditions[19]. Since then cases have been mainly sporadic.

Infantile myoclonic epilepsy (infantile spasms, salaam attacks) is a form of epilepsy with onset usually in the first year of life. It often leads to a psychotic state and dementia[20,21]. The attacks, which consist of a sudden flexion of the arms while the head simultaneously drops forward, may be frequent at the height of the condition, when there may be scores or even hundreds of attacks per day. They usually die out during the second year of life. The end result is usually a severely mentally retarded child, but some of these children present with a psychotic picture. The degree of withdrawal may resemble that seen in infantile psychosis, though the history usually distinguishes the conditions. The withdrawn behaviour sometimes leads to the suspicion that the child is deaf.

There are various known causes of infantile spasms, including brain damage at the time of birth, reaction to immunisation, and such other conditions as tuberous sclerosis, inborn errors of metabolism and cerebral agenesis; but in many cases no cause can be discovered, and the condition comes on after a period of normal development.

Treatment using adrenocorticotrophic hormone (ACTH) appears to be of value and lessens the chance of the child being left with severe brain damage.

Lead encephalopathy results from the ingestion of excessive amounts of lead. It may cause brain damage and mental retardation. In children it is often associated with pica, the eating of substances not normally regarded as edible; old lead paint is the commonest danger. The use of lead, or lead paint, in toys does not normally occur nowadays, though it occasionally happens in error. Lead is also used in car batteries, in the structure of buildings and in industry, and lead poisoning has been known to occur in children playing with materials on rubbish dumps and in old buildings. Lead can be absorbed through skin and lungs as well as through the gastrointestinal tract.

In mild cases there may be a behaviour disorder with irritability, restlessness, inability to concentrate and loss of interest in things. In severe cases the behaviour disorder may be of psychotic intensity. Loss of appetite, vomiting, abdominal pains, constipation, headaches and sleeplessness may occur. There may be pallor due to the anaemia lead poisoning causes. Lead poisoning may lead to dementia, sometimes sufficient to cause severe mental handicap.

The diagnosis is supported by finding basophilic stippling in the red cells, a 'lead line' in the gums and increased density on X-rays of the ends of long bones, but all these things may be absent even though there are behavioural symptoms due to lead intoxication. Raised levels of lead are found in blood and urine, and there is excretion of copro-porphyrin in the urine. Lead poisoning should be treated in a specialised centre; all sources of lead must immediately be removed and the excretion of lead promoted by chelating agents. In the absence of treatment and if exposure to lead continues, the condition is of course progressive.

(b) PROGRESSIVE CAUSES

Tuberous sclerosis (or epiloia) is a rare condition due to a dominant autosomal genetic trait. Sporadic cases also occur. Multiple tumours and malformations in the brain are associated with epilepsy and mental deterioration. There may also be behavioural symptoms, and withdrawal, of psychotic intensity. A characteristic rash develops on cheeks, nose, chin and forehead.

Hepato-lenticular degeneration (or Wilson's disease) is inherited as an autosomal recessive trait and is a disorder of copper metabolism. Various parts of the body are affected; the damage to the brain may cause a psychotic syndrome or milder psychological symptoms. Involuntary movements, emotional lability, fits and a dementing process are characteristic features. These children can sometimes be helped by restricting copper intake, and by administration of penicillamine to increase the excretion of copper.

Huntington's chorea is a degenerative disease of the nervous system which is inherited as a dominant trait. Onset is usually during adult life, but may occur in childhood. The first symptoms tend to be involuntary choreiform movements, or a dementia. In the early stages, however, disturbed behaviour may dominate the clinical picture, there being emotional lability, hyperactivity and excitement, irritability and delusions as well as intellectual deterioration. No treatment is known which cures the process but anti-Parkinsonian drugs such as benztropine or orphenadrine may control the involuntary movements.

In the *disorders of sphingolipid metabolism* (lipidoses) fatty substances (sphingolipids) accumulate in the brain and other parts of the body. These disorders are usually inherited and due to recessive genes. Various different lipids may be involved. A variety of neurological symptoms occur, for example blindness and fits. Onset may be at any time during childhood with progressive deterioration, leading eventually to death occurring over a period which may be months or years. Sometimes the condition presents, not with neurological symptoms, but as a progressive disintegrative psychosis; or it may closely resemble infantile psychosis. Deterioration may be slow and cases are on record in which the diagnosis was unsuspected until revealed by post-mortem examination upon death some years later[15]. Tay-Sachs disease (or amaurotic family idiocy) and metachromatic leukodystrophy are particular forms that may present with psychiatric symptoms, and eventually progress to dementia and death.

Diffuse cerebral sclerosis (Schilder's disease) describes a group of conditions in which the white matter of the brain degenerates. Some forms, the leukodystrophies, are genetic in origin. The myelin sheaths of the nerve fibres are lost (demyelination) and this is followed by the growth of fibrous tissue (gliosis). Several forms have been described, with onset from infancy onwards. In the early stages there may be bizarre, unpredictable and variously disturbed behaviour, often with apparent loss of contact with the environment. Cortical blindness or deafness, in which the brain is unable to make normal use of the nerve impulses reaching it, may also occur. A falling-off in the performance of school work may be the presenting symptom. Labile and inappropriate emotional responses are sometimes early features. The course is progressive and the early symptoms are followed by profound dementia. No treatment is known which will arrest the disease process.

Dementia infantilis (Heller's syndrome) is a term first used by Heller[22] in 1930 to describe a dementing process, often associated with disturbed, restless, psychotic behaviour, starting at about the age of 3 or 4. The term is little used nowadays and the cases Heller described appear to have been examples of progressive disintegrative psychosis.

TREATMENT OF DISINTEGRATIVE PSYCHOSES

In few cases is it possible to affect the underlying disease process although, as indicated above, in lead poisoning the lead present in the body can be removed, sometimes with clinical improvement. Otherwise treatment is mainly symptomatic and palliative; measures which may help in particular disorders have already been mentioned.

Non-progressive cases often benefit from the treatment methods which are helpful in infantile psychosis (pages 89 to 90). It is also important to realise that considerable recovery may occur after encephalitis. Improvement may continue to be evident for as long as a year. In addition the normal processes of growth and maturation continue.

Epilepsy is common in cases where there is an organic disorder of the brain. Anticonvulsants should be used to achieve as complete control as possible (pages 229 to 231). Hyperactive behaviour should be controlled using either a phenothiazine drug (page 231) or haloperidol (page 231). Drug treatment may also be needed for sleep disorder (page 234).

Casework help for the family (page 221) is always required, and in the case of progressive disorders, long-term residential care may eventually become necessary. Special education is often required.

OUTCOME

In non-progressive disorders the long-term outlook depends largely on the severity of any brain damage that is evident. Social and language skills may improve with maturation, combined with behavioural treatment and an appropriate educational programme. Progressive cases seem to be commoner, however, and have a poor outcome. In many cases a state of dementia, often becoming severe, develops, followed by death – though this may not occur until well into adult life. The rate of deterioration varies widely.

Schizophrenic Psychoses of Later Childhood and Adolescence

In later childhood, and particularly in adolescence, there occur psychoses which more clearly resemble schizophrenia as it is seen in adult patients[4,23]. These are quite distinct from infantile psychoses.

PREVALENCE

Childhood schizophrenia is rare. In child psychiatric practice, children with such psychoses are seen less often than children with psychosis of earlier onset, and in only very few adult schizophrenic patients (probably less than one per cent) do symptoms date back to before puberty. Onset before age 7 is very uncommon. After puberty, however the incidence increases greatly and the fifteen- to twenty-year age range is a common period for the onset of schizophrenia.

CAUSES

The causes of childhood schizophrenia are not known but genetic predisposition probably plays a part, as in adult schizophrenia. No metabolic or biochemical abnormality has as yet been shown to be causal, nor have any psychological factors or environmental stresses been proved responsible, though it has been suggested that certain patterns of family behaviour can cause schizophrenia in children.

DESCRIPTION

The clinical features resemble those of adult schizophrenia. Many of these children (87 per cent in one study[4]) are reported to have been odd (shy diffident, withdrawn, timid or sensitive) before the develop-

ment of the psychotic symptoms. There is a history of delayed development, especially of speech, in nearly half, but this contrasts with
infantile psychosis in which this is almost invariably present.

At the onset there is a change of personality and an alteration of
the contact the child makes, on an emotional level, with the environment. There may be progressive withdrawal from contact with people,
with a violent reaction if attempts are made to counter this, but the
degree of withdrawal is less marked than in infantile psychosis.
Emotional reactions to people and situations may be inappropriate,
or flat. Thinking tends to become loose and woolly, with a falling-off
in the standard of school work as an early manifestation. This thought
disorder is a major symptom of schizophrenia and takes various forms.
There is often loosening of the constraints normally present on thought
association. Thus the subject may when talking turn from one subject
immediately to another apparently unrelated one (the so-called
'knight's move'). Various other disorders of the form and stream of
thought such as thought blocking, when thoughts suddenly come to
a stop, or thought insertion, when the subject experiences the insertion
of what are felt to be alien thoughts into the mind, may be present.

There may be abnormalities of motor function with underactivity
or overactivity, but especially with bizarre movements and posturings.
Also evident may be disturbances of volition such as passivity and lack
of drive, stubbornness, negativism, or impulsive outbursts of aggressive
or in other ways inappropriate behaviour. Delusions are often present
but may be difficult to distinguish from fantasies. Hallucinations,
usually auditory, are common and they, and delusions also, probably
account for many of the preoccupations of these children (with
people's spectacles, the time, motor vehicles and so on).

There is a lack of agreement among psychiatrists about the precise
criteria which should be used in making a diagnosis of schizophrenia.
There are considerable variations between different centres and different countries. Schneider, a German psychiatrist, described certain
'symptoms of the first rank' each of which he believed was diagnostic
if it occurred in clear consciousness. These have been conveniently
summarised by Kendall[24].

1. Auditory hallucinations taking any one of the specific forms:
    (i) Voices repeating the patient's thoughts out loud or anticipating
        them.
    (ii) Two or more hallucinatory voices discussing, or arguing
         about, the patient who is referred to in the third person.
    (iii) Voices commenting on the patient's thoughts or behaviour,
          often as a running commentary.

2. The subjective experience of alien thoughts being put into the patient's mind by some external agency, or of own thoughts being taken away (thought insertion or withdrawal).
3. The experience that the patient's thinking is no longer confined within his or her own mind, but is instead shared by or accessible to others (thought broadcasting).
4. The experience of feelings, impulses or acts being experienced or carried out under external control, so that the patient may feel like a robot or like someone who is hypnotised.
5. The experience of being a passive and reluctant recipient of bodily sensations (haptic, thermic or kinaesthetic) imposed by some external agency.
6. Delusional perception – a delusion arising fully fledged on the basis of a genuine perception which would be regarded as commonplace by others.

Although these symptoms are reliable as indications that a diagnosis of schizophrenia is appropriate, they are absent in 20 per cent or more of cases. Moreover they can be hard to elicit in withdrawn children.

The behaviour of schizophrenic children is often changeable and unpredictable. Thus impulsive and overactive behaviour may alternate with withdrawn and underactive behaviour. Behaviour may also become socially inappropriate, with sexual exposure or talking or shouting at people inappropriately. Regressive behaviour such as wetting, soiling and infantile behaviour at mealtimes may also appear.

Paranoid schizophrenia (in which the patient falsely believes he or she is being persecuted) is seldom seen in childhood, but becomes commoner in adolescence.

While schizophrenic psychoses may occur in mentally retarded children, most schizophrenic children are of average intelligence, some higher. They continue to perform in intelligence tests at or about the average level long after the onset of their illness, but usually become increasingly retarded educationally because in their disturbed state they are unable to benefit from schooling.

TREATMENT

Symptomatic improvement, with reduction in the severity of symptoms such as impulsivity, aggressiveness and hallucinations, can often be obtained by administration of phenothiazine tranquillisers such as chlorpromazine, fluphenazine and perphenazine. Haloperidol is also sometimes helpful. (For doses, see Chapter 14.) Supportive psychotherapy may be symptomatically helpful, and it may be possible to find an educational regime (perhaps in a special school or hospital unit) from which the patient can gain benefit. Family therapy (page 222) has been advocated for schizophrenia but there is a lack of evidence of its efficacy.

OUTCOME

It is doubtful whether any of the above measures alter the long-term course of the disease which is usually progressive. Symptomatic improvement on phenothiazine drugs may be considerable however, and with maintenance treatment some patients can live a useful life in the community. Occasionally remission occurs but more often there is deterioration leading to the need for long-term care in hospital. There have, however, been few long-term follow-up studies of schizophrenic children and data are scanty.

Affective Psychoses

Affective psychoses are conditions in which a psychotic process is characterised primarily by a deviation from normal of the mood (or *affect*). This may be in the direction of depression or of elation (as in *mania*). In adults, disorders sometimes occur in which there are periodic changes in mood between psychotic depression, normality and psychotic elation. In certain cases these gross periodic mood changes occur regularly and with little apparent relationship to environmental events. This condition, *manic–depressive psychosis*, is very rare before puberty, though a few cases have been reported[25,26]. Indeed mania, and its lesser form hypomania, are rarely seen in children. Depression is more common, though not as a feature of manic–depressive psychosis. Clear-cut depressive and manic psychoses are commoner in adolescence, though even in this age range manic conditions are rare.

   Depression of mood frequently occurs in children faced with environmental stresses. When the depression can be understood in terms of the stress the child is facing, a diagnosis of psychosis is not appropriate. When the depression is disproportionately severe, however, and is not appropriate in terms of the reality the child is facing, the condition may be termed 'psychotic depression'. Thus the differentiation is a matter of clinical judgement involving assessment of both the child's mental state and his life situation. George, the boy whose case is described on page 73, was close to the borderline between neurotic depression and psychosis. Had he attempted suicide instead of running away from home he might have been called psychotic.

CAUSES

Manic–depressive disease appears to have a biological cause, and sometimes periods of depression and mania alternate regularly for many years, regardless of the subject's environmental circumstances. The underlying causes are not fully understood, but biochemical changes in the brain are involved. It may be that similar processes can cause attacks of depression, without mania, but how often this happens in children is not known. What is clear, however, is that most depressed children are facing considerable stress. There is often an unhappy family situation, a lack of security, and an atmosphere of instability and pessimism among family members. Sometimes there is gross parental strife or a broken home. Parental rejection or scape-goating of the child is common. Difficulties at school or in relationships with other children may contribute. What causes the sad or unhappy child to become psychotically depressed – that is to lose his reality contact – is not understood, but constitutional, possibly genetic factors, seem to play a part.

DESCRIPTION

Psychotic depression is commoner after puberty than before it. The main feature is depression of mood, persisting in spite of variations in environmental circumstances. The moods of most children and adolescents are quite labile. Children are easily upset, and they cry readily, but they quickly overcome upsets. In the depressed child there is a more longstanding and less changing mood of sadness, though fluctuation in severity from day to day, or at different times of day, may occur. The child may express unjustified feelings of guilt, needlessly blaming himself for the misfortunes of others. One depressed twelve-year-old girl said that her 'nervous state' was responsible for her father's difficulties at the office, mother's anaemia and general ill-health and the bad behaviour of her brother and sister. The feeling that life is not worth living may be expressed, and there may be suicidal thoughts, or even acts. There is sometimes slowing of thought and speech and also of motor activities (psycho-motor retardation). School refusal may occur, the ordinary stresses of school being more than the depressed child can cope with. The chronically depressed child may become hostile and rebellious, and antisocial or frankly delinquent behaviour may develop. Sleep difficulties are usual in depression. They may take the form of difficulty in getting to sleep, restless and disturbed sleep, or wakening early in the morning.

In a valuable review Garfinkel and Golombek[27], express the view that 'depressive equivalents', such as boredom, restlessness, fatigue, poor concentration, behaviour problems and physical symptoms (aches, pains, sickness and so on) are commoner than frank depression in children. Instead of being depressed verbally, depression may be 'acted-out' by, for example, running away, delinquency, promiscuity, truancy or bullying.

DIFFERENTIATION FROM OTHER CONDITIONS

There is a lack of agreement among psychiatrists about when 'depression' should be diagnosed in unhappy, sad prepubertal children. The rare case of the severely depressed child, perhaps with suicidal thoughts and psychomotor retardation, presents little problem. But much commoner is the child with a continuing, though fluctuating, mood of sadness, perhaps with other neurotic or behavioural symptoms, who is facing stress of some degree in one or more areas of his life. How far the latter type of child should be regarded as suffering from an 'illness' similar to depression in adults (about which also there is controversy) is an open question. It is important because it has implications for treatment. Some psychiatrists, like Frommer[28], consider a substantial proportion of their child patients, even those under five, to be depressed. Pearce[29] studied 547 children aged 3–17, attending a child psychiatric clinic, after excluding those with organic or schizophrenic psychoses, IQs below 50, or equivocal symptoms of depression. He found that 23 per cent of the group had 'the symptom of depression'. These children were significantly older and more often postpubertal and were more often inpatients. Relationships within the family were more disturbed than with people outside it. Symptoms found significantly more often in children with depression than in those without it included morbid anxiety, sleep disturbance, irritability, suicidal tendencies, eating disturbances, school refusal, phobias, alimentary disorders/abdominal pain, ruminations/obsessions, hypochondriasis and altered perception. The author comments that these symptoms 'show a remarkable resemblance' to those of depression in adults. Depression in girls was found harder to distinguish than depression in boys, since fewer factors discriminated between depressed and non-depressed girls.

On the other hand Graham[30] advocated caution in making this diagnosis and points out that in the Isle of Wight epidemiological study sadness and misery occurred in roughly equal proportion in both the children with conduct disorders and those with neurotic conditions. He states that there is no evidence that such sadness and misery are related genetically or psychopathologically to adult depression. 'Pure' depression was found in only three children in the population studied (a rate of less than 0·2 per cent).

It seems best at present to regard depressed mood as a common accompaniment of other psychiatric symptoms and disorders of children, but not a frequent manifestation of anything resembling the depressive 'illness' of adult life. In the pre-school period the latter concept is particularly questionable. Depression in adolescence is discussed further in Chapter 13, page 191.

The term *anaclitic depression* was coined by Spitz[31] many years ago to describe a condition of misery, crying, withdrawal and failure to thrive in babies and young children suffering from severe deprivation of parental care. This was apparently an environmentally-determined reaction to a lack of care, and probably nothing to do with the depressive psychoses of later life.

TREATMENT

The treatment of depression in childhood requires full assessment of the child's condition and environment. Where the condition is a reaction to an obvious stress, this should be removed, if possible, or modified. In many cases the cause of the depression lies in the family, for example in the scapegoated child, and an approach by family group therapy (see page 222) is required. In other circumstances the child benefits from psychotherapy. The role of antidepressant drugs (see page 232) is unclear, but many psychiatrists believe them to be of value in seriously depressed children, and especially adolescents.

Suicide in Children

Suicide is probably rare in pre-pubertal children, at least in Great Britain. Shaffer[32] obtained information about all the recorded suicides in children aged 10 to 14 in England and Wales over a seven-year period and found none below age 12. On the other hand some authors believe that there is under-reporting of childhood suicide[27]. They assert that death by suicide in childhood is often reported as accidental to avoid the stigma attached to suicide. While this may be true in North America, Shaffer cites good evidence that this is not the case in England and Wales.

In Shaffer's study there were 21 boys' and 9 girls' deaths. This is an annual suicide rate of 1 child out of every 800,000 in the 10–14-year age range. The commonest method of suicide was coal-gas poisoning, followed by hanging and drug overdose. Shaffer noted two personality stereotypes in the series. One consisted of children who had led a solitary existence, were of superior intelligence and appeared to have been culturally distant from their less well educated parents. Their mothers were mentally ill. Before their death they had seemed depressed or withdrawn, and some of them had stolen or stayed away from school.

The second group, which included several of the girls, consisted of children judged impetuous or prone to aggressive or violent outbursts, as well as being suspicious, and both sensitive to and resentful of criticism.

In most of the cases there had been prior antisocial behaviour and in 46 per cent previous suicidal behaviour was reported. The commonest precipitant was a disciplinary crisis.

Suicidal attempts and threats are much more common than completed suicides. Attempted suicide should be regarded as serious and always justifies careful psychiatric evaluation of the child and his family background. Often there is an element of depression though this may clear, usually only temporarily, after the attempt, if the child is in hospital and is being treated solicitously by the family. Attempted suicide has been found to be associated with severe disturbances in children's emotional and family relationships; parental rejection is common. Long and difficult treatment involving the whole family may be needed and repeated suicidal attempts often occur[33]. Suicidal behaviour in adolescence is discussed on page 192.

OUTCOME

Most depressed children recover either with treatment or spontaneously, though the depression may last several weeks or months, especially if suitable treatment is not instituted. The outlook is closely related to how far it is possible to remove or lessen whatever environmental stress the child is facing. If there is chronic, severe stress or family relationships are grossly disturbed and cannot be repaired, the outcome may depend on whether the child can be found a happier place in which to live. If the stress continues the depression may become chronic, with serious risk to future personality development.

Acute and Subacute Confusional States

In these conditions there is diffuse impairment of brain function with a state of delirium or confusion. Episodes are generally short-lived. The condition is usually reversible following the removal of the cause, though irreversible changes may occur. (The term 'acute confusional state' is used differently in the GAP classification – page 29 where it is applied to a special form of psychosis in adolescence).

The commonest causes are systemic infections, intracranial infections, metabolic disturbances, acute brain injury and chemical intoxications caused by drugs or other toxic ingested substances. Similar states are sometimes seen in epilepsy. Children, especially in their first few years of life, are particularly prone to develop delirious states during an illness causing a high fever. Common examples are pneumonia, measles (and other acute infectious fevers) and meningitis, but in all these antibiotics have greatly reduced the incidence of psychiatric complications. All sedative drugs, if taken in sufficiently high doses, may cause delirium, as may atropine and related substances. Of importance because of their illicit use by young people are amphetamine drugs, cannabis, lysergic acid diethylamide, heroin, other opiates and cocaine.

The main symptoms of delirium are clouding of consciousness, confusion, disorientation (for time, place and person) and vivid, often frightening fantasies or hallucinations. Memory is impaired. Restlessness, fearfulness or anxiety, increased suggestibility and rapid variation in the state of consciousness are also common features. Orientation may be difficult to assess in children, and this criterion cannot apply in infants who have not yet achieved normal orientation for time, place and person. The vivid fantasies reflect the normal tendency for young children to indulge readily in fantasy. It is often difficult to be sure whether or not the patient is actually hallucinated. When they occur, hallucinations tend to be mainly visual.

Confusional states vary in severity and in acuteness. Sometimes the child is confused and disorientated, but the complete syndrome is not present. Convulsions are a common feature of these states in the first five years of life, but do not usually presage continuing epilepsy.

The treatment of these conditions is that of the underlying cause.

References

1. Kanner, L. 'Autistic disturbance of affective contact'. *Nervous Child*, **2**, 217–250, 1943.
2. Kanner, L. 'Early infantile autism'. *Journal of Pediatrics*, **25**, 211–217, 1944.
3. Kolvin, I. *et al*. 'Studies in the childhood psychoses'. *British Journal of Psychiatry*, **118**, 381–419, 1971.
4. Rutter, M. 'Infantile autism and other child psychoses'. In *Child Psychiatry: Modern Approaches*, ed. M. Rutter and L. Hersov. Oxford: Blackwell, 1976.
5. Wing, J. K., O'Connor, N. and Lotter, V. 'Autistic conditions in childhood: a survey in Middlesex'. *British Medical Journal*, **3**, 389–392, 1967.
6. Rutter, M. 'Autistic children: infancy to adulthood'. *Seminars in Psychiatry*, **2**, 435–450, 1970.

7. Rutter, M. and Lockyer, L. 'A 5- to 15-year follow-up of infantile psychosis'. *British Journal of Psychiatry*, **113**, 1169–1182, 1967.

8. Bartak, L., Rutter, M. and Cox, A. 'A comparative study of infantile autism and specific developmental receptive language disorder'. *British Journal of Psychiatry*, **126**, 127–145, 1975.

9. Rees, H. M. N. 'Assessment and treatment of language disordered children'. In *The Residential Psychiatric Treatment of Children*, ed. P. Barker, London: Crosby Lockwood Staples, 1974.

10. Marchant, R., Howlin, P., Yale, W. and Rutter, M. 'Graded change in the treatment of the behaviour of autistic children'. *Journal of Child Psychology and Psychiatry*, **15**, 221–227, 1974.

11. Hermelin, B. and O'Connor, N. *Psychological Experiments with Autistic Children*. Oxford: Pergamon, 1970.

12. Szurek, S. A. and Berlin, I. N. (eds). *Clinical Studies in Childhood Psychosis*, New York: Brunner/Mazel, 1973.

13. Currie, K. H. and Brannigan, C. 'Behaviour analysis and modification with an autistic child'. In *Behaviour Studies in Psychiatry*, ed. C. and S. J. Hutt. Oxford: Pergamon, 1970.

14. Lovaas, O. I., Koegel, R., Simmons, J. Q. and Long, J. S., 'Some generalisations and follow-up measures on autistic children in behaviour therapy'. *Journal of Applied Behavioural Analysis*, **6**, 131–166, 1973.

15. Creak, M. 'Childhood psychosis: a review of 100 cases'. *British Journal of Psychiatry*, **109**, 84–89, 1963.

16. Corbett, J., Harris, R., Taylor, E. and Trimble, M. 'Progressive disintegrative psychosis of childhood'. *Journal of Child Psychology and Psychiatry*, **18**, 211–219, 1977.

17. Norouha, M. J. 'Cerebral degenerative disorders of infancy and childhood'. *Developmental Medicine and Child Neurology*, **16**, 228–241, 1974.

18. Wilson, J. 'Investigation of degenerative disease of the central nervous system'. *Archives of Disease in Childhood*, **47**, 136–170, 1974.

19. Barker, P. 'History'. In *The Residential Psychiatric Treatment of Children*, ed. P. Barker, London: Crosby Lockwood Staples, 1974.

20. Jeavons, P. and Bower, B. D. *Infantile Spasms. A Review of the Literature and Study of 112 Cases*. London: Heinemann, 1964.

21. Jeavons, P., Harber, J. R. and Bower, B. D. 'Long-term prognosis in infantile spasms. *Developmental Medicine and Child Neurology*, **12**, 413–421, 1970.

22. Heller, T. 'About dementia infantilis' (translation). *Journal of Nervous and Mental Disease*, **119**, 471–477, 1954.

23. Vrono, M. 'Schizophrenia in childhood and adolescence'. *International Journal of Mental Health*, **2**, 7–116, 1974.

24. Kendall, R. E. 'Schizophrenia: the remedy for diagnostic confusion'. *British Journal of Hospital Medicine*, **8**, 383–390, 1972.

25. Anthony, E. J. and Scott, P. 'Manic–depressive psychosis in childhood'. *Journal of Child Psychology and Psychiatry*, **1**, 53–72, 1960.

26. Varsanis, J. and Macdonald, S. M. 'Manic–depressive disease in childhood'. *Canadian Psychiatric Association Journal*, **17**, 270–281, 1972.

27. Garfinkel, B. and Golombek, H. 'Suicide and depression in childhood and adolescence'. In *Psychological Problems of the Child and his Family*, ed. P. Steinhauer and Q. Rae-Grant, Toronto: Macmillan, 1977.

28. Frommer, E. 'Depressive illness in childhood'. In *Recent Developments in Affective Disorders*, ed. A. Coppen and A. Walk. Ashford, Kent: Headley Brothers, 1968.

29. Pearce, J. B. 'The recognition of depressive disorders in children'. *Journal of the Royal Society of Medicine*, **71**, 494–500, 1978.
30. Graham, P. 'Depression in pre-pubertal children'. *Developmental Medicine and Child Neurology*, **14**, 340–349, 1974.
31. Spitz, R. A. 'Anaclitic depression'. *Psychoanalytic Study of the Child*, **2**, 113–117, 1946.
32. Shaffer, D. 'Suicide in childhood and adolescence'. *Journal of Child Psychology and Psychiatry*, **15**, 275–291, 1974.
33. Connell, P. H. 'Suicidal attempts in childhood and adolescence'. In *Modern Perspections in Child Psychiatry*, ed. J. G. Howells. New York: Brunner/Mazel, 1971.

CHAPTER SEVEN

Enuresis, Encopresis and the Hyperkinetic Syndrome

In the past, enuresis, encopresis and the hyperkinetic syndrome have been classified as 'developmental disorders', that is disorders of development in specific, limited areas of function which often occur in the absence of any other serious disorder[1]. The 1975 revision of the *International Classification of Diseases*[2], however, limits the category of 'specific disorders of development' more strictly, omitting these three common problems; instead enuresis and encopresis, appear under 'special symptoms or syndromes not elsewhere classified', while the hyperkinetic syndrome has a specific code with 5 sub-categories. The GAP classification's (see page 29) category, 'developmental deviations', has a sub-category, 'deviations in maturational patterns' which covers enuresis and encopresis as primary conditions. This classification does not have a single category for hyperkinetic disorders.

For convenience these three common and important developmental problems are considered together in this chapter.

Enuresis

Bedwetting, or *nocturnal enuresis*, often occurs on its own. It may be accompanied by daytime wetting, or *diurnal enuresis*; less commonly diurnal enuresis occurs on its own. Most children achieve day and night continence by three to four years of age, usually being dry by day before they are dry at night. Persistent enuresis beyond age 5 is abnormal.

Prevalence studies show bedwetting to be very common. About ten per cent of children still wet their beds at age five; the percentage falls to about five at age ten and one to two per cent continue during their teens. These are average figures from Britain, different studies having produced different results, probably because different criteria for calling a child enuretic have been used[3]. There are also big differences between countries. In Australia and North America the rate is three times that in Sweden, where the prevalence is about 8 per cent at age 5. The British rate is thus nearer the Swedish one, than that of the 'bed-sodden states of America'[4]. The prevalence generally drops with increasing age, but some studies have shown an increase between the ages of five and seven, especially in boys. This is presumably due to the appearance, between these ages, of cases of secondary enuresis, that is enuresis appearing after the child has become dry. The prevalence of daytime wetting is considerably lower than that of nocturnal wetting; about 2 per cent of 5-year-olds are wet by day once a week or more, though about 8 per cent are wet at least once a month.

The *causes* of enuresis are imperfectly understood, and probably vary from case to case. Genetic factors seem to play a part. Enuresis tends to run in families and a study of twins by Bakwin has shown that monozygotic twins are concordant for enuresis about twice as often as dizygotic twins[5]. Physical causes are rare and most enuretics have no demonstrable physical abnormality except for small bladder capacity. It has been shown, however, that enuretics have on average smaller maximum bladder capacities than non-enuretics; that they pass urine more frequently than non-enuretics; and that their bladders are only functionally and not structurally small. Enuresis may also be associated with urinary infections, especially in girls, and occasionally there is structural abnormality of the urinary tract. Other rare causes are nocturnal epileptic fits and conditions causing the production of excessive quantities of urine (for example, diabetes). Most physical causes lead to diurnal as well as nocturnal enuresis.

There is an association between enuresis and emotional disorder, though most enuretic children are not disturbed. Enuresis can, like soiling, be a part of a pattern of regression (see page 114). Enuresis can also be a symptom of a more general disturbance such as neurosis, psychosis, or adjustment reaction. It has been suggested that early disturbing events (family break-up, temporary separation from mother, birth of a sibling, accidents, operations, hospital admission, moving house) can cause enuresis. MacKeith[6] believes that there is a 'sensitive' period for learning bladder control (one-and-a-half to four-and-a-half years) and that if something happens to interfere with learning or training at that time, subsequent learning will be more difficult.

Unusually deep sleep has been said to contribute to nocturnal enuresis, but satisfactory evidence that enuretic children do sleep especially deeply is lacking, though this theory, like most of the others, has not been disproved. Another theory is that delayed maturation of the nervous system (or certain parts of it), which may be partly genetically determined, is important. This would account for the findings of twin studies and the fact that there is a positive family history in up to 70 per cent of cases of primary enuresis. It might be expected that delayed biological maturation would be more likely to lead to continuing enuresis if combined with family disorganisation, inconsistent training or other stresses producing anxiety. Delay in achieving bladder control is also a feature of mental handicap, and is usually marked in the presence of severe retardation.

The causation of enuresis, and other aspects of the condition, are discussed in the book *Bladder Control and Enuresis*[3] and also by Shaffer[7].

Clinical picture: Most cases of nocturnal enuresis are of the primary variety. The child has never become dry at night. The only symptom, initially at least, is the passing of urine while asleep. In due course this may be complicated by feelings of anxiety or guilt, particularly if the child is blamed or punished for his wetting. Depending on the family's attitudes towards the symptom, a secondary emotional disorder may develop. Indeed enuresis causes great unhappiness and distress to some children, and this is perhaps its main psychiatric importance. Many children are blamed for it and some are severely punished. It can prevent holidays, visits to relations and friends, and participation in camping activities.

Some bedwetters (about a fifth) have increased frequency of micturition by day but do not actually wet themselves during the day. In other cases there is both increased frequency and daytime wetting. The presence of these features, however, is more often associated with the existence of other evidence of anxiety or emotional disorder. The presence of infection of the urinary tract is also more likely if wetting occurs both by day and by night.

Investigation and treatment should go hand in hand. In primary enuresis carefully taken histories from child and parents will establish that the enuresis is the outstanding problem, and that any other emotional symptoms are a consequence of the wetting. It is important to adopt an optimistic outlook while taking the history and to let the family feel that the problem is a common one, and not too serious, despite the inconvenience it may cause. Many parents, and children, are unaware of the frequency of the complaint. The self-blame both often show must be dispelled as far as possible. The history must be considered to see whether there is evidence of any physical abnormality of bladder or urethra. The abdomen and external genitalia should be examined, and the urine tested, especially for evidence of infection. X-ray examination of the urinary tract is done routinely in some clinics, but is probably only necessary if there is evidence to suggest a physical abnormality. The latter is unlikely if the wetting is purely nocturnal.

When there is no evidence of physical or emotional disorder, as in most cases, the choice of treatment lies between drug therapy and treatment with the pad and buzzer. Either method should be combined with support and reassurance for the family. The symptom is usually best talked about as 'a delay in learning to control the bladder while asleep' (or 'when excited', etc.) rather than as a serious disease. It should be made clear that the child wets himself involuntarily. (Deliberate, that is consciously intended, wetting is rare and is almost always a symptom of a general disturbance such as a conduct disorder.)

The only drugs which have been shown to be effective are tricyclic drugs such as imipramine, amitriptyline, nortriptyline and related compounds. Imipramine has been shown, in controlled trials, to be effective in a significant number of cases, though the response rate falls well short of 100 per cent, and the relapse rate is high. It should be given initially in a dose of 25 mg at night, increasing if necessary to 50 mg. The mode of action of the tricyclic drugs is uncertain. They are also antidepressants, but it may be that they are effective in enuresis as a result of their side-effects on the autonomic nervous system (see page 233), rather than because of their antidepressant action. It does seem, however, that some children thought not to be disturbed show behavioural changes for the better while on imipramine for enuresis, and a few show adverse psychological effects including irritability and depression[8]. If there is response to medication it should be continued at least until the child has been dry for a continous period of a month. A very cautious reduction in dosage can then be tried. Any sign of relapse should lead to an increase to the former dosage. The total duration of treatment needed is usually several months.

Conditioning with the pad and buzzer apparatus is often used as the treatment of first choice[7,9]. The apparatus consists essentially of two metal sheets, one at least being perforated, which are placed in the bed and attached to a buzzer or bell. The wire gauze or foil-covered sheets are arranged so that there is a sheet (flannelette or cotton) between them, and another one on top of the upper one. If only one of the foil-covered sheets is perforated, this should be the upper one. The wires are then attached, with the metal sheets in such a position that they will become wet as soon as the child starts to pass urine. The arrangement is shown in Figure 1. The wires lead to a buzzer or bell which is best placed at a sufficient distance from the bed,

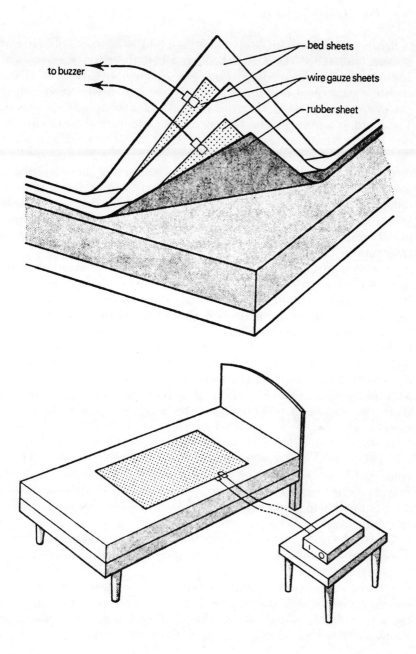

Figure 1

preferably at the bottom, to prevent the child switching it off without getting out of bed. It is switched on when the child goes to bed, and as soon as the sheet separating the two metal pads gets wet the circuit is completed and the buzzer sounds. It is better for the child not to wear pyjama trousers; this ensures quick wetting of the sheets. The child is woken by the buzzer and should then get out of bed, turn off the buzzer, pass urine and, ideally, re-set the apparatus using dry sheets. Sometimes in the initial stages it may sound two or even three times in the course of a night. In such cases there is often a particularly quick response to the treatment. Use of the apparatus should be continued at least until the child has been dry continuously for three weeks. Even after this period relapse may occur, but relapses usually respond quickly to a second course of treatment. In occasional cases more than one further course of treatment is needed.

Certain points are important in this treatment. It is essential to get the child's active co-operation. Without it treatment is seldom successful. It is often best for the child to set up the apparatus, switch it on and keep a record of wet and dry nights, rather than have the parents do these things. Some children, if not adequately prepared, are frightened of the machine; others are suspicious of it or hostile towards it. It is easy for a child to sabotage its use, so any feelings such as these must be explored and dealt with before treatment is started. If after a few discussions a child of seven or older does not accept the treatment there may well be an emotional disorder needing treatment in its own right.

The apparatus can seldom be used effectively in children below age six. Sometimes it is necessary to wait until a year, or even two, later before adequate co-operation can be gained. Children of six to seven may be better moved into, or near, their parents' bedroom, so that a parent can help them re-set the buzzer and rearrange the bed after they have woken.

If any relapses are treated promptly along the lines suggested, a good response to conditioning treatment is usually obtained. Success rates of 80 per cent or better may be expected. In refractory cases imipramine 25–50 mg at bedtime, or amitriptyline in the same dose, may be combined with use of the buzzer. Other measures such as restricting the amount the child drinks, or lifting during the night, should be avoided. They tend to delay the conditioning process.

Buzzer ulcers are an occasional complication of the use of the buzzer. They may occur if current passes between the electrodes through the skin. This can occur if the apparatus and drawsheet become disarranged so that the electrodes touch the skin. It can also occur when conduction through the skin is facilitated because the skin is wet with urine or, possibly, sweat. It may happen in the presence of urine if (a) there is insufficient urine to trigger the alarm so that a small current passes for a considerable time; (b) the buzzer fails to operate because the battery is partially exhausted; or (c) the child fails to wake up when the alarm sounds, so that buzzing continues until exhaustion of the battery causes the relay to cease operating, whereupon the electrodes again become live. Modern buzzer design has largely eliminated these problems, but it is important to ensure that a flat battery is never used.

Outcome: As the figures for prevalence show, there is a tendency for children to grow out of their enuresis, though the spontaneous recovery rate is not sufficient to justify therapeutic inaction. Active treatment, particularly of primary enuretics in the age range six to nine, usually gives excellent results. If treatment is left till later the results tend to be less satisfactory. Sometimes secondary emotional disorder interferes with treatment, though it can usually be overcome. Children with impoverished and disorganised homes, especially when they share a bed with one or more siblings, are difficult to treat. Even if the child can be got into a bed on his own, systematic and correct use of the buzzer may be hard to achieve. Drug therapy may be easier. Occasionally it is justifiable to admit children from such backgrounds to a hospital or other institution for conditioning therapy.

Encopresis (Faecal soiling)

Encopresis, or faecal soiling, is the passing of faeces in the clothes. Usually the underpants are soiled, but the symptom sometimes occurs at night with soiling of pyjamas, nightdress or bedclothes. A child is normally 'clean', that is continent of faeces, by the age of three. Some otherwise normal children do not achieve continence until a little later, but soiling beyond the age of four is abnormal.

Soiling has been classified into 'continuous' and 'discontinuous' varieties. 'Continuous' means that the soiling has been present from birth. In discontinuous soiling the symptom appears after a period of continence.

Prevalence: Bellman[10], in a study in Sweden, found a prevalence rate at age 7 of 2·3 per cent in boys and 0·7 per cent in girls, a boy:girl ratio of 3·4 to 1. In the Isle of Wight[11] survey of 10- and 11-year-olds, the prevalence was 1·3 per cent in boys and 0·3 per cent in girls. Clinical studies also show a much higher rate in boys than girls. The prevalence falls practically to zero by age 16[10].

Causes: Soiling is more often a manifestation of emotional disorder than is enuresis, but physical disease is sometimes the cause. It may be due to failure on the parents' part to provide suitable, consistent toilet training. Children have to learn to defaecate at the appropriate time and place. If there is no consistent pattern of training they may not learn this by the normal age. This may happen in disorganised and chaotic families, which usually show their social incapacities in other ways too[12]. It can also happen in understaffed or badly run institutions, such as orphanages. In due course the child's persistent soiling may lead to angry, punitive and rejecting attitudes on the part of the parents, or parent substitutes, who do not realise that the soiling is due to their own failure, or inability, to provide suitable training. Soiling due to inadequate training is usually of the continuous variety.

Mental handicap is another common cause of continuous soiling. Severely retarded children are always slow to achieve bowel control, and many of the most handicapped never do so. Less severely retarded children tend to be later than normal in achieving continence, depending partly on their environment and toilet training. Retarded children living in large, understaffed hospitals for the mentally handicapped are at a particular disadvantage.

Soiling due to emotional causes, usually though not always discontinuous, is seen more often in child psychiatric clinics than the 'inadequate training' type. It is a common presenting problem. The rareness of the 'poor training' variety in clinics is probably due in part to the failure of families in which it occurs to make use of clinic facilities.

Emotionally determined soiling may be regressive or aggressive in type; a combination of the two is also possible.

Regression is commonly observed in children who are acutely anxious or under stress. It is a return to an early, more dependent stage of emotional development. The child who was previously independent may start clinging to mother, or cry excessively, or have temper tantrums, or demand to be fed, having previously grown out of such behaviour. Soiling and enuresis may also occur. Soiling is particularly likely to occur in the child who has fairly recently achieved faecal continence. In older children a greater degree of regression will be needed to produce this type of soiling. Regression may be caused by a variety of circumstances, but there is usually a marked upheaval in the child's emotional life. Common causes are the birth of a sibling (with perhaps the sudden loss of mother's attention), the illness or death of a parent, admission to hospital or an acute, frightening experience. In many of these cases a diagnosis of adjustment reaction (see pages 124) is more appropriate than one of developmental disorder.

Aggressive soiling is usually a manifestation of a disturbed relationship between parents (most often mother) and child[12]. The mother often has an obsessive and controlling personality, and a high regard for order and cleanliness. Toilet training has typically been started early, perhaps within the first few weeks of life. Success at a surprisingly early age, even well before the first birthday, may be reported. It is thus particularly distressing for the mother when, as a toddler or after starting school, the child begins to soil. This is also what is, unconsciously, intended by the child whose behaviour has been obsessively controlled by mother. Normal outlets for aggression may have been denied him and he has been expected always to be clean, tidy and perfectly behaved. Unconsciously, however, he feels very angry with his mother. His appreciation of her emotional Achilles' heel, namely bowel control, is also unconscious but leads to the soiling as a devious way of expressing his angry feelings. It has also been reported that these children are immature and show excessive dependence on their mothers, their fathers often playing little part in the families[13]. The mothers often have a great fear of constipation and may use laxatives to excess. Their preoccupation with bowel function may date back to their own childhood experiences.

Aggressive soiling may be retentive or non-retentive. In retentive soiling there is not just a refusal to defaecate at a place and time desired by the parents, but refusal to pass faeces at all. This leads to constipation, retention of faeces, enlargement of the large intestine which becomes filled with a mass of faeces, and then overflow incontinence. A physical disability has thus been added to the original psychological one. The condition will, if untreated, persist even if the emotional disorder resolves. It has been called 'psychogenic mega-colon'[14].

Soiling can be organically caused. *Hirschsprung's disease* is a rare condition in which the nerve ganglia are congenitally absent from a section of the colon. This section is therefore unable to contract normally and thus move the faeces on. The colon behind it becomes loaded with faeces and dilates, leading to overflow incontinence. An *anal fissure* may, by causing pain on defaecation, lead to inhibition of the passage of faeces, again with retention and overflow. This also may persist after the fissure has healed. Constipation from other causes may act in a similar way. These conditions must be considered before the soiling is accepted as psychogenic.

Description: Continuous soiling due to lack of proper toilet training usually occurs in children who appear in other ways poorly cared for. They are often dirty and badly dressed. There may be other evidence of poor social training. Truancy from school may be reported and progress at school is often unsatisfactory. The families usually face, or through their social inadequacy have acquired, many other problems. These may include bad housing, a burden of debt, unemployment or a criminal record. The child's soiling may be just one feature, though perhaps the most prominent and troublesome, of a general pattern of immature behaviour. Soiling due to mental handicap is readily distinguished by its association with general retardation of development.

Regressive soiling may occur in children from any social class. The symptom is usually readily recognised as due to some acute or continuing emotional stress. There may be regression in spheres other than bowel function. There may also be other evidence of anxiety. The anxiety is, however, understandable in the light of the stress the child is facing. (If it were disproportionate, a diagnosis of a neurotic condition might be more apt. Some short-lived episodes of regressive soiling reactive to acute stress are appropriately classified as adjustment reactions.) The symptom is closely allied to the diarrhoea some adults experience before examinations, interviews and the like.

Aggressive soiling usually occurs in the obsessive, bowel-conscious family setting described above. In contrast to the first category these children are clean, often too clean, well dressed and inhibited in their behaviour. They tend to be bright, successful pupils at school, in contrast to the typical 'continuous' soiler who usually is not. They appear ashamed of their soiling and may attempt to conceal it, for example by hiding or destroying underpants. They are often reluctant to discuss it though they may allude to it in play or drawings. There may be retention of faeces. This is ascertained by digital examination of the rectum. When there is overflow incontinence, faeces leaking from the rectum may be visible. It may also be possible to feel faecal masses on palpation of the abdomen. There may be few associated symptoms, the child being a generally socially conforming individual. Nevertheless there are sometimes other features which also represent expressions of the child's hostility. The commonest is food refusal. Failure to eat sufficiently is complained of by parents in about half these cases. The child usually appears adequately nourished, but is not eating enough to satisfy mother (or father). He is, as it were, rebelling by means of both ends of the alimentary tract. There is, by contrast, an absence of the rough play and self-assertiveness of a degree which would be normal at the child's age.

In some children who soil there may be both aggressive and regressive features. In the following case there were factors evoking both anxiety and hostility towards the parents.

David was referred for psychiatric assessment at age eight, the main symptom being soiling. His birth had been normal, he was described by his mother as an easy baby to bring up, and she said toilet training was completed by his first birthday. He gave mother no trouble as a toddler and at five he went to school without difficulty. When David was six his sister died after a short illness. This upset both David and his mother, who had always been an anxious woman. She became depressed and was admitted briefly to hospital for psychiatric treatment.

On examination David was a quiet, inhibited, very clean and well-dressed boy. There was little spontaneous conversation or play, but he was polite and 'correct' in his behaviour.

Mother, by contrast, was a big, talkative, anxious and dominating woman. She tried to decide and control every activity of David, over-protecting him yet at times getting very angry with him, usually for minor, or even imagined, misdeeds. She did not bring father to the clinic but reported that he worked well in a steady job and was a good provider.

David was admitted to hospital for treatment. He was found to be chronically constipated and was given Senokot regularly. He settled quickly and after about two weeks became more self-assertive in his play and showed some aggressiveness towards the other children. His soiling had completely stopped within three weeks of admission. He did well in the clinic school.

Mother's behaviour was very disturbed. She visited daily for long periods, preventing David taking part in some of the activities arranged for the children. She was often highly critical both of David and of the hospital staff, yet she spoilt him by bringing him food and expensive presents. She seemed grossly over-anxious about him. Father visited less often, and was a quiet man who behaved normally and appropriately when with David.

Despite mother's doubts about the treatment, her lack of trust in the hospital staff, and her apparent need for a mutually dependent relationship with David she allowed him to remain in the hospital for seven weeks. David was then allowed home for a weekend, but his mother could not bring herself to let him return after this.

Mother proved a most difficult person to help. She was chronically anxious, had episodes of severe depression, was suspicious of the family and neighbours, and of the hospital staff's efforts to help her and David, and expressed much guilt about her daughter's death. She had apparently brought David up in a rigid, obsessive way. David had conformed until the death of his sister. He, and mother, then became acutely anxious and various types of regressive behaviour, particularly soiling, appeared. Mother reacted angrily and David could only assert himself by continued refusal to conform in the matter of bowel control.

It was perhaps a little surprising that after discharge David did not start to soil again, according to his mother's account, but it was clear that family relationships remained disturbed and mother required further psychiatric treatment.

Investigation: A detailed history from the parents and mental and physical examination of the child are often all that is needed to establish the type of soiling. Its severity must also be ascertained. This may be anything from slight staining of underclothes to the passage of all faeces in the clothes. It is important also to discover whether or not there is any retention of faeces.

Diagnosis tends to be most difficult in long-standing cases, particularly when there is faecal retention and over-flow incontinence. The origin of the symptom may then be impossible to discover. If it was physical, emotional disorder may have appeared secondarily, due to parental disapproval and the child's anxiety and guilt. If it was emotional, the child's negativistic refusal to defaecate may have been complicated by long-standing constipation and dilation of the colon.

X-ray examination of the abdomen may help. The most useful procedure is visualisation of the large intestine by means of a barium enema. This may show a narrow length of undilated colon with a great increase in size of the colon proximal to it, indicating Hirschsprung's disease. In this rather rare condition any emotional disorder will be secondary to the physical condition. In psychogenic cases, the whole length of the colon is dilated.

Treatment: This depends on the cause, the presence or absence of constipation or faecal retention, the age of the child and the duration of the condition. If there is no evidence of constipation or retention of faeces, no physical treatment of the bowel condition itself is required. If there has been a failure to provide normal toilet training, the child usually responds to a period of consistent, firm and kind training. This can be done in the hospital or in some other residential setting. Though it can be more difficult, it may sometimes be better to get the parents to do it at home. The family may need intensive help, not only with toilet training their children, but also in overcoming other social difficulties. Behaviour modification programmes can be helpful in these cases[15].

Regressive soiling in the acutely anxious or insecure child does not usually require treatment in itself. It is best made light of, while attention is directed to removing the cause of the child's anxiety. If this is impossible, psychotherapy may help the child cope with the stress he faces. This is discussed further in Chapter 15, as is drug therapy which may occasionally be of use.

When soiling is due to a disturbed relationship with an obsessive parent, as outlined above, psychotherapy is needed. With younger children, treatment aimed primarily at altering the parents' attitude to the problems, and thus the handling of the child, may be the main need. Sometimes an approach by family therapy (see page 222) is helpful.

Constipation, if present, must be dealt with. It often responds well to regular administration of a laxative such as Senokot. One to four tablets daily are usually required. If there is also much retention of faeces enemas and/or suppositories may be needed. (The view, propounded by a few psychiatrists, that physical measures should never be used because the soiling will clear up when the emotional problem has resolved, is not commended.)

In the more severe cases of retentive soiling, the child is usually best admitted to hospital for treatment[16]. This is certainly so if physical treatment other than the oral administration of laxatives is needed. Even then, enemas and suppositories should only be given after a good relationship with the child has been established by the nurse, and after due explanation of the treatment to the child. Otherwise the treatment may be regarded, unconsciously at least, as a further aggressive attack. Thus while the constipation may get better the basic emotional problem may worsen. Indeed, physical measures must only be carried out as part of a wider plan of treatment dealing also with the emotional problems.

Most children who soil become clean within two or three weeks of admission to hospital, provided that if there is faecal retention, this is relieved. If the soiling continues it may be because the hospital staff are dealing with it in a punitive or hostile way, or because the disturbed interaction with the parent is continuing. For example, one boy for several weeks handed his mother his soiled pants to take home and wash, unknown to the staff.

The parents always need help, whether or not the child is admitted to hospital. Usually the mother has the greater need. Once a trusting relationship with her has been established, the whole question of constipation and its dangers may be discussed. It can be difficult to get this viewed in proper perspective by these bowel-conscious people. When this has been done, at least partially, the discussion can go on to the child's symptoms. Ultimately the parent has to be led to an understanding of the soiling as a means of self-expression, or protest, or as a manifestation of anger, in a child who feels unable to express these feelings in other, normal ways. Difficult as open aggression may be for these parents to accept, they need to see that its expression can be a sign of improvement. Simple explanation of these points is seldom sufficient. Discussion over a period of time, in the context of a trusting relationship with the doctor or social worker, is required. Group therapy can be helpful in this process[13].

Psychotherapy with the child is more often needed in older children (over 8 or 9) with chronic and well-established soiling. Such children are often less sensitive to changes in parental attitudes.

The *outcome* of encopresis depends on its type. Regressive soiling generally disappears quite quickly, especially if the child is admitted for inpatient treatment. Aggressive soiling, especially when accompanied by retention, is harder to treat and may take longer to stop. In most cases the soiling has ceased by the mid-teens[10], but it appears that some of these children later show their unresolved aggressive feelings in other ways.

Hyperkinetic Syndrome of Childhood

The glossary of the ICD[2] described the essential features of the hyperkinetic syndrome as short attention span and distractibility. The GAP classification (see page 29) does not have a single category for hyperkinetic disorders, which can be classified under 'developmental deviations' (when there is no evidence of brain damage), 'chronic brain syndromes' or 'reactive disorders', according to the circumstances. When using the ICD as a multi-axial scheme (see page 27), however, the first axis diagnosis will be hyperkinetic syndrome, and associated organic and psychosocial factors would be classified in axes 4 and 5 respectively.

The *prevalence* of the hyperkinetic syndrome varies according to diagnostic criteria used, the age of the children being investigated, the method of investigation and the population studied. North American prevalence rates are generally higher than British ones; this is probably due to the use in most British studies of the criterion that hyperactivity must be present in an interview situation. By contrast questionnaire and rating scale data, which have tended to be used in North American studies, give higher prevalence rates. Safer and Allen[17], reviewing the literature, conclude that parents report 35–50 per cent of boys and 20–25 per cent of girls as hyperactive, and elementary school teachers report 40 per cent of their students as restless and one-third inattentive. But when only 'a prominent degree of hyperactivity and inattentiveness' is considered, the prevalence falls to 5–10 per cent. If learning disability is an added criterion the prevalence is about 5 per cent. The boy:girl ratio is a about 3:1 or even 4:1, so that the prevalence in elementary school is: boys, 8–9 per cent; girls, 2–3 per cent. These are mainly North American figures; by contrast in the Isle of Wight epidemiological study[11] of 10- and 11-year olds only 2 cases of hyperkinetic syndrome were found in 2199 children (0·1 per cent). By this age hyperactivity has often lessened, however.

Various *causes* have been suggested for the hyperkinetic syndrome. There is evidence that genetic factors play a significant role and that polygenic inheritance is the most likely mechanism[18]. Some children with the hyperkinetic syndrome have an organic brain disorder[19], but most do not and many brain-damaged children are not hyperactive. Hyperkinetic children tend to have been very active babies[17] and it is possible that some are children at one end of a normally distributed range of activity levels; such children might be especially at risk if growing up with parents who reacted adversely to a child with that temperamental trait.

Sometimes the terms 'minimal brain damage' or 'minimal brain dysfunction' are applied to hyperactive children and at times the terms are used almost as if they were interchangeable. Thus Wender, one of the main proponents of the concept of minimal brain dysfunction (MBD)[20], even quotes descriptions of hyperactive children when describing 'MBD'. On the other hand he states that children with MBD may be underactive; also that many of them show no neurological abnormalities of any sort. In addition over 100 clinical manifestations are attributed to MBD, making the concept virtually useless as a diagnostic entity. It is small wonder it has been described as a 'myth'[21]. Confusion is avoided if the term is not used.

Description: This syndrome consists of sustained motor hyperactivity and restlessness. The ability to concentrate is impaired, with a short attention-span. The children are abnormally distractible, but attend only briefly to the distracting stimulus. Associated symptoms often include learning problems, antisocial behaviour and a tendency to emotional outbursts. The learning difficulties are due in part to the disorder of attention which is an essential part of the syndrome, but in some cases seem to have other causes as well. If antisocial behaviour is marked, the condition will be more appropriately termed a conduct disorder, but minor forms of antisocial behaviour are almost invariably complained of by the mothers of hyperkinetic children, especially aggression and disobedience. The emotionalism is often manifest through temper tantrums, but other manifestations of anger, unhappiness, joy or annoyance may appear and disappear with bewildering frequency.

The child may be reported to have been overactive as a baby, or even *in utero*, but often the symptoms first become obvious when the child begins to walk. The parents then find these children are constantly on the move, concentrate poorly and are prone to interfere with furniture, ornaments, the contents of drawers and so forth, to an unusual extent. Normal methods of control are ineffective. Sleep disturbance is sometimes reported in younger hyperkinetic children, but many of them sleep well: apparently their activity has exhausted them by bedtime, though they are liable to waken early in the morning.

A helpful review of this syndrome has been provided by Cantwell[22].

The *assessment and treatment* of hyperkinetic children are closely related. Treatment must be preceded by assessment of the type of excessive motor activity present; the situations in which it is more, or less, prominent; and any associated problems such as learning difficulties or current retardation in school progress. The latter may be due to the impairment of concentration and shortening of attention-span caused by the hyperactivity, but it is important also to discover whether there are associated perceptual or motor difficulties, or mental handicap.

This syndrome is one of the few child psychiatric disorders in which drugs can be of real value. The choice lies between methylphenidate, various amphetamine derivatives, phenothiazine drugs and halo-peridol. The treatment must be carefully monitored and may need to continue for several years. Other treatment approaches may be of help. It is sometimes possible to lessen hyperactivity by behaviour modification techniques designed, for example, to condition attention or concentration, or to extinguish hyperactivity directly. When anxiety appears to be significant factor, psychotherapy may be of value. Where there is a learning problem a remedial education programme will be needed, and sometimes placement in a special class is helpful. Despite the often good response to drug treatment, it is important that a comprehensive treatment plan, dealing with all facets of the case, is formulated.

Help for the family is as important as treatment of the child, and in many cases there are problems of mothering. Some modern houses are singularly unsuited to the containing and management of hyper-active toddlers, and much support and advice may be needed. Anxious and obsessional parents in particular tend to find these children difficult.

The treatment methods mentioned, including drug dosages, are discussed further in Chapter 15.

Outcome: Hyperactivity tends to lessen with increasing age, and has usually ceased by puberty, but the outlook for associated learning disorders is less good, and that for antisocial behaviour worse still[23].

A significant proportion of hyperkinetic children develop antisocial disorders in adolescence. Children who have not shown antisocial behaviour do better, on the whole, than those who have. (But see also page 184.)

References

1. Rutter, M., Lebovici, S., Eisenberg, L., Sneznevskij, A. V., Sadoun, R., Brooke, E. and Lin, T. Y. 'A tri-axial classification of mental disorders in childhood'. *Journal of Child Psychology and Psychiatry*, **10**, 41–61, 1969.
2. World Health Organisation. *International Classification of Diseases*, 1975 Revision. Geneva: WHO, 1977.
3. Kolvin, I., MacKeith, R. C. and Meadow, S. R. (eds). *Bladder Control and Enuresis*. London: Heinemann, 1973.
4. 'Enuresis' (editorial). *British Medical Journal*, **1**, 1977, 4.
5. Bakwin, H. 'Enuresis in twins'. *American Journal of Diseases of Children*, **121**, 222–225, 1971.
6. MacKeith, R. 'A frequent factor in the origin of primary enuresis: anxiety in the third year of life'. *Developmental Medicine and Child Neurology*, **10**, 465–470, 1968.
7. Shaffer, D. 'Enuresis'. In *Child Psychiatry: Modern Approaches*, ed. M. Rutter and L. Hersov. Oxford: Blackwell, 1976.
8. Werry, J. S., Dowrick, P. W., Lampen, E. L. and Vamos, M. J. 'Imipramine in enuresis: psychological and physiological effects'. *Journal of Child Psychology and Psychiatry*, **16**, 289–299, 1975.
9. Dische, S. 'Management of enuresis', *British Medical Journal*, **2**, 33–36, 1971.
10. Bellman, M. 'Studies on encopresis'. *Acta Paediatrica Scandinavica*, Supplement 170, 1966.
11. Rutter, M., Tizard, J. and Whitmore, K. *Education, Health and Behaviour*. London: Longman, 1970.
12. Anthony E. J. 'An experimental approach to the psychopathology of childhood encopresis'. *British Journal of Medical Psychology*, **30**, 146–175, 1957.
13. Hoag, J. M., Norriss, N. G., Himeno, E. J. and Jacobs, J. 'The encopretic child and his family'. *Journal of the American Academy of Child Psychiatry*, **10**, 242–256, 1971.
14. Pinkerton, P. 'Psychogenic megacolon in children: the implications of bowel negativism'. *Archives of Disease in Childhood*, **33**, 371–380, 1958.
15. Sluckin, A. 'Encopresis: a behavioural approach described'. *Social Work Today*, **5**, 643–646, 1975.
16. Pinkerton, P. 'Inpatient treatment of children with psychosomatic disorders'. In *The Residential Psychiatric Treatment of Children*, ed. P. Barker, London: Crosby Lockwood Stapes, 1974.
17. Safer, D. J. and Allen, R. P. *Hyperactive Children: Diagnosis and Management*. Baltimore: University Park Press, 1976.
18. Morrison, J. and Stewart, M. 'Bilateral inheritance as evidence for polygenicity in the hyperactive child syndrome'. *Journal of Nervous and Mental Disease*, **158**, 226–228, 1976.
19. Werry, J. S. 'Organic factors in childhood psychopathology'. In *Psychopathological Disorders in Childhood*, ed. H. C. Quay and J. S. Werry. New York: Wiley, 1972.

20. Wender, P. *Minimal Brain Dysfunction in Children*. New York: Wiley, 1971.
21. Schmitt, B. D. 'The minimal brain dysfunction myth'. *American Journal of Diseases of Children*, **129**, 1313–1319, 1975.
22. Cantwell, D. 'Hyperkinetic syndrome'. In *Child Psychiatry: Modern Approaches*, ed. M. Rutter and L. Hersov. Oxford: Blackwell, 1976.
23. Mendelson, W., Johnson, N. and Stewart, M. A. 'Hyperactive children as teenagers: a follow-up study'. *Journal of Nervous and Mental Disease*, **153**, 273–279, 1971.

CHAPTER EIGHT

Other Clinical Syndromes

Adjustment Reactions

The ninth edition of the ICD[1] defines adjustment reactions as 'mild or transient disorders ... without any apparent pre-existing mental disorder'. The term is applied to circumscribed or situation-specific disorders which are generally reversible. They are usually related to major stresses, and may last a few days or up to a few months. In the GAP classification[2] these are termed 'reactive disorders'.

The ICD distinguishes three main types of adjustment reaction: those with depression (either brief or prolonged depression reactions), those with disturbance mainly of other emotions and those with disturbance of conduct. Provision is also made for a mixed type.

Adjustment reactions may take many forms. Since they are distinguished more by their mildness and transient nature, no typical clinical picture exists. They are therefore best described by means of examples.

Susan was referred at age 15, and was seen at the request of the juvenile court. She had been born in Jamaica. Her parents had migrated to England when she was three, but she had remained in Jamaica with her grandmother, joining her parents at age 12.

It seemed that Susan had never had any problems in Jamaica where she was happy, had a warm relationship with her grandmother, and progressed well at school. From the time she came to England, however, she had been unhappy. She said this was partly because she found the work and atmosphere at school different from that which she was used to, but mainly because of the situation at home. Her parents had been strangers to her when she arrived but had expected both love and obedience from her. Susan had found it difficult to provide either on demand. She said of her mother, 'She treats me different, she don't like me, she treats me like a dog.' She believed she was brought over simply to look after the four younger children born in England, who seemed to have a secure, warm relationship with the parents.

After some months of increasing unhappiness at home Susan ran away and was missing, and also absent from school, for two months. It transpired she had been living with a 17-year-old distant cousin during this time. Her parents reported unfavourably on her behaviour at home and she refused to return there.

On being placed in a group home Susan settled down well, behaved normally, showed no signs of emotional disorder and said she was happy.

COMMENT

There was no evidence that Susan suffered from any serious psychiatric disorder. Her condition was rather a transient, reversible reaction to migration from one culture to another combined with her arrival to live with a family who did not give her the support, security and understanding she needed. Her symptoms rapidly subsided with a change in environment. Her condition is an example of an adjustment reaction with a depressive element that was quite prolonged.

Timothy was referred by the family doctor at age 4 years 9 months. He had been showing aggressive behaviour since the birth of the only other child in the family, a sister two years younger. His mother described him as rude, fidgety and 'not a happy child – very highly strung'. The family were living in a new estate of owner-occupied houses, many of which were still under construction. Father was a young executive in an industrial company which was going through a financially difficult time. He worked long hours, arrived home late, tired and bad-tempered, and gave mother little support. He had had an emotionally deprived family background. While mother said she came from a warm, close family, all the other members of it lived in another part of the country.

At interview Timothy was a good-looking, well-dressed, friendly boy. He spoke freely, had a remarkably good vocabulary for his age and was pleasant and likeable in his attitude. In conversation he did give some indication of rivalry with his sister, but said he was happy at school, where he was nearing the end of his first term, and he appeared in other respects a normal, healthy child.

The problem was formulated as that of a boy living in a socially isolated family. His young mother (aged 24) was looking after two essentially healthy children with little help from her husband or anyone else. Consequently she had been unable to give Timothy enough support and attention, a situation which was exacerbated when the sister was born. Treatment consisted of five interviews with the parents and two with Timothy. The main work was done with the parents. It aimed to help them understand Timothy's needs and, perhaps more important, each other's. They were well-motivated people of high intelligence and seemed to benefit considerably from these few interviews spread over six months. After this time Timothy's symptoms had disappeared, Karen, the sister, had started at a pre-school playgroup and the parents felt the problems were resolved.

COMMENT

This was a mild adjustment reaction, fitting best in the sub-group 'with mixed disturbance of emotions and conduct', although the problem was really the family's. Brief intervention yielded good results.

Quentin was referred at age five after his mother had been told by his head teacher that he would not respond to discipline and therefore could not attend school. The school staff complained, among other things, that Quentin went into the girls' toilets in spite of being told not to and had repeatedly tried to climb over a wall, a thing which was forbidden because there was a busy road on the other side. The head teacher consequently feared for Quentin's safety and was not willing to be responsible for him in the circumstances.

Quentin's mother was unmarried. Quentin was her only child and had lived what seemed to have been an isolated life with her and his maternal grandparents before starting school. He had a mild speech defect and was a little hyperactive, but the main problem seemed to be that he had been much indulged and overprotected by his mother and especially by his grandparents who had mainly looked after him. These circumstances seemed to be the main reason for his difficult behaviour on starting school.

Quentin was admitted for a short period of inpatient assessment and treatment. He showed only mildly difficult behaviour, and this quickly ceased; he made good progress in the unit school and was discharged to attend a different school.

COMMENT

Although this boy had been indulged and overprotected, his personality development was fundamentally sound and he was of above average intelligence. In many schools he might have adjusted more easily, and psychiatric referral was probably as much a reflection of anxiety on the part of the family and school staff, as of disturbance in Quentin himself.

These cases illustrate some of the stresses that may lead to adjustment reactions. Other common stresses are the departure or return of a parent, bereavement, serious illness in a family member and social or academic difficulties at school.

Personality Disorders

Some children show seriously maladaptive personality characteristics from an early age. While many psychiatrists are reluctant to use the term personality disorder in children and adolescents, who have the capacity for further development, in some instances the deviation is so pronounced and long-standing that the diagnosis is justified.

A diagnosis of personality disorder implies that the individual has developed inappropriate ways of dealing with daily tasks, with interpersonal relationships or with the handling of stressful situations. In many cases there are difficulties in all these areas.

The *causes* of personality disorder are unclear. In many cases the modelling of inappropriate parental behaviour patterns seems to be a factor, and there is often also unsuitable, inconsistent or even largely absent parenting. The relationship of these disorders to such factors is, however, by no means direct, and in many instances genetic and other biological factors are probably important. Extreme variations of temperament (see page 21) may play a part, as may a bad 'fit' between the temperamental style of the child and the parents' temperaments.

Dockar-Drysdale[3,4] and Balbernie[5] have written extensively about 'unintegrated' children. Their work is based largely on that of Winnicott[6]. They believe that many children with personality disorders have lacked 'primary experience'. Describing what he means by this, Balbernie[5] states, 'the mother in nurturing and care, provides regular, ordered, complete experiences of well-being through which a child learns that it does survive separation'. Lacking this experience children act out their anxiety, do not feel guilt, lack regard for others' feelings and fail to value themselves. To quote Balbernie[5] again 'the basis of well-being is the experience of a basic sense of natural order that is internalised'. This has not been provided for unintegrated children.

Several categories of unintegrated children are described including 'frozen children', whose primary experience has been interrupted when they and their mothers would be starting to separate out. They survive 'without boundaries to personality, merged with their environment and unable to make any real relationships or to feel the need for them'.

Also described are 'archipelago children' who have achieved the first step towards integration, but whose 'ego-islets' have 'never fused into a continent', that is a whole person.

Two other categories are 'false-selves' and 'caretaker-selves'. Describing the 'false-self' Winnicott[6] writes:

The false-self sets up as real and it is this that observers tend to think is the real person. In living relationships, work relationships, and friendships, however, the false-self begins to fail. In situations in which what is expected is a whole person the false-self has some essential lacking. At this extreme the true self is hidden.

Winnicott[6] describes types of false-selves approaching more closely a state of health. This leads to the 'caretaken-self' which is built upon identifications. Inside this caretaker is the child's 'little self', carefully concealed. There may then, for example, be a delinquent 'caretaker' stealing, without conflict, on behalf of the 'little self'.

In *distinguishing* personality disorders from other conditions, the absence of a distorted intellectual view of the world is important. While personality disordered individuals may be self-centred and may handle situations in most unsuitable ways, they do not hold delusional beliefs as psychotic individuals do. The distinction between personality disorders and conduct disorders is more difficult, since children and adolescents with personality disorders often display antisocial behaviour. The important point is the presence of serious, long-standing difficulties of the types mentioned above as a basis for the antisocial behaviour. Indeed both children and adults with personality disorders are particularly prone to develop other conditions, for example neurotic disorders, depressive conditions or behavioural problems, as well as conduct disorders.

It is generally wise to use the diagnostic category 'personality disorder' sparingly. The term describes a long-standing state, not just recent behaviour.

The term 'borderline state' is sometimes used to describe conditions which approach psychotic severity but in which clear-cut evidence of lack of reality sense is not present[7]. In some of these cases there is a fluctuating condition, the subject appearing at times to be operating in touch with reality, while at other times this does not seem to be so. Those who use this term might well apply it in Thomas's case, but the term is not included in either the ICD or GAP schemes of classification, although the draft DSM III (see page 30) has a category 'unstable personality disorder' for patients with 'unstable interpersonal relationships, unstable mood and an unstable sense of identity'. It is probable that many so-called borderline states might be better understood as personality disorders. Further discussion of 'borderline' states in adolescence can be found in the book on the subject by Masterson[8].

Table 1 summarises the sub-categories of personality disorder listed in the two diagnostic schemes we are considering. Categories have been matched as closely as possible, but the definitions and descriptions differ, and there is no category in the GAP that corresponds strictly to the group 'with predominantly sociopathic or asocial manifestations', of the ICD.

TABLE I: CATEGORIES OF PERSONALITY DISORDER

GAP	ICD	Main Clinical Features
Compulsive	Anankastic	Rigid, inflexible, obsessive, ritualistic, perfectionistic.
Hysterical	Hysterical	Over-dramatic, flamboyant, labile mood, suggestible.
Anxious	—	Chronically tense and apprehensive.
Overly dependent	Asthenic	Helpless, clinging, passively compliant, lacking vigour.
Oppositional	(Asocial*)	Aggressive through negativism, stubbornness, procrastination.
Overly inhibited	—	Passive, shy, lacking initiative, untalkative.
Overly independent	—	Active, ebullient, challenging limits, pseudoadult.
Isolated	Schizoid	Distant, detached, cold, introspective, unresponsive.
Mistrustful	Paranoid	Suspicious, jealous, sensitive to slight or imagined insults.
Tension-discharge disorders (i) Impulse-ridden (ii) Neurotic	Explosive (Sociopathic or asocial*)	Readily express anger, violence, hate, affection, either verbally or physically. May relate in shallow fashion. Demand immediate gratification.
Sociosyntonic	—	Aggressive or antisocial but consonant with social or ethnic group.
Sexual deviation	Sexual deviations and disorders.	Sexual feelings or behaviour seriously and chronically anomalous.
—	Affective	Show lifelong mood deviation or alternation.

*These ICD categories do not correspond very closely with the GAP ones.

It will be clear that personality disorders are a very varied group of conditions. The following brief case histories can give only a limited idea of the wide range of possible ways they may be manifest.

Thomas had always been a difficult child, his mother said. His first weeks of life were interrupted by an operation for pyloric stenosis, and he was a difficult, negativistic baby and toddler. More serious, however, was his lonely, asocial behaviour. As he grew up he would not talk to other children or to strangers. He violently resisted school at age five, kicking and screaming, and resisting doing anything he was asked. Transfer to a school for slow-learning children, and then a year in a children's convalescent hospital under the care of a psychiatrist did little to help him.

At age nine Thomas appeared a good-looking boy, well-dressed, but timid and anxious. He failed to respond to most questions, and the few answers he did give were either very short verbal ones or consisted of nodding or shaking the head.

During a subsequent 2-year period of first inpatient and then daypatient treatment, Thomas made little progress. He remained quiet, isolated and passively resistant, though he could become acutely physically and verbally aggressive, for example when a physician approached him to take a sample of venous blood for a test. He persistently resisted participating in psychological tests.

The family situation was difficult in that there was much marital strife, Thomas being the focus of many parental disagreements. The parents were divorced when Thomas was 11, and soon afterwards his mother remarried. Thomas, however, remained a passive, non-communicative, friendless boy without contacts outside his home.

COMMENT

Thomas's personality had been odd, and his relationships with his family unusual, from infancy. When he was seen for assessment a gross, long-standing disorder was present, having many of the features of the isolated personality type described in the GAP, or the schizoid type of the ICD. A diagnosis of psychosis was considered, but could not be supported. While Thomas showed many of the features of elective mutism (page 138), his disorder also involved his whole personality functioning and his social and educational development. His early experiences and family relationships seemed to have combined with biological factors to produce the problem. A failure of early bonding with his mother (see page 2) may also have been important.

Laura was first seen at age 13, at which time her mother said she could no longer cope with her. She was stealing money both in the house and outside it, lying, staying out late and associating with friends her mother had forbidden her to see. When she was asked to mind her two younger half-siblings she acted irresponsibly.

Laura had had many changes of home. For her first few months she lived with her mother and father. When they separated she was placed with an aunt who was later convicted of child abuse: the charges related to the aunt's own children, but Laura said she too had been beaten repeatedly. At age 5 Laura returned to live with her mother, who was now divorced. For the next eight years she lived an unstable existence. At times she was in the care of child welfare agencies, at others she was with her mother, who had a large number of brief relationships with different men. These men would live in the home from a period of a few days up to a few months, before the relationship broke up.

Laura was admitted to a residential treatment centre for assessment and treatment. She proved a difficult child to get to know. She was emotionally cold and aloof, so that staff never knew what she was thinking or feeling. At various times she ran away, sometimes to her father. She truanted from school, stole money and other children's property and told lies. She was also suspected of having clandestine meetings with boys with whom she had been told not to associate. Staff found that the biggest problem in helping Laura was getting emotionally close to her. She seemed always to give the response that seemed most expedient. This often involved lying. It was impossible to get to the real Laura, they felt. Her life seemed to be a sort of store-front, with little or nothing behind it – or at least nothing that could be discovered. She did, however, from time to time reveal fantasies about her family, especially her father. She said that *he* loved her, and that only circumstances beyond his control stopped him having her to live with him. In fact he had only had about half-a-dozen contacts with her in the previous 10 years, but on two or three occasions when she had run away to him at his place of work he had given her a friendly reception and even bought her lunch.

It proved possible to bring about changes in Laura's behaviour by setting up environmental contingencies: for example she responded to monetary fines for certain behaviours. These changes were not permanent, and when the fines were discontinued, her behaviour relapsed. Behaviour change based upon her relationships with people, and on identifications, did not seem possible.

COMMENT

The central feature of Laura's disorder seemed to be an inability to form warm, close relationships with people. Her personality problem seemed to fit best into the group with predominantly sociopathic or asocial manifestations of the ICD. It is probable that a major causative factor was her lack of a loving, stable relationship with a mother-figure during her first few years of life. She had many features of Winnicott's[6] 'false-self' children (see page 128).

Terence was first referred for psychiatric assessment at the age of twelve. He had been abandoned by his mother as a baby and admitted to the care of the local authority. He spent his first five years in a residential nursery, and then moved to a group home, where there were several changes of houseparents.

The presenting problems were Terence's tendency, since age six, to spy upon female staff members when they were undressing or having a bath, and an incident in the early hours of one morning. On this occasion he went into the older girls' bedroom, got into the bed of one of them and started exploring with his hand the breasts and genitals of this girl, greatly to the alarm of the girl and the staff.

At interview Terence was a big boy for his age, in early puberty, but passive and reluctant to discuss freely the presenting problems. When confronted with his voyeuristic acts he always maintained they would not be repeated. He had learned his lesson and would discuss the subject no further. Invariably, however, the acts were repeated. Various treatment attempts, including psychotherapy and drug therapy, failed. Terence seemed lacking in any motivation for treatment.

Terence was subsequently moved to another, smaller home where at first he seemed to settle. But after a few months, similar problems again arose. He was referred back to the author at age 16, after appearing in court charged with sexually assaulting girls. He admitted that he had approached girls 'mauling them and feeling their breasts', as he put it. He was unable to make any normal contact with girls. The staff of the home where he was then living reported that they had the utmost difficulty in getting him to go to the local shops because most of the assistants were teenage girls with whom he was too shy to talk.

Terence did obtain a job in a local factory, where there were a number of girls. He dealt with this situation by having nothing whatever to do with the girls – not even talking to them. In other respects there was no evidence of psychiatric disorder.

Although Terence was successful in keeping out of trouble with the police over a period of six months, he was later convicted of further sexual offences.

COMMENT

This boy's psychosexual development took an abnormal course at least from the age of six. It is probably significant that he had spent all his infancy and childhood in institutions, and had been looked after mainly by female staff. How important was the lack of a normal family life and of suitable identification figures, and how major a part was played by constitutional factors, it is impossible to say. Not all boys brought up in similar circumstances show this sort of deviant psycho-sexual development, so constitutional vulnerability was probably important. In any event, by the age of 16 Terence showed signs of an established pattern of 'sexual deviation' as defined in the GAP and the ICD.

The *treatment* of children with personality disorders is difficult and it is likely that by the time such a disorder is established only radical, intensive, long-term measures have any hope of success. Only a few therapists and treatment centres have concentrated on trying to help such children; among such centres in Britain are the Mulberry Bush School and the Cotswold Community. For further information on this work the reader should consult especially the work of Barbara Dockar-Drysdale[3,4], and Richard Balbernie[5].

The British Department of Health and Social Security also proposed, in 1971, to set up *youth treatment centres*[9]. These were designed for what were described as 'severely damaged boys and girls' who 'show grossly impaired capacity for making relationships and a paucity of satisfying life experiences'. The publication proposing the centres listed the following characteristics of the children they were intended to treat. They are a useful summary of the characteristics of probably the most difficult group of personality disorders, though of course some disorders take other forms, for example, withdrawal (as in the case of Thomas mentioned above) or deviant psychosexual development (as in Terence's case).

(a) They exhibit a markedly diminished sense of responsibility to an extent that staff find frustrating and alarming, since the normal capacity to respond co-operatively to help seems to be so seriously impaired.

(b) They lack restraint, inhibitions and development of the more mature reactions that are found in some measure in the majority of approved (i.e. 'training') school boys and girls.

(c) They lack concern, guilt or anxiety about the consequences of their behaviour.

(d) They are capable of explosive violence which may appear un-directed and unmotivated, and they may show an altered state of consciousness with violence.

(e) They may exhibit marked symptoms of instability which are often distressing and bizarre and undermine staff confidence in handling and management.

(f) Their conduct at times may be potentially dangerous to themselves, other children, the staff and the outside community.

(g) They may present, during adolescence, acute behavioural crises which in many cases follow on long-standing behaviour difficulties displayed less acutely throughout childhood.

(h) They show a grossly impaired capacity for making relationships and a paucity of satisfying life experiences.

At the time of writing little information has been published about the results of treatment in these centres.

The *outcome* in children with personality disorders tends to be poor, at least unless intensive long-term treatment is available. Prevention may offer more hope and is discussed in Chapter 17.

Tics and Gilles de la Tourette's Syndrome

Tics, sometimes known as *habit spasms*, are repeated, sudden movements of muscles or groups of muscles, not under the voluntary control of the subject and serving no obvious purpose. They most often affect the face, and eye-blinking tics are one of the commonest types. A variety of facial contortions may occur and muscle groups in other parts of the body may be affected too. Thus the whole head and neck may be suddenly and briefly moved in one direction or contorted. Trunk and limbs may display similar movements. A feature of tics, as opposed to the involuntary movements seen in the various forms of chorea, is that the same movements occur repeatedly, in severe cases scores or hundreds of times a day. When they involve large movements, especially of the trunk and limbs, tics can constitute a serious handicap. Vocal tics are similarly sudden and involuntary vocalisations. They may consist simply of noises, or actual words may be vocalised.

Prevalence. About five per cent of seven-year-old children have a history of tics. They are often considered to be of 'nervous' or 'emotional' origin but in reality their cause is unknown. Causes that have been suggested include emotional tension, brain damage or developmental abnormality; explanations derived from learning theory have also been put forward. There may well be multiple factors involved. Tics are commoner in children than in adults and in younger children than in older ones.

Description. A survey of 100 ticquers seen at the Maudsley Hospital, London, provided much information about the condition[10]. Seven per cent of children seen in the child psychiatric department had tics. Boys predominated in a ratio of more than three to one. The tics most commonly started about age seven. The face was the most frequently affected part of the body. Isolated tics of other parts were less common. The ticquers showed certain emotional symptoms significantly more often than the general clinic population of disturbed children. These were 'gratification habits, speech disorders, disorders of defaecation (including encopresis) and obsessional and hypochondriacal symptoms'. By contrast, tempers and aggression, truanting, fighting and depression occurred less often in ticquers. These findings could mean that the tics (and the symptoms that go with them) are means of expressing anxiety and aggression in individuals who have difficulty in expressing these emotions more directly. Moreover, many of the ticquers were found at later follow-up to be anxious even though the tics had improved.

The *Gilles de la Tourette syndrome* consists of the combination of motor tics, usually severe, with involuntary vocal and verbal utterances, often obscene (sometimes known as coprolalia). The vocal tics may take the form of impulsive enunciation of words spoken by others (echolalia). The condition starts in childhood and may persist into adult life, though it sometimes resolves. It is not certainly established that sufferers from this condition have anything other than particularly severe forms of tic syndrome, though some authors believe they do[11].

In the *treatment* of mild tics the general management should consist of a supportive attitude, combined with the removal or alleviation of any circumstances causing anxiety in the child. The tics should be made light of, and parents encouraged to ignore them. They should be explained as a somatic manifestation of anxiety. In more severe and persistent cases, including Tourette's syndrome, drug treatment is usually helpful. The most useful drug is haloperidol, but quite high doses (up to 6 mg per day) may be needed[12]. Phenothiazines are also sometimes effective and may be tried in the few cases which do not respond to haloperidol. Further information about these drugs is given in Chapter 16. Psychotherapy has also been recommended, but its efficacy is uncertain; if there is serious associated emotional disorder however it may be helpful. Claims have also been made for various forms of behaviour therapy, but again their effectiveness is unproven.

The *outcome* is quite good. The Maudsley study suggests that most children's tics improve, and 40 per cent had recovered at follow-up five years after psychiatric consultation. There seemed to be a tendency to anxiety and neurosis in the patients followed up. Tourette's syndrome presents a more difficult treatment problem, but the symptoms often remain in abeyance if the subject is maintained on haloperidol.

Stuttering

Stuttering (or stammering) is the repeated interruption of the flow of speech by repetition, prolongation or blocking of sounds. In children aged two to four there are often hesitations, repetitions of the first sounds of words or phrases, and irregularities of the rhythm of speech. This is known as 'clutter' and sometimes precedes true stuttering, though in many cases the child grows out of it and comes to speak normally.

Stuttering may also appear after speech has been acquired. It is present in about one per cent of school children in Britain. It usually starts before the age of ten. It is three to four times commoner in boys than in girls. Its causes are not fully understood but hereditary predisposition, other constitutional factors (notably brain injury and mental retardation), emotional stress and anxiety may play a part. The consensus of current opinion seems to be that there is an underlying disorder of neurological maturation, and that faulty learning processes contribute also. Disturbed parent–child relationships may affect the learning of fluent speech. As a group, stutterers are late in starting to talk and below average in intelligence. There is often a family history of the condition. Nevertheless there are many exceptions to these generalisations. The syndrome has been well described by Andrews and Harris[13].

The severity of stuttering varies from occasional repetition of speech sounds to severe blocking of speech which seriously interferes with communication. The severity may vary greatly from time to time. Some children can speak freely at home but stutter at school. Some can sing freely but talk with a stutter. Some are obviously worse when anxious, but others are not. Anticipatory anxiety may be present and avoidance behaviour often develops. At first the avoidance may simply be of certain letters or sounds but it may spread to involve particular places or social situations, so that the subject's whole life pattern is affected. Sometimes stuttering children become isolated at school, and their communication difficulty may affect their ability to take part normally in lessons and other activities.

Usually stuttering is not a part of a more widespread psychiatric disorder, and in most cases the contribution of emotional disorder appears small, at least as regards the basic cause, though anxiety may exacerbate the condition. Neurotic symptoms or antisocial behaviour sometimes seem to develop as a reaction to stuttering.

The *treatment* of stuttering is usually undertaken by speech therapists. The psychiatric contribution to it is limited. Techniques intended to relieve anxiety, promote relaxation in the child and encourage self-confidence may help. Various specific techniques are recommended for the symptom, for example 'syllabic speech', in which stutterers are taught, usually in a group, to speak slowly and deliberately, syllable by syllable. Psychotherapy should probably be reserved for cases in which there is associated emotional disorder in child or family. Drugs, particularly haloperidol, may help, especially in the more severe cases[14]. Approaches to treatment, and other aspects of the syndrome, are discussed by Wingate[15].

Many children who stutter outgrow the symptom, but in some cases it persists into adult life.

Elective Mutism

In elective mutism the child refuses to talk in certain circumstances, often at school, yet talks freely elsewhere, especially at home. It is generally considered a rare condition, occurring in 1 per cent or less of referrals to child psychiatry clinics. No populations study was on record until Brown and Lloyd published a survey of all 6072 children who enrolled in infant school in Birmingham, England one September[16]. These were children aged about 5. Forty-two were still not speaking in class after 8 weeks in school, a prevalence rate of 7·2 per 1000 children. The number of mute children fell steadily during the subsequent four terms; at 64 weeks after starting school only one child remained silent at school. The condition is thus fairly common as an initial reaction to school, but is rare as a persistent problem. Similar findings were reported by Bradley and Sloman[17]. They found 26 electively mute children in a total sample of 6865 Canadian kindergarten children, with a highly significant excess of children from immigrant families.

The *causes* of elective mutism are not fully understood. The family backgrounds of the children vary from obviously disturbed to apparently normal. Brain damage and intellectual handicap are usually absent. Psychoneurotic conflict has been suggested as a cause, with an abnormally close tie to the mother, great dependency needs and regression to an infantile 'oral' level of behaviour as a psychological defence. Explanations based on learning theory have been suggested[18]. There is evidence of a family history of shyness more often than in 'control' cases[16]. The condition is probably a complex disorder to which genetic and other personality factors, emotional disorder, deviant learning processes and problems of family dynamics may all contribute.

The main *clinical feature* is the child's failure to talk, at school, in the consulting room and usually in most places other than home. Yet at home the child talks freely. There is usually no defect of speech and language. Other behavioural abnormalities may be present. Brown and Lloyd[16] found that children who were mute at school showed other behaviour patterns which distinguished them from speaking children: they were more likely to stop an activity when the teacher approached and to avoid playing with other children, and less likely to draw, go to the toilet or approach the teacher's table.

In the doctor's office or therapist's playroom these children usually behave as negatively non-verbally as they do verbally. They may passively decline to sit down when invited to do so, or to engage in any play activity. Some will shake or nod (usually shake) their heads in reply to questions, others deny the examiner even this response. At the same time they can usually be seen looking around the room, apparently taking everything in. They can be extraordinarily stubborn, remaining silent for session after session for months, even years. Yet given the right conditions (for them) they can speak freely. One girl who was making good, if non-vocal, progress at school was observed on closed circuit television to be talking freely and in a relaxed way when alone with her family; but as soon as a staff member entered the room she became silent and remained so as long as he was in the room.

It has been suggested that there are different types of electively mute children. Reed[19] described four cases. Two were 'hyper-relaxed' and made little response to any kind of stimulus, being generally negativistic and immobile. The other two showed much tension and anxiety. He thought that the first group, which could be called 'manipulative', might have learned mutism as an attention-gaining and evasive form of behaviour, while the second, which might be called 'phobic' used mutism as a fear-reducing mechanism.

Treatment of the established, long-standing case can be very difficult. Brown and his colleagues, in a review of treatment[18], list the following approaches which have been tried: suggestion, persuasion, coercion, psychodynamically oriented play therapy, speech therapy, family therapy and behaviour therapy. All have met with only equivocal success. This does not of course apply to the mute child recently arrived at school, who is likely to start to speak within a few terms at most, but to the case which has persisted longer than this. It seems that the most effective treatment may be behaviour therapy, but only for Reed's second group, the 'phobic' cases. The 'manipulative' group often show a stubborn resistence to any treatment[18].

Outcome. Elective mutism is usually a self-limiting condition, becoming manifest when a child first attends school. Severe, chronic cases are rarer and outcome data are scanty, but total mutism apparently does not persist into adult life. The 'phobic' group seem more responsive to treatment than the 'manipulative' group, but in both cases the outcome in terms of adjustment in adult life is unknown.

Epilepsy

While epilepsy is not a psychiatric condition, it is often associated with such a disorder. It can also directly cause disturbed behaviour. It consists of recurrent attacks of lost or altered consciousness, associated with the abnormal activity of groups of brain cells. This may be reflected in an abnormal electroencephalogram (EEG), not only during attacks but also between them. The fits are often accompanied by abnormal muscle movements, or abnormal behaviour.

In many cases the *cause* is not known. In such cases the disturbance of brain function often appears to arise in the central part of the brain and spread to the cerebral cortex on both sides, causing a generalised fit. Local damage or disease affecting a particular part of the cerebral cortex may cause a localised or focal attack, and such a focal attack may spread to become a general one.

Major fits (or *grand mal* epilepsy) usually start suddenly and with little warning, but a few children experience a brief aura lasting a few seconds. This may consist of an abnormal sensation or the twitching of muscles. The first stage is usually the tonic one. There is a general contraction of muscles, the child falls to the ground (unless already lying down) and becomes unconscious. The limbs and trunk muscles are held stiffly, the face becomes first pale, then blue (or cyanosed) as a result of not breathing. The pupils are dilated and unresponsive. The tonic phase usually lasts from twenty seconds to one minute. It is followed by the clonic phase, in which there are repetitive, to-and-fro, purposeless movements of the muscles, especially of the limbs and face. Cyanosis continues. This phase may be as short as the tonic phase, but can last several minutes. It is followed by a similarly variable period of unconsciousness, which often leads into a state of sleep from which the subject can be roused. On waking up, the patient has no memory of the period of the fit and often complains of headache. Sometimes the patient is incontinent of urine or, less often, faeces, during an attack. Injury may also occur, a common form being biting the tongue or lip. When one major fit follows another without consciousness being regained in between, this is known as *status epilepticus*. This is a serious condition requiring urgent medical intervention.

Minor fits, often known as *petit mal*, are common in children, affecting girls more often than boys. They consist of brief periods of un-consciousness, lasting only a few seconds. The child does not usually fall down, even if standing, but may drop things held in the hand. Activities such as talking, writing or playing cease for the duration of the attack, but are then often resumed where they were left off, though the child may have lost the thread of the conversation. Frequency can vary from less than once a month to several hundred times a day. Most children with minor fits grow out of them by puberty, but they are sometimes replaced by major fits. There is a characteristic EEG pattern which is often (but not invariably) seen in children with minor fits.

Focal epilepsy is usually due to a localised disorder of an area of the cerebral cortex, or tissues closely connected to it. There are localised convulsive movements of a group of muscles (for example of the face, hands, arms or legs), or an abnormal sensory experience, without complete loss of consciousness. There may be some alteration of consciousness, however. Sometimes the attacks spread to become typical major fits. Temporal lobe epilepsy is a form of focal epilepsy, arising in the temporal lobe of the brain. It may cause abnormal behaviour which can sometimes be difficult to recognise as epileptic. The behaviour appears purposive and can be quite complicated, like running around, screaming and shouting. It can take the form of aggressiveness and severe temper. If consciousness is obviously altered at some point, or if the child is drowsy or has a headache at the end of the attack, diagnosis may be easier. It is in children who do not obviously show these features that the distinction between epilepsy and a conduct disorder can be hard to make. To compound the problem, the two can co-exist, as in the case of Rowland, described below.

In *akinetic attacks* (or *drop attacks*) there is a sudden, brief loss of muscle power or tone, causing the subject to fall down on to the knees. There is often no obvious loss of consciousness, and it may be thought that the person affected has just stumbled. The EEG pattern is different from that typical of minor fits.

The psychiatric importance of epilepsy in children is considerable[20]. Apart from the inconvenience of repeated loss of consciousness, the child's schoolmates or siblings, or adults, may witness major fits, and become frightened, anxious or hostile. Some activities such as swimming or cycling may have to be curtailed. The condition may provoke anxiety or rejection in parents, relatives or teachers. The child may himself come to feel he is 'bad', or imperfect, or at least 'different', or even that the fits are in some mysterious way his own fault. These difficulties are, however, mainly due to the attitudes of others and are thus not inevitable.

In addition to the psychological repercussions of the condition, disturbed behaviour can itself be caused by epilepsy, especially of the temporal lobe variety as explained above. Moreover, some epileptics have other neurological or intellectual handicaps which may add to their difficulties (though many are otherwise normal and of average or higher intelligence). Thus an epileptic child may be faced with a variety of difficulties, giving a greater risk of psychiatric disorder than in his non-epileptic peers. Medication given to control fits can also have unwanted side effects, and adversely affect behaviour and cognitive function.

Helen was referred to a clinic at the age of six. She was said to have developed normally until the age of three. She then had a major epileptic fit, after which she lost, over a few months, the few words she had acquired. She became noisy and hyperactive, and rocked back and forth in her chair. She ceased playing with other children.

On admission to hospital she was hyperactive, played and rocked repetitively, appeared to understand speech, but did not herself speak. Four weeks later she had a series of epileptic attacks during the night. When these were controlled she was left with a spastic paralysis of the left face, arm and leg. This progressed during the next few weeks to involve the right side.

An air encephalogram (in which air is injected into the ventricles of the brain to show them up on X-ray) showed widespread degeneration of the brain tissues.

COMMENT

Helen had a degenerative brain disorder. This was not at first obvious, but the quite rapid progresssion and the investigations which were done as a result, made the diagnosis plain. Her disturbed behaviour was due mainly to her cerebral condition. Her family was a stable one, and environmental factors played a minimal role in her condition.

Rowland was referred at the age of eleven. He complained of 'horrible feelings'. These consisted of acute, irrational fear, particularly of dying, lasting a minute or so. He would get up to ten attacks a day; they also sometimes occurred when he was in bed at night. He sometimes described the attacks as 'a fear of God'. He also had episodes in which his face felt 'funny' and he complained of getting thoughts of dying, of being about to swear and of possible future actions which he was then unable to control. For example, he said he had thought he might fall down on the way to school which he later found he could not help doing.

Rowland's parents complained of difficult, uncontrollable, vicious and very naughty behaviour. This had been increasing in severity since the age of six. He would get very angry with people, wander off and truant from school. He once tried to strangle his younger brother. He also had nocturnal 'turns', occurring in the early morning, in which he twitched and made choking and snorting noises.

Rowland was the oldest of three siblings. The others were well. So also were the parents, physically, though they were anxious and distressed about Rowland's behaviour. Both pairs of grandparents lived near and so also did a number of aunts and uncles. Many of this extended family gave the parents advice, and also interfered in their dealings with Rowland. Thus if he was refused something by his parents he would usually get it from another relative. This appeared to have contributed to Rowland's behaviour getting out of control.

At about 5 a.m. during Rowland's first night in hospital he was observed by the nursing staff to have a typical major epileptic fit; he also had several during subsequent nights. He continued to have attacks of irrational fear by day, as well as episodes of altered consciousness lasting fifteen to twenty seconds, in which he felt unable to move. During these nothing abnormal was noticed by the staff. He was at times aggressive to other children and had violent temper outbursts. On the Wechsler children's scale his intelligence quotient was in the average range. He was about three years retarded in reading. No abnormal physical signs were found on examination and an X-ray of his skull was normal. An EEG showed abnormal electrical discharges in the right temporal lobe of the brain, more marked during sleep, supporting the clinical diagnosis of temporal lobe epilepsy.

The nocturnal fits ceased, and Rowland's 'feelings' improved, when treatment with anticonvulsant drugs was started. His behaviour remained very disturbed and aggressive, however. He continued to try to manipulate the hospital staff as he had his family at home, asking one member for something which had been refused by another; or giving one member a false account of what another had said or done. When he was thwarted in this he would become angry, though over the course of a few months he began to accept firmer control, and after six months his behaviour was greatly improved.

COMMENT

Rowland clearly had a brain abnormality. There may well have been a small area of damage to the right temporal lobe, though there was no history of any illness or accident which might have caused this. The problem was probably made more difficult by the five-year delay in diagnosis, during which Rowland was subject to conflicting discipline and control at home, and became progressively more disturbed in his behaviour and retarded in his school work. One reason for the delay in diagnosis was that father's sister had epilepsy; this had caused in father a great fear of the condition, and a firm denial that Rowland had it, despite the nocturnal attacks. Even after the diagnosis was made in hospital it took father a while to accept it. Earlier diagnosis and treatment, and help for the family in handling Rowland, might have avoided some of the more disturbed antisocial behaviour, for instance the truanting and aggressiveness to siblings. Thus the clinical syndrome Rowland presented was the outcome of a combination of intrinsic, organic factors and of social, environmental ones.

It is of interest that an EEG done a year before admission was normal, which illustrates the important point that such a negative finding by no means excludes the diagnosis of epilepsy.

A helpful review of epilepsy in childhood is that of Brett[21].

The *investigation* of a child with epilepsy starts with the taking of a full history. The diagnosis of epilepsy must always rest primarily on the clinical picture, that is the history and the accounts given by eye-witnesses and by the individual himself of his subjective experiences. The next step is a careful physical examination. Further tests which may be useful are an X-ray examination of the skull and an EEG. As in other disorders, a careful investigation of the child's family and school situation should also be carried out.

Treatment usually consists of a combination of anticonvulsant drugs[21] and help to child and family in accepting the nature and consequences of the disorder. Major fits can often be controlled by drugs such as phenytoin, primidone or sulthiame. Another useful drug is carbamaze-pine, which can be particularly useful in treating temporal lobe epilepsy. Ethosuximide is the drug of choice for minor fits. Pheno-barbitone is an effective anticonvulsant but often has undesirable side-effects in children, and may cause behaviour disorders to worsen. Akinetic attacks often respond to nitrazepam. For drug doses and details, (see pages 229 to 231).

As important as administering the right drugs are the support and help given to the child and the family as a whole. The nature of the disorder should be explained in appropriate terms and any queries or doubts in the minds of child or family should be discussed. This may need to be done repeatedly. There is a considerable folklore about epilepsy, some of it most alarming to those afflicted with it. The aim of management should be to enable the child to live as normal a life as possible, though some restrictions, for example on swimming and cycling, may be necessary. As optimistic a view as is justified should be taken in each case. The point that the condition is a common one should be stressed. Progress should be regularly reviewed, including the child's educational performance and adjustment in school. Medica-tion is usually continued until the child has been free of fits for at least two years. The importance of taking the medication regularly must be stressed.

Sometimes assessment or treatment in hospital is necessary, and a few epileptic children require long-term residential education[23]. In a very few cases surgical removal of a damaged section of brain tissue, especially when there is a circumscribed area of scarring in the temporal lobe, can be of value. Detailed neurological assessment is essential first.

Outcome. Many children with epilepsy outgrow it, but the fits may persist into adult life. The nature of the attacks may change as the child gets older. Minor fits are often replaced by major ones, though sometimes minor fits disappear completely. Fits can usually be controlled completely or to a substantial extent by use of anticonvulsant drugs.

References

1. World Health Organisation. *International Classification of Diseases*, 1975 Revision. Geneva: WHO, 1977.
2. Group for the Advancement of Psychiatry. *Psychopathological Disorders in Childhood*. Report no. 62. New York, 1966.
3. Dockar-Drysdale, B. *Therapy in Child Care* (collected papers). London: Longman Green, 1968.
4. Dockar-Drysdale, B. *Consultation in Child Care*. London: Longman, 1973.
5. Balbernie, I. 'Unintegration, integration and level of ego functioning as the determinants of planned "cover therapy", of unit task and of placement'. *Journal of the Association of Workers for Maladjusted Children*, **2**, 6–46, 1974.
6. Winnicott, D. *The Maturational Process and the Facilitating Environment*. London: Hogarth, 1960.
7. Grenker, R., Werble, B. and Drye, R. C. *The Borderline Syndrome*. New York: Basic Books, 1968.
8. Masterson, J. S., *Treatment of the Borderline Adolescent; Developmental Approach*. Wiley-Inter-Science, New York, 1972.
9. Department of Health and Social Security. *Youth Treatment Centres*. London: HMSO, 1971.
10. Corbett, J. A., Matthews, A. M., Connell, P. H. and Shapiro, D. A. 'Tics, and Gilles de la Tourrete's syndrome: a follow-up study and critical review'. *British Journal of Psychiatry*, **115**, 122–141, 1969.
11. Brunner, R. D. and Shapiro, A. K. 'Differential diagnosis of Gilles de la Tourette's syndrome'. *Journal of Nervous and Mental Disease*, **154**, 328–334, 1972.
12. Greenberg, L. M. and Stephans, J. H. 'Use of drugs in special syndromes'. In *Psychopharmacology in Childhood and Adolescence*, ed. J. M. Wiener. New York: Basic Books, 1977.
13. Andrews, K. and Harris, M. *The Syndrome of Stuttering*. London: Heinemann, 1964.
14. Rantala, S. L. and Petri-Larmi, M. 'Haloperidol in the treatment of stuttering'. *Folia Phoniatrica*, **28**, 354–361, 1976.
15. Wingate, M. E. *Stuttering: Theory and Treatment*. New York: Irvington, 1976.
16. Brown, B. and Lloyd, H. 'A controlled study of children not speaking at school'. *Journal of the Association of Workers for Maladjusted Children*, **3**, 49–63, 1975.
17. Bradley, S. and Sloman, L. 'Elective mutism in immigrant families'. *Journal of the American Academy of Child Psychiatry*, **14**, 510–514, 1975.
18. Brown, B., Fuller, J. and Gericke, C. 'Elective mutism: a review and a report of an unsuccessfully treated case'. *Journal of the Association of Workers for Maladjusted Children*, **3**, 27–37, 1975.
19. Reed, G. F. 'Elective mutism in children: a re-appraisal'. *Journal of Child Psychiatry*, **4**, 99–107, 1963.
20. Bayley, C. *The Social Psychology of the Child with Epilepsy*. London: Routledge and Kegan Paul, 1971.
21. Brett, E. M. 'Epilepsy in childhood'. *British Journal of Hospital Medicine*, **9**, 177–186, 1973.
22. Parsonage, M. 'Anti-epileptics'. *British Journal of Hospital Medicine*, **9**, 615–626, 1973.
23. Pond, D. 'Residential psychiatric treatment of children with epilepsy and brain damage'. In *The Residential Psychiatric Treatment of Children*, ed. P. Barker. London: Crosby Lockwood Staples, 1974.

CHAPTER NINE

Specific Delays in Development

Certain children show delayed development in one or more specific areas of function. These conditions are thought to be related to delayed biological maturation, though usually there is no proof of this. The ninth edition of the ICD (see page 27) has a special coding for specific delays in development. These are defined as delays in development of particular functions relative to the child's general level of development. Thus when delayed development of one function is part of a picture of generally retarded development it would not be classified here; it would qualify only if this delay were disproportionately great.

The sub-categories listed in the ICD are:

1. Specific reading retardation.
2. Specific arithmetical retardation.
3. Other specific learning difficulties.
4. Developmental speech/language disorder.
5. Specific motor retardation.
6. Mixed developmental disorder.

In the past, other conditions have been considered 'developmental' including enuresis, encopresis and the hyperkinetic syndrome (Chapter 7). They share with the conditions dealt with in this chapter a higher incidence in boys than in girls and frequent occurrence in the absence of other psychiatric disorder.

Specific Reading Retardation

Reading difficulties are common and in societies with a high literary level they are serious and handicapping disorders. Although they may occur on their own they are also significantly associated with psychiatric disorder, especially conduct disorders.

The prevalence of reading retardation depends on the age group and population studied and the criteria used to define the retardation. Reading attainment is in general related to intelligence level; brighter children tend to learn to read faster than duller ones. While the reading quotient cannot always be expected to equal the intelligence quotient (see Chapter 14) statistical techniques exist which enable predictions of expected reading age (see page 199) to be calculated from a child's age and IQ[1]. By this means *specific* reading retardation can be calculated[2]; it is distinct from general reading backwardness, which simply means that the child is not reading up to the level expected for his age.

In the Isle of Wight epidemiological study of 9- and 10-year-old children a prevalence of specific reading retardation, defined as a reading level 28 months or more below that expected for age and IQ, was found to be about 4 per cent. The prevalence of reading backwardness (28 months or more behind the level expected on the basis of age alone) was about 6·5 per cent[3]. The Isle of Wight consists of rural areas and small towns, and the prevalence of reading problems appears to be higher in large cities, especially poor inner city areas. A study in inner London, using the same criteria as were used in the Isle of Wight, showed specific reading retardation to be present in about 10 per cent of ten-year-olds, while the rate of general reading backwardness was 19 per cent[4]. A higher prevalence of reading problems in inner city children has also been found in American studies[5].

Specific reading retardation is considerably commoner in boys than in girls, the boy:girl ratio in the Isle of Wight study being 3·3 to 1, as opposed to 1·3 to 1 in the general reading backwardness group.

The *causes* of specific reading retardation are not fully understood. It appears that in most cases they are multiple. The predominance of boys suggests biological susceptibility, perhaps genetically determined. Other factors which may contribute include difficulty in distinguishing right from left, other minor neurological disorders, delayed language development and current speech difficulties[2]. Social factors indirectly play a part since the condition is commoner in inner city children and there is also much variation from school to school[4]. An association has also been reported with large family size[6]. Thompson has reviewed the aetiology of reading disabilities paying particular attention to the concept of maturational delay[7]. It is not surprising that children who have had difficulty learning spoken language also find it hard to learn the associated written symbols.

How well a child learns to read or write, or to do arithmetic, depends also upon how well he is taught, how regularly he attends school and what his motivation to learn is. The latter is largely a function of his relationship with whoever is teaching him, which may also be affected by emotional factors. Frequent changes of school or teacher, especially if teaching methods change too, can contribute. Cultural factors are also involved. The child from a home in which books and written material are much valued and used is better placed than one in whose home there is a dearth of books and no interest in reading; an extreme case is the family in which the parents are illiterate. All these factors will tend to cause reading delay in any child, but especially in the biologically vulnerable.

The *clinical picture* of specific reading retardation is that of a child with a history of a serious delay in learning to read, perhaps following delay in the acquisition of speech and language skills, while development in other areas has been relatively normal. Writing, and particularly spelling, are also impaired, and the spelling difficulty may be more severe than the reading problem, persisting after the child has learned to read.

Ingram has distinguished two main types of reading and spelling difficulty[8]. In the first, the child has difficulty in identifying and differentiating the written symbols, in orientating them in space and in perceiving the position of each one among the other symbols (letters or words). These are referred to as 'visuo-spatial' difficulties.

The second group consists of children with so-called 'audiophonic' difficulties. Such children have difficulty in recognising the sound symbols represented by the written material, and also in building the symbols up into meaningful words. They find spelling similarly difficult because they cannot easily identify the syllables of which a word is composed, and thus they may get the syllables in the wrong order.

A third and more handicapped group consists of children who have both visuo-spatial and audiophonic difficulties.

The term *developmental dyslexia* is sometimes applied to these disorders, but using such a term has the disadvantage that it may give those without detailed knowledge the idea that the condition is a sort of 'disease', which it is not. There is no objection to saying a child is dyslexic, providing it is realised that this is just a way of saying in Greek that he has a reading problem. More important is the making of a functional diagnosis which takes account of all relevant factors, biological, social, emotional and educational.

Assessment and *treatment* of children with these problems are the special province of the educational psychologist and remedial teacher. Various of the tests described in Chapter 14 may be used in elucidating the nature of the child's difficulties. This is a necessary preliminary to working out a programme of remedial help. In severe cases individual remedial teaching is usually needed. Secondary emotional disorder may be present, and the child who finds he cannot read may eventually 'give up', leading to school difficulties, including truancy. The relationship between conduct disorder and reading disability has been mentioned in Chapter 4.

The *outcome* depends on the severity of the disorder and the help available to the child in school and at home. Many children overcome their reading problems, with or without help. Some seem eventually to reach a state of 'learning readiness', but much later than normal. Children who have had reading disability are often left, as adults, with spelling difficulties and poor writing. If reading difficulties are not correctly diagnosed and treated in good time, emotional and behavioural difficulties may appear, combined with progressive failure at school.

Specific Arithmetical and other Learning Difficulties

From time to time children are seen who show specific retardation in areas other than reading. Spelling difficulty has been mentioned as a common accompaniment of reading retardation, but other specific learning difficulties have been less intensively studied than reading problems.

Arithmetical difficulties are probably the next most common problem. The term 'developmental dyscalculia' has been used to describe specific difficulties in the development of arithmetical skills. Slade and Russell[9] described four adolescents who had all had severe difficulty with arithmetic from an early age such as could not be accounted for by a generally low level of intellectual functioning. Of the four basic arithmetical processes, the greatest disability seemed to be in multiplication, though all processes were affected.

Arithmetical difficulties are generally less handicapping than reading problems, but may also lead to secondary emotional disturbance. They also require skilled psychological assessment and remedial teaching.

Speech and Language Disorders

A baby's first sounds are undifferentiated crying. By two months this has become differentiated so that it varies according to the circumstances in which it occurs (for example, when hungry, cold, or in pain). Within a month or two the baby also starts to babble, and during the following months the variety of sounds, consonants and vowels, increases. Babbling is made up of a succession of sounds produced spontaneously by the infant. Many of these sounds will be incorporated into words when speech is acquired.

By about nine months the child's use of consonant–vowel combinations, takes on a communicative function; these combinations are used for calling, for responding and for expressing intentions.

The development of language is a very complex process. The child must acquire the ability to observe objects and events in the environment before coming to understand them and express them in language. The development of language is thus closely tied up with cognitive, that is thinking, capacities. The learning of the meaning of words is closely related to concept development. Subsequently the child has to understand and learn sentence forms (syntax) and also acquire the skills necessary to request, protest, label and express other intentions (pragmatic abilities).

The first spoken words usually appear around the age of one, but children usually attempt to communicate very simple vocalisations and gestures before that. The first words are often ones like 'dada' and 'mama', which may simply be bits of babble reinforced by the attention and approval given them by the parents. The subsequent acquisition of vocabulary is closely tied in with the child's perception, for example, of shape, and the words heard and used in relation to them. Thus at first all round objects may be labelled 'ball'. At the same time the child is trying actively to work out how language is put together, so that with every attempt at communication he is, in a way, testing an hypothesis. This applies to the acquisition of words, phrases and sentences. It is clear that even young children 'make up' new words using rules they have inferred, as when they produce words like 'sheeps' or 'gived' which they will not have heard used by others. Such errors are often corrected by parents and others with whom the child talks. Much the same applies to phrase and sentence construction, and indeed the learning of syntax starts almost from the acquisition of the first words. When the child finds that what he says is not understood properly he has to try again, perhaps after receiving some help or instruction from the person to whom he is talking. It is largely by such give-and-take that the child learns to master the complexity of verbal language. For all this there must be, of course, a background of neurological readiness.

During the second year an increasing, but relatively small, number of words is acquired, many of them the names of objects. Short phrases appear about the middle of the second year, sentences and simple questions about age two. At first small groups of words, mainly nouns and verbs, are produced, for example 'mummy come', 'doggie naughty'. 'No' and 'yes' are often incorporated into phrases like 'apple no' or 'Johnnie apple no', which express their meaning quite well in a sort of verbal shorthand. Phrases of this type are often acquired during the second year and gradually sentences with a more normal structure replace them. Adjectives are used increasingly to qualify nouns, and pronouns are used with greater correctness. Subsequently the finer points of syntax are gradually mastered, though this is a process which continues well into and through the child's primary school days. The use of adverbs, prepositions and conjunctions appears relatively late, though normally before the child starts school at five.

The child's vocabulary increases rapidly in the third and fourth years. At the same time articulation, the accuracy with which words are pronounced, improves. At first the child's attempts at many words may be poor. Parents usually understand them before outsiders do.

Vocabulary and sentence structure are culturally determined. In most countries there are regional variations in speech patterns. There are usually also social class differences, only partly determined by intelligence. Thus 'normal' speech development in a labourer's child would be likely to differ from the 'normal' for a university lecturer's child, as regards both vocabulary and syntax. In some English-speaking families the double negative ('I don't want no more tea') is accepted usage, and naturally this is what the child growing up in such a family will learn.

Between the ages of two and seven there are equally important changes in children's capacity to comprehend spoken language. This also is learnt in an organised way. Thus it appears that children at first interpret sentences by assuming that the first noun is the subject/actor of the sentence[10]. This leads to the child learning to interpret the subject-verb-object sequence as representing actor-action-recipient. This strategy works well as in 'the boy chases the girl', but later the child must learn to refine and change the strategies used to deal, for example, with 'the boy is chased by the girl'. Gradually children learn to cope with sentences of increasing complexity, as they hear them used.

Further information on language development is to be found in the book *Language Development: Structure and Function*[11].

ABNORMALITIES OF SPEECH AND LANGUAGE DEVELOPMENT

Language, articulation or both may be affected. Language disorders are abnormalities of the use or understanding of words and combinations of words (though language can be non-verbal, as in the use of gesture and mime). The deficit may be receptive or expressive, or both functions may be affected. Disordered articulation is referred to as *dysarthria* – used when there is a disorder of the structure or function of the muscles or other organs responsible for the production of the speech sounds; or *dyslalia* – the unduly prolonged persistence of infantile modes of pronunciation.

The *prevalence* of severe language disorders is estimated by Rees[12] to be about one per thousand live births. But, according to Ingram[8], about four per cent of five-year old children have such defective articulation that when they go to school their teachers cannot understand them.

Causes: Children may fail to develop language because of deafness, severe mental handicap or gross sensory deprivation. The term 'specific developmental language disorder' is not usually applied to such conditions. While total deprivation is rare, relative language deprivation is commoner. This may occur in large, badly run institutions such as orphanages, and also in some poorly endowed, underprivileged families, where retarded language development may be a cultural phenomenon.

In most children with specific language delay the main cause appears to be abnormality of the central nervous system. The necessary neurological apparatus has not developed normally, or at least is not functioning correctly. In the presence of such an abnormality a degree of deprivation of language experience (resulting from any of the causes mentioned above) may have a particularly damaging effect. Often the cause of the neurological abnormality cannot be discovered, but sometimes there is a history of cerebral trauma at birth or soon afterwards. In many cases there appear to be genetic factors, and a family history of late speech development, other speech difficulties, and reading and spelling problems is common.

The main *clinical feature* is that the child is late starting to talk. The first words (except perhaps 'dada' and similar items of babble) are acquired late, sentence construction is delayed and when words are produced they are abnormal. The extent to which the child can understand speech varies a lot. In severe instances there is little or no understanding of speech. This condition has also been called 'congenital auditory imperception.' It can be demonstrated by electroencephalographs that there is a normal response in the cerebral cortex to sounds, but they are not meaningful to the child. In such cases there will also be an expressive disorder which, however, may exist without a receptive one, or at least without a severe one.

Diagnosis depends on the late acquisition of speech in the presence of normal, or relatively normal, development in other spheres. Deafness and psychosis must also be considered. Audiometric examination and specialist opinion may be necessary for this. Various special tests are also available. Figure 2 shows the processes of language comprehension and expression. Any of the stages may be affected, language disordered children having difficulty in the decoding-encoding area.

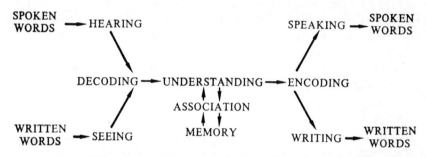

Figure 2. The comprehension and expression of language

Treatment is difficult, especially in severe cases. If there is a severe receptive language problem, speech may never be acquired, though it may be possible to teach a few sterotyped phrases. Where the difficulty is mainly expressive a concentrated training programme, perhaps using operant conditioning techniques (see Chapter 16), may be of value. Fortunately many cases are relatively mild and the result of delayed neurological maturation. Such children tend to develop speech in due course and, when ready, can be helped by speech therapy[13]. Their language capacity may, nevertheless, remain somewhat impaired so that they have difficulty learning to read and write.

DISORDERS OF ARTICULATION

Abnormal articulation may be due to a neurological condition affecting the control of the muscles responsible for speech, as in cerebral palsy; it may be due to a structural abnormality of the larynx, palate or tongue;

it may be a developmental condition (and indeed is always present along with severe language disorder); or it may have emotional causes.

The latter two groups are the main ones of psychiatric importance, though severe dysarthria from any cause may have psychiatric consequences.

Developmental articulatory disorders are often simply the persistence of infantile modes of articulation beyond the period of life at which they usually disappear. They may be due to delayed neurological maturation; the frequent combination with language delay tends to support this.

The *clinical picture* is of a child who speaks freely and appears to understand speech normally (unless there is also a language disorder), but is himself hard to understand because the words he uses are ill-formed. Longer words are more difficult than shorter ones, parts of words (often the ends) may be missed out, and consonants tend to be more affected than vowels. Usually the parents can understand the child better than can outsiders. Indeed the parents, being used to the child's mode of pronunciation, may not realise the severity of the disorder.

Treatment is primarily the sphere of the speech therapist, though ideally a team including a psychiatrist, a paediatrician and an otologist should be involved in the management of the more severe cases. In many milder cases there is spontaneous recovery.

Emotionally determined immature articulation occurs quite frequently in children showing other evidence of delayed emotional maturation. There may be overprotection by the parents. Sometimes the child talks normally when away from the mother, relapsing into 'baby talk' when with her. The same process may occur when the young child is faced with severe stress causing regression in other spheres, as in regressive soiling. The diagnosis in these cases depends on a general assessment. If there is a clear history of normal, or at least better, articulation in certain circumstances, this supports the diagnosis. So also does the presence of emotional immaturity in other spheres, with over-dependence on parents, or at least a need or wish for such over-dependence. Some of these disorders are more appropriately categorised as adjustment reactions. Treatment is likely to involve some combination of psychotherapy with the child and help for the family (see Chapter 15). The *outcome* depends on the nature of the underlying psychiatric problem.

Specific Motor Retardation

Some children's motor development is specifically retarded, relative to their development in other spheres. This can take the form of severe clumsiness which may interfere with a child's school work, games or physical education. If unrecognised or unsympathetically handled it can lead to great unhappiness or to secondary emotional disturbance. This condition is sometimes known as 'developmental apraxia'[14]. Characteristically these clumsy children are late in developing motor skills such as dressing, feeding and walking. They usually experience difficulty in writing and drawing, and even in copying. They perform badly at ball games, tend to break crockery and are poor at handicrafts. Sometimes there is also defective articulation. On the other hand intelligence is normal, even above average, on verbal tests. In verbal work the child usually does well, but because of his inability to put what he knows down in writing he may be regarded as dull, or even mentally handicapped. Sometimes he is regarded as lazy and the view is taken that he could do better if he tried.

Clumsy children do not usually show evidence of any abnormality in the motor pathways controlling voluntary movement. That is to say, they can carry out all normal movements but coordination of them to perform a particular task is defective. The condition is analogous to developmental reading disorder in which the subject can see writing but cannot organise it into the meaning it represents.

Children with this condition may present at psychiatric departments, sometimes with secondary emotional disorders. Careful history-taking usually indicates the diagnosis which can be confirmed by asking the child to write and draw. Administration of the Wechsler Intelligence Scale for Children (see Chapter 14) usually reveals a much lower performance than verbal IQ. These children's standards of reading are usually better than their writing ability. Similar clumsiness also occurs in children with severe mental handicap, but in these cases it is but part of generally retarded development and thus not a specific developmental disorder.

Treatment necessitates first the recognition of the disability and its explanation to child, family and teacher, and then the provision of special teaching and training. Modification of the school routine may be needed, especially along the lines of relieving the child of attempting games and other motor tasks which are clearly too difficult for him.

A full account of this syndrome, including two population surveys and information on the various neurological disorders which may cause clumsiness, is to be found in the book *The Clumsy Child*[15].

Mixed Developmental Disorders

Mixed developmental disorders consist simply of combinations of the various conditions described above. The coexistence of reading, spelling and language disorders is particularly common, but various other combinations also occur.

References

1. Yule, W. 'Predicting reading ages on Neal's analysis of reading disability'. *British Journal of Educational Psychology*, **37**, 252–255, 1967.
2. Rutter, M. and Yule, W. 'The concept of specific reading retardation'. *Journal of Child Psychology and Psychiatry*, **16**, 181–197, 1975.
3. Rutter, M., Tizard, J. and Whitmore, K. *Education, Health and Behaviour*. London, Longman, 1970.
4. Berger, M., Yule, W. and Rutter, M. 'Attainment and adjustment in two geographical areas'. *British Journal of Psychiatry*, **126**, 510–519, 1975.
5. Eisenberg, L. 'Reading retardation: psychiatric and sociological aspects'. *Pediatrics*, **37**, 352–365, 1966.
6. Rutter, M. 'The concept of "dyslexia"'. In *Planning for Better Learning*, ed. P. Wolff and R. C. MacKeith, London: Heinemann, 1967.
7. Thompson, L. J. 'Learning disabilities: an overview'. *American Journal of Psychiatry*, **130**, 393–399, 1973.
8. Ingram, T. T. S. 'Psychomotor development and its disorders'. In *A Companion to Medical Studies* (Vol. 3, Part 2), ed. R. Passmore and J. S. Robson, Oxford: Blackwell, 1974.
9. Slade, P. D. and Russell, G. F. R. 'Developmental dyscalculia: a brief report on four cases'. *Psychological Medicine*, **1**, 292–298, 1971.
10. Bever, T. G. 'The cognitive bases of linguistic structures'. In *Cognition and the Development of Language*, ed. T. R. Hayes. New York: Wiley, 1970.
11. Dale, P. S. *Language Development: Structure and Function*. Hindsdale, Ill.: Dryden Press, 1976.
12. Rees, H. M. N. 'Assessment and treatment of language-disordered children'. In *The Residential Psychiatric Treatment of Children*, ed. P. Barker, London: Crosby Lockwood Staples, 1974.
13. Lahey, M. and Bloom, L. 'Planning a first lexicon: which words to teach first'. *Journal of Speech and Hearing Disorders*, **42**, 340–369, 1977.
14. Walton, J. N., Ellis, E. and Court, S. D. M. 'Clumsy children; developmental apraxia and agnosia'. *Brain*, **85**, 603–612, 1962.
15. Gubbay, S. S. *The Clumsy Child*. London: Saunders, 1975.

CHAPTER TEN

Psychosomatic Disorders

Psychosomatic disorders are physical conditions in which emotional factors play an important part. There is evidence that emotional factors play some part in most, perhaps all, disease processes, but in predominantly 'physical' conditions their part is relatively small. Even in such clearly organic disorders as pneumonia or appendicitis, however, the individual's emotional state and attitudes towards treatment and recovery can, it seems, affect progress. But these are not psychosomatic disorders as usually defined. Pinkerton has described psychosomatic disorders as those in which disordered psysiology and psychopathology 'are so intimately interwoven that both components actively and concurrently contribute to the natural course of the disorder'[1]. Examples are bronchial asthma, infantile eczema, ulcerative colitis, peptic ulcers, migraine, the periodic syndrome and obesity.

Related to psychosomatic disorders, but somewhat different, are what Pinkerton calls 'pseudosomatic' disorders. These are disorders in which, although the condition presents as a physical problem, no organic disorder can be shown to be present. Examples include many cases of enuresis and soiling (Chapter 7), tics and various sleep and feeding disorders. *Anorexia nervosa* is also included in this group by Pinkerton, but is nevertheless considered in the present chapter.

A third, though distinct, group of related conditions are those Pinkerton calls 'somatopsychic states', in other words disorders in which there is a basis of organic pathology which causes psychological consequences, so that psychiatric treatment may be needed. This is the case in many children with serious physical handicaps. Important examples include epilepsy (see Chapter 8), brain damage and its consequences (Chapter 2), diabetes, cystic fibrosis, congenital heart conditions, some skin diseases, head injury and various forms of *spina bifida*.

A fuller discussion of psychosomatic medicine is to be found in the book *Childhood Disorder: A Psychosomatic Approach*[2].

Causes

The effects of the emotions on bodily functions are familiar to all of us. Thus people can be 'scared stiff' or 'shaking with laughter'. When anxious or frightened they may lose their appetite or feel the urge to urinate or defaecate: in extreme cases they may actually do these things. Some people's peptic ulcers get worse when they are worried or under stress. In psychosomatic disorders these factors combine with constitutional weakness, or an individual's tendency to react in a particular way, to produce the disorder.

The reasons for these constitutional weaknesses are not fully understood, but it appears that genetic factors play a part in at least some of these disorders. Thus bronchial asthma and eczema tend to run in families, though the exact mode of inheritance is not established. Migraine has been found to occur in the families of about three-quarters of the sufferers from the condition, and it is also said to be more frequent in the families of subjects with bronchial asthma than it is in the general population.

In particular disorders other factors, for example infective and allergic ones, play a part too. This is well illustrated in bronchial asthma.

Minuchin and his colleagues[3] have proposed an explanation of psychosomatic disorders based on systems theory. They believe that certain types of family organisation favour the development and maintenance of children's psychosomatic symptoms, which in turn play a major role in maintaining family homeostasis (see page 24). They consider that for a severe psychosomatic disorder to develop the child must be physiologically vulnerable, the family must show four characteristics in its transactional patterns – enmeshment, overprotectiveness, rigidity and lack of conflict resolution – and the sick child must play an important role in the family's pattern of conflict avoidance. These enmeshed families, in which everyone is deeply involved with and responsive to everyone else, show a high degree of protectiveness between all family members.

The rigidity of these families is shown in reluctance to change in response either to outside circumstances or to internal events, such as a child reaching adolescence. The enmeshment, overprotectiveness and rigidity combine to cause these families to have very low thresholds for conflict. These conflicts are not resolved. Instead each family has its own particular way of avoiding conflict; this is brought into action again and again and involves the continuation of the child's psychosomatic problem.

Minuchin and his co-workers report excellent results from treatment directed at these family difficulties in cases of intractable asthma, anorexia nervosa and 'superlabile diabetes' – that is children with diabetes which frequently gets out of control in association with emotional factors[3]. The book *Psychosomatic Families*[4], by this group, deals more fully with this work, and contains extensive descriptions of therapy in cases of anorexia nervosa.

Description

Psychosomatic disorders are best described by means of examples, and bronchial asthma is a good one. It consists of attacks in which there is constriction of muscles in the walls of the smaller air passages in the lungs. In addition to the contraction of the muscles, liquid secretions often accumulate in the air passages, and the walls of the passages swell. The secretions cannot be coughed up as they normally would be, and so cause further blockage. Breathing out is more difficult than breathing in, because the negative pressure created by the expansion of the chest wall during inspiration tends to dilate the air passages. The reverse happens on expiration. Thus the lungs tend to get over-filled with air and they and the whole chest are over-expanded.

The muscles of the air passage walls are supplied by nerves of the autonomic nervous system. This network of nerves, with connections in the brain, is responsible for the correct ordering of certain physiological functions, for example heart rate, blood pressure and the diameter of the air passages in the lungs. It is not under conscious control. As well as responding to the needs which arise in activities such as exercise (in which more blood supply to the muscles and more oxygen supply to the blood are required), the system is also sensitive to emotional changes. This is a relatively primitive physiological reaction. Thus the startled or frightened animal has to be ready for 'fight or flight'; and a quick physiological response to danger was probably important for survival in our ancestors, if not in man today. A means thus exists for changes in the lungs and blood vessels and other tissues to occur as a result of alterations in the emotional state of a person.

The diameter of the air passages can also be affected by at least two other factors. One of these is infection, whether by bacteria or viruses. The other is allergy. By an allergy is meant an adverse bodily reaction to a substance which may be present in the environment, and which is not normally harmful. (A good example of an allergic condition is hay fever, in which the subject may be sensitive to certain grass pollens. When these are present in the atmosphere the patient gets red and running eyes, and also inflammation and irritation of the nasal passages with sneezing and nasal discharge). Pollen and many other allergens can also irritate the air passages in the lungs, causing production of liquid secretions and thus their blockage. Infections have a similar effect.

There are therefore three possible precipitants of an attack of asthma: infection (which may start as a cold or bronchitis), exposure to an allergen, and emotional factors. A particular asthma patient may be more sensitive to one or other of these, but their effects tend to be cumulative. An attack of asthma becomes more likely with increasing severity of any of the precipitating conditions; if two or three operate at the same time it is more likely still, and will probably be more severe.

Asthma is often preceded by infantile eczema. This is a skin disease in which there is widespread eruption with inflammation and irritation, coming on during the first year of life. If severe, it is a serious condition with risk to the baby's life. It is often replaced, at least partially, by asthma after a year or two. Thus by the age of three or four the asthma may be the bigger problem, though the two often co-exist and the 'asthma-eczema syndrome' is common in children. The onset so early in life is in itself suggestive of a constitutional weakness in the child. It seems that these patients are constitutionally vulnerable individuals who may react in at least two ways (eczema and asthma) to at least three types of stress.

Paula was referred for psychiatric opinion at the age of eight. She was the younger of two siblings, the other being a boy of thirteen, in good health. She had had eczema in infancy; she had been in hospital several times for this. The eczema and hospitalisations had caused her family great anxiety. She still had some areas of relatively mild eczema but her skin condition had greatly improved.

Asthma had started in the second year of life. At first a diagnosis of 'bronchitis' was made, and it was not until the age of about four that the condition was labelled asthma. This in itself caused the parents much concern as the maternal grandfather had been, so mother said, a lifelong asthmatic who died of the condition at the age of fifty-four.

Paula was referred by a paediatrician because of the increasing frequency of attacks which were causing her to miss a lot of school. At interview Paula appeared a bright, attractive girl of about average intelligence. She talked freely, gave a good account of her life situation and acknowledged, but made light of, her asthma. Some patches of mild eczema were visible on her arms.

She maintained that she liked school, but went on to say that very often her mother would not let her go because of her bad chest.

Paula's parents gave a slightly different account of things. They said that the asthma tended to be worse when Paula was supposed to be going to school. They felt unable to be firm with Paula over school attendance, and indeed over other things too, for fear she might have an asthmatic attack and perhaps die, as her grandfather had done. Moreover Paula had had some severe attacks of asthma at school time, requiring the presence of the family doctor and the administration of drugs to help terminate the attack.

The school report indicated that Paula did quite well despite her frequent absence, but did not mix much with the other children.

It rapidly became clear that the parents', and especially mother's, anxiety and fear of Paula dying were important features. Paula had only to develop a mild cough to be kept off school. Mother over-indulged Paula, and was seldom firm with her lest she precipitate the asthma.

Paula's anxiety about her asthma, gradually emerged in psychotherapeutic interviews. She spoke of her dreams, the subjects of which (not identified as herself) died or nearly died, and then recovered or came back to life. She also played in an animated way with the family figures in the doll's house. The children were frequently being cared for in bed by the parents, but were also at times aggressively defiant towards the parents (which Paula never was in real life).

Paula, her mother and sometimes father, were seen weekly over a period of about three months, then less often. Paula played and talked out her fears and fantasies in individual sessions and gradually came to link them consciously with her asthma and its consequences. The parents were able to discuss their great anxiety and fear about Paula, indeed at first mother talked of little else. They gradually came to understand how anxiety and protectiveness increased Paula's anxiety. Supported by the therapist the parents became better able to be firm with Paula over things like bedtimes and her demands for toys and presents, as well as over going to school. To their surprise, Paula's cough and asthma became better, not worse. After about two months' treatment mother arrived one day and said, 'I've come to the conclusion she's been having me on a string all these years.'

COMMENT

There was clearly a constitutional predisposition to asthma, perhaps with a genetic basis, in Paula's case. Allergic factors were not prominent, but there was a history of exacerbations when she had minor colds which (as the parents said) 'went straight to her chest'. Hence the anxiety about her cough. Paula's ill-health had come to dominate the family, and Paula shared the parents' anxiety and fear of her dying. She also came unconsciously to use the asthma as a means of getting her way and avoiding things like going to bed or to school. She thus almost had a vested interest in it. Treatment of child and parents brought gratifying results, with a great reduction in asthmatic attacks in the next two years and with only occasional absences from school, as compared with an absence rate of over fifty per cent previously.

Similar processes occur in other psychosomatic conditions. In *ulcerative colitis* there is apparently a constitutional weakness predisposing to inflammation and ulceration of the large intestine. Emotional factors seem more important in some cases than others, infection can play a part and so possibly can 'auto-immune reactions' (reactions thought to be due to normal substances present in certain tissues of the body). There is also evidence that the condition is more frequent in Jews than in other races, suggesting a genetic basis (though possibly the racial incidence may be due to dietary habits). The condition usually present with diarrhoea, abdominal pain, passage of blood with the faeces and other symptoms such as fever, loss of appetite and weight, nausea and malaise; there may also be depression, irritability and difficult behaviour. The interplay of emotional and other factors in this often serious, and even fatal condition, is complex and demands that psychiatric and other treatments are closely integrated.

Migraine consists of recurrent headache, usually unilateral, often preceded by visual disturbances and accompanied by vomiting[5]. It is a common disorder (about one person in five has an attack at some time during his life), and again genetic, allergic, emotional and perhaps other factors combine to cause the spasm, and then dilatation, of arteries in the head which cause the symptoms. Onset is often during adolescence, but the condition does occur in children also.

The *periodic syndrome* occurs in the first decade of life. Attacks of headache may be accompanied by photophobia, abdominal pain, vomiting, and a miserable whimpering appearance in the child. Any one of these symptoms may predominate. No organic disease is found on investigation and the condition is probably a variant of migraine, having similar causes. One variety of it is called 'cyclical vomiting'. This seems often to be associated with emotional problems within the family[6].

Other psychosomatic conditions include peptic ulcer (commoner in adults than children), and possibly deprivation dwarfism[7], in which growth failure is associated with environmental, especially family, stress – though in such cases under-nutrition may often be a major factor[8].

It is also probably appropriate to regard *obesity* as a psychosomatic disorder, though its cause, in that majority of cases in which no organic disease is found to be responsible, is not properly understood. It does seem, however, that emotional and social factors can, in predisposed children, play a part in causing obesity[9]. Certain individuals apparently have a high count of adipose cells. This may be genetically determined but there is evidence that it may also be caused by over-nutrition in the early months of life. The deprived, unwanted child may eat excessively as a compensation for lack of affection. A mother who, perhaps unconsciously, feels guilty about her rejecting or aggressive attitude towards a child may over-feed the child in an attempt at compensation. Over-feeding may also be motivated, again unconsciously, by a parent's desire to keep the child in a close and dependent relationship. It may thus be but one aspect of a disturbed parent–child relationship, the child being used to fulfil the parent's own needs to have a mutually dependent relationship. Despite these points however it seems that obese children as a group are not seriously disturbed or deviant[10].

Emotional problems can also result from obesity, which may have endocrine, metabolic or other physical causes. The fat child may be teased and so come to feel self-conscious. It can be hard to get children to keep to a reducing diet when one has been prescribed. This can lead to tension and even strife between family members, though severe problems of this sort usually prove to result from pre-existing family relationship difficulties. In some instances it may be hard to discover whether obesity is the cause or the effect of the family problem, or whether it has simply become the focus of a problem which would have been centred around something else had the child not been obese.

Janice was referred at the age of eight. She was the youngest of three girls. The pregnancy had been unwanted, but mother gradually became reconciled to it in the hope that she would have a son. The father, a country postman, seemed to play little part in the family. Mother had apparently been critical of Janice from birth onwards. At the time of referral she complained of Janice's poor school progress and rather gross obesity. Investigation showed Janice to be of above average intelligence, and the teacher said she was doing well at school, if anything better than her sister. Mother said Janice would not keep to her diet, stealing biscuits from the kitchen and money from the house to buy sweets. There was a running battle betwen mother and daughter, and Janice if anything got fatter.

Janice attended weekly for psychotherapy. She proved a friendly girl with a talent for drawing, through which she gave various indications of her feelings of rejection by, and of anger towards, her mother. Mother was seen weekly by a social worker, to whom she expressed her disappointment at having a third daughter and also a husband who, she felt, had contracted out of the family. Once mother was engaged in discussing these problems, a big improvement in the family emotional climate followed. Janice's school progress ceased to be a problem in mother's eyes and it was reported that Janice no longer ate food illicitly; she got only a little thinner, however.

COMMENT

The obesity was being used by child and mother as a focus for their mutually hostile feelings, based probably on mother's long-term rejection of Janice. Whether it was primarily caused by the psychological problem (its failure to disappear being due to incomplete resolution of the emotional problem), or whether it was due to other causes, and exacerbated by the emotional problem, was not clear. This case history is typical of children with psychosomatic disorders referred for psychiatric help in that there was a contribution the psychiatric clinic was able to make, but psychiatric help on its own did not solve the problem.

The *treatment* of psychosomatic disorders involves the removal, amelioration or prevention of any of the causative factors in a particular case. Thus infections and allergies are treated, or contact with the substances to which the child is allergic is avoided. Appropriate medical treatment is given; in asthma, for example drugs which dilate the air passages in the lungs are given, combined as necessary with antibiotics, oxygen or breathing exercises.

The extent to which psychiatric help is needed will vary with the relative importance of emotional factors in the particular case, but the emotional state of child and family must always be taken into account when the treatment plan is worked out. Some psychosomatic disorders, for example asthma and ulcerative colitis, can be life-threatening and may *cause* anxiety and fear in child and family, as well as being in part caused by emotional factors. Psychotherapy may be required by child, parents or the whole family. Increasingly the whole family is being taken as the unit for treatment, as these disorders come to be seen as playing a role in the maintenance of a dysfunctional family system (see page 24). The various forms of treatment are discussed further in Chapter 15.

Outcome: It is difficult to generalise about the outcome in such a diverse group of disorders, varying as they do in their nature, causation and severity. In most cases, however, treatment leads to good results if a comprehensive formulation is made, and a similarly comprehensive treatment plan, taking in all aspects of the child's and family's problems, is carried out.

Anorexia Nervosa

In anorexia nervosa there is severe and prolonged refusal to eat with progressive loss of weight, but without evidence of physical disease. The disorder occurs mainly in adolescent girls.

Causes: In most instances, anorexia nervosa is a neurotic condition; less often there is depression of psychotic intensity, and occasionally the condition is an early manifestation of schizophrenia.

In the neurotic cases – over three-quarters of the total -- there is usually complex psychopathology involving the family as well as the patient. The condition tends to occur in families in which there is much emphasis on food and eating. The latter is perceived by the patient as necessary for growing up and becoming sexually mature, and a major feature of the patient's psychopathology is usually a fear of growing up. The unconsciously intended purpose of the refusal to eat is to remain in a pre-pubertal state. As Crisp puts it[11], 'the search for security and self-esteem has proved incompatible with growth, which has therefore come to be stifled and avoided'. It is also generally agreed[11,12,13], that there are usually serious family problems. Many cases of anorexia are hysterical neurotic reactions to family stress.

Liebman and his colleagues[12] believe that the parents deny their problems and avoid dealing with them by concentrating on the child patient's symptoms. The families have the characteristics described on page 158. Generational boundaries are weak and the parents are divided and ineffective, while individuals in the family are given little autonomy or privacy. These rigid systems cannot resolve conflicts, solve problems or deal effectively with stressful, frustrating situations.

Description: Anorexia nervosa is a disease of adolescence rather than of childhood. It is nearly confined to girls but occasional cases occur in boys. It usually starts after menstruation begins, though sometimes there have been only one or two periods prior to the onset of the anorexia and it may occur before puberty. Menstruation ceases as the patient loses weight.

The condition often begins as 'normal' dieting arising from the patient's feeling that she is too fat, which is sometimes the case at the onset. The dieting, however, develops into a profound aversion to food with consequent severe and progressive weight loss. In many cases there develops a serious state of starvation with danger to life; it sometimes leads to death. Yet the subject typically shows a total lack of concern about her symptoms, as in hysterical illness generally. She is often abnormally active (this does not apply in the minority of depressed patients) and, at least in the early stages, adopts a superficially gay manner and enjoys feeding food to, or preparing it for, others. She will not eat it herself, however, and she may resort to all sorts of subterfuges to dispose of what she is supposed to eat. There are often disturbances of body-image. As the condition progresses, the physical effects of starvation come to dominate the picture.

Once anorexia nervosa is established *treatment* is an urgent matter, for this is one of the few child psychiatric disorders which may lead directly to a fatal outcome. It also differs from most other child psychiatric conditions in that toleration of the symptom while the underlying psychological problem is treated may not be possible.

In severe cases admission to hospital is required, preferably before there has been deterioration of the patient's physical health. Bed rest is often advised as an initial step until weight gain has started. Psychotherapy for the patient and the family are also necessary. A variety of psychotherapeutic regimes have been used, but the team working at the Philadelphia Child Guidance Clinic and Children's Hospital claim particularly good results from their family therapy programme[3,4]. In addition various drug regimes have been suggested, involving particularly chlorpromazine and insulin[14]; while these help patients gain weight during the acute stage they do not deal with the underlying psychopathology. Behaviour therapy programmes (see page 227) can also be useful, as is pointed out in a helpful review of the treatment of anorexia nervosa[15]. Behaviour therapy principles are indeed used by the Philadelphia group in their programme[12].

Outcome: Anorexia nervosa is not an easy condition to treat successfully but in most cases recovery occurs, though this may only follow long and difficult treatment. Unfortunately relapse is quite common and sometimes there is recurring anorexia for years. This is probably due to incomplete resolution of the underlying emotional disorder. One 5- to 20-year follow-up of children treated when under the age of 16, suggested that outcome is closely related to personality type, 'hysterical-manipulative' patients, the biggest group, doing best, while those with obsessive personalities did less well and those with schizoid personalities did worst[16].

References

1. Pinkerton, P. 'Inpatient treatment of children with psychosomatic disorders'. In *The Residential Psychiatric Treatment of Children*, ed. P. Barker. London: Crosby Lockwood Staples, 1974.
2. Pinkerton, P. *Childhood Disorder: A Psychosomatic Approach*. London: Crosby Lockwood Staples, 1974.
3. Minuchin, S., Baker, L., Rosman, B. L., Liebman, R., Millman, L. and Todd, T. C. 'A conceptual model of psychosomatic illness in children'. *Archives of General Psychiatry*, **32**, 1031–1038, 1975.

4. Minuchin, S., Rosman, B. L. and Baker, L. *Psychosomatic Families: Anorexia Nervosa in Context.* Cambridge, Mass: Harvard University Press, 1978.
5. Bille, B. 'Migraine in school children'. *Acta Paediatrica*, **51**, supplement 163, 1962.
6. Davenport, C. W., Zoule, J. P., Kuhn, C. C. and Hanison, S. T., 'Cyclic vomiting'. *Journal of the American Academy of Child Psychiatry*, **11**, 66–87, 1972.
7. Silver, H. K. and Finkelstein, M. 'Deprivation dwarfism'. *Journal of Pediatrics*, **70**, 317–324, 1967.
8. Whitten, C. F., Pettit, M. G. and Fischhoff, J. 'Evidence that growth failure from maternal deprivation is secondary to undereating'. *Journal of the American Medical Association*, **209**, 1675–1682, 1969.
9. Bruch, H. 'Obesity' (part II). In *Eating Disorders, Obesity, Anorexia Nervosa and the Person Within.* London: Routledge and Kegan Paul, 1974.
10. Sallade, J. 'A comparison of the psychological adjustment of obese vs. non-obese children'. *Journal of Psychosomatic Research*, **17**, 89–96, 1973.
11. Crisp, A. 'Diagnosis and outcome of anorexia nervosa'. *Proceedings of the Royal Society of Medicine*, **70**, 464–470, 1977.
12. Liebman, R., Minuchin, S. and Baker, L. 'An integrated treatment program for anorexia nervosa'. *American Journal of Psychiatry*, **131**, 432–436, 1974.
13. Bruch, E. *Eating Disorders.* New York: Basic Books, 1973.
14. Dally, P. and Sargant, W. 'A new treatment of anorexia'. *British Medical Journal*, **2**, 293–295, 1966.
15. Van Buskirk, S. S. 'A two-phase perspective on the treatment of anorexia nervosa'. *Psychological Bulletin*, **84**, 529–538, 1977.
16. Goetz, P. C., Succop, R. A., Reinhart, J. B. and Miller, A. 'Anorexia nervosa in children: a follow-up study'. *American Journal of Orthopsychiatry*, **47**, 597–603, 1977.

CHAPTER ELEVEN

Problems of Young Children and their Families

Certain problems occur in young children that are difficult to fit into the usual diagnostic categories. While the ninth edition of the *International Classification of Diseases*[1] has tried to deal with this difficulty by means of several special diagnostic groups (e.g. 'special symptoms or syndromes not elsewhere classified' and 'disturbances of emotions specific to childhood and adolescence'), it is nevertheless convenient to consider some problems of young children separately. Psychotic, including autistic, conditions have been dealt with in Chapter 6, hyperactivity, enuresis and encopresis in Chapter 7 and speech, language and motor developmental disorders in Chapter 8. Various other disorders described elsewhere in this book may occur in this age group, but this chapter will consider some common problems of pre-school age children which are not covered in other chapters.

In this age range the family is particularly important as the child has relatively little contact with people outside it. Independent reports, for example from teachers, are not usually available and a self-report from the child is not as easy to obtain as it may be at a later age. The intimate involvement of child and family in this age period means that the child is particularly susceptible to tensions and problems in the family group, and that careful assessment may be necessary to determine whether the problem is essentially a disorder of the child's development or is primarily a manifestation of family dysfunction. These are not mutually exclusive, however, and elements of both may be present. Consequently a careful assessment of the child's level of development and emotional state is necessary, as well as assessment of the family as a whole.

While the conditions described here usually have their onset in the first five years life, and are mainly prevalent in that age group, they may persist into middle childhood.

Prevalence

There have been few studies of the prevalence of behaviour problems in young children, but Richman and her colleagues report a survey of 3-year-old children in a North London Borough[2]. They found that 7 per cent had moderate or severe behaviour problems and a further 15 per cent had mild problems. There were no significant sex differences in overall prevalence rates, but overactivity and wetting and soiling problems were more frequent in boys, and fearfulness in girls. Children with delayed language development are not included in these figures, and the survey did not cover 'immigrant' families. As the authors point out, prevalence figures of this type can be misleading since young children are highly reactive to the environment, and considering them in isolation from their parents is artificial.

These findings are similar to those of an earlier study in Newcastle-on-Tyne, in which 8 per cent of under-five were considered to have behaviour problems[3]. Further information about the behaviour and problems of pre-school children can be found in the book *Four Years Old in an Urban Community*[4].

Common Problems

Temper tantrums are normal in toddlers (see page 4) but may become a problem if they are severe and persistent. This is likely to happen if they are reinforced by attention and gratification. This in turn is likely to happen in unstable families in which other aspects of the care of the children are unsatisfactory. They are thus often part of a more widespread disturbance.

Since temper tantrums are the expression of a rather primitive rage reaction at being frustrated, their escalation or cure depend upon how situations that are frustrating for the child are handled by the parents and other care-givers. Firm but kind limit-setting in an emotionally warm, accepting context will usually bring about a rapid improvement. Inconsistent or hostile attitudes, and especially the intermittent re-inforcement of the tantrums by giving into them, will tend to cause them to worsen. At the same time some children seem constitutionally more prone to tantrum behaviour than others, and children seem to differ in the ease with which tantrums can be extinguished.

SLEEP PROBLEMS

Failure to sleep as and when expected by the parents may simply be due to unrealistic expectations by the parents, or a lack of knowledge of the amount of sleep needed by a child of the age in question. Moreover, the amount of sleep needed by different children seems to vary considerably. Failure to conform to a regular pattern of sleeping behaviour may occur in chaotic and disorganised homes where there is no regular bedtime and a bedtime routine is not adhered to, so that the child does not have the opportunity to learn a set pattern of sleeping and waking behaviour. Failure to sleep, with crying, is common in babies, but normally settles after a few months if feeding and the general care of the infant are satisfactory. Persistence of the trouble into the toddler years is quite common, however.

In many instances the child is in other ways mentally and physically healthy and the trouble is transient, clearing up after some weeks or months.

Night terrors can be alarming to parents who have not seen them before, but are common in perfectly healthy toddlers. These children wake up in a frightened, even terrified, condition. They are inaccessible and do not respond when spoken to, nor do they appear to see their surroundings. Instead they may appear auditorily or visually hallucinated, talking to and looking at people and things not actually there. They may be difficult to comfort at first, and the period of disturbed behaviour and altered consciousness may last up to fifteen minutes, occasionally even longer. Eventually the disturbance subsides, with or without comfort from a parent, and the child goes back to sleep. There is usually no memory of the incident when the child wakes up in the morning.

Night terrors have been shown to occur on waking from 'stage 4' (deep) sleep. They persist into later childhood in 1–3 per cent of children[5]. There is evidence that they are associated with dream content, which as revealed by sleep talking, touches on an area of intense emotional conflict for the subject; also that severity is related to the duration of stage 4 sleep[6].

Nightmares are unpleasant or frightening dreams. The child does not wake up, nor necessarily become overtly disturbed while having a nightmare. If woken up the child reacts normally and there is no period of altered consciousness or inaccessibility such as occurs in night terrors. Nightmares occur in 'REM' (that is 'rapid eye movement', or light) sleep.

Sleep-walking, or somnabulism, may accompany either nightmares or night terrors. Apparently the content of the dream or terror is acted out in a state of sleep or altered consciousness.

All forms of sleep disturbance are liable to be exacerbated by physical or emotional disorder. Nightmares and restless sleep are common in acute febrile illnesses. The possibility of nocturnal epilepsy must also be considered, since some epileptic children with major fits have their attacks only at night. It is important in these cases to get as accurate a description as possible of what happens (see pages 139 to 144 for further information on epilepsy).

Very often no evidence is found of any other abnormality. The sleep disorder can then usually be regarded as a transient phase in development, and the parents reassured accordingly. It may indeed represent a reaction to the normal anxieties of the toddler period, during which the child has to meet and cope with many new experiences and situations. Sometimes, however, there is evidence of emotional disorder in the child or in the family group. In that case treatment for a neurotic disorder (see Chapter 5) or for the family problem as a whole (see page 222) may be needed. It has also been suggested that the drug diazepam (page 231) may be of value in the treatment of night terrors[5].

A fuller review of young children's sleep disorders is that of Anders and Weinstein[7].

FEEDING PROBLEMS

Feeding problems are common in young children, in whom they sometimes occur in the absence of other significant problems. Children may eat, or be thought by their parents to eat, too little or too much; they may be excessively particular over what they eat (or 'faddy'); or they may eat items not normally regarded as edible (this is known as 'pica').

It has been mentioned in Chapter 7 that *food refusal* may be present in cases of soiling. It may also occur on its own. The psychopathology is often similar to that present in children who soil. The parent is attempting to control the child, often in a rigid, obsessive way. The child reacts by refusing to eat what the parent considers an adequate diet. The parent may have an exaggerated idea of the importance of adequate nutrition, and perhaps unrealistic fears of what will happen if the child does not eat enough. The child is unconsciously or consciously aware of this and so chooses this particular symptom, while showing a total lack of concern about the 'problem'. Such children are usually perfectly satisfactorily nourished, and so have been receiving adequate diets, though it may not be very easy to persuade the parents of this.

The management needed resembles that used in case of negativistic soiling. The food refusal itself should be ignored. A lot of work may require to be done with the parents to enable them to understand and accept this. Where the parent (most often it is the mother) has very set, abnormal attitudes on the matter of feeding, the problem may have its roots in her own childhood.

Special food should not be prepared, and no attempt should be made to persuade the child to eat. An ordinary menu should be offered on a 'take-it-or-leave-it' basis. If this is done, children normally select a diet which provides adequate nourishment. (This does not of course apply to suffers of anorexia nervosa, a disorder of adolescents – see page 164.)

The outcome is usually satisfactory. In many cases food refusal is simply a phase in development, particularly in toddlers who are trying to assert their individuality and are rebelling against constraints they find are placed on their behaviour. Where parental attitudes or the family environment are seriously disturbed, the outlook may be less good, but this is because of the background problems rather than the food refusal. In cases of this sort treatment by a family group approach may be helpful (see page 222).

Food fads often occur in children with food refusal. Many types of food are refused, which may cause anxiety to the parents. Nevertheless these children are usually well nourished and thus appear to be receiving an adequate diet. Relatively mild food fads are extremely common in normal, healthy children. They are probably largely a means whereby children instinctively select a balanced diet suited to their present nutritional needs.

Pica is the eating of items not usually regarded as edible, for example paper, soil, paint, wood and cloth. Many other materials may be involved. The symptom has many causes, including adverse environmental factors and emotional distress; it is often associated with distorted developmental patterns, brain damage and mental retardation, but is sometimes seen in children of normal intelligence[8]. The children often have relationship difficulties. The condition is frequently associated with iron deficiency anaemia (due to a generally poor diet) and lead poisoning, which itself can cause anaemia. Lead poisoning often results from eating old paint containing lead; it can lead to severe brain damage (see page 93).

Associated sleep and behaviour problems are common, and the families tend to be disorganised and poor. In severe cases treatment usually involves admission to hospital as well as intensive work with the family. Bicknell has provided an excellent review of the condition[8].

BREATH-HOLDING SPELLS

Breath-holding spells occur commonly in pre-school children. They usually start before age 2, but seldom before 6 months. Livingstone[9] reports a mean age of onset of 12 months and a peak frequency between ages 2 and 3. The spells usually die out by age 5 or 6.

Breath-holding spells are usually precipitated by some minor upset or frustration. This is followed by crying which increases in intensity until the child reaches a state of rage. Breathing then stops, usually in expiration, and cyanosis becomes manifest in blueness of the face, especially around the lips. Occasionally the period of breath-holding leads to a major epileptic fit (see page 140), but in most cases the child starts to breathe again in half a minute or so and recovery quickly occurs. The three distinguishing factors are a precipitating factor, violent crying and cyanosis[9]. The spells seem to be used by some children to alarm their parents, who may reinforce them by a show of concern and indulgence. They are better treated calmly and with as little fuss as possible. The outcome is usually good and there is no increased incidence of epilepsy in these children.

THUMB-SUCKING AND NAIL-BITING

Both these behaviours are common in young children, though nail-biting also occurs frequently in older children, and in one population survey was found to reach a peak at 9 years in boys and eleven years in girls[10]. Thumb- and finger-sucking are normal in babies and gradually lessen during the second and subsequent years. Persistent thumb-sucking usually has little significance on its own but may be one feature in a pattern of regressive behaviour in a child who is anxious or under stress. It often requires no treatment, but if necessary can usually be stopped by simple reminders, rewards or even sanctions. Occasionally it becomes a severe, compulsive behaviour associated with rocking or masturbation, and more active treatment is required. Severe thumb-sucking can cause dental malocclusion in older children and may merit treatment for this reason.

Nail-biting is also usually a tension-reducing habit and tends to occur in anxious and tense children. Direct treatment is not usually needed, but the underlying condition may need treatment in its own right. Nail-biting often disappears at puberty if it has not done so previously.

References

1. World Health Organisation. *International Classification of Diseases*, 1975 Revision. Geneva: WHO, 1977.
2. Richman, N., Stevenson, J. E. and Graham, P. J. 'Prevalence of behaviour problems in 3-year-old children: an epidemiological study in a London borough'. *Journal of Child Psychology and Psychiatry*, **16**, 277–287, 1975.
3. Miller, F. J. W., Court, S. D. M., Walton, W. S. and Knox, E. K. *Growing Up in Newcastle-on-Tyne*. Oxford University Press 1960.
4. Newson, J. and Newson, E. *Four Years Old in an Urban Community* London: Allen and Unwin, 1968.
5. Keith, P. R. 'Night terrors'. *Journal of the American Academy of Child Psychiatry*, **14**, 477–489, 1975.
6. Fisher, C., Kahn, E., Edwards, A., Davis, D. M. and Fine, J. 'A psychophysiological study of nightmares and night terrors'. *Journal of Nervous and Mental Disease*, **158**, 174–188, 1974.
7. Anders, T. F. and Weinstein, P. 'Sleep and its disorders in infants and children'. *Pediatrics*, **50**, 312–324, 1972.
8. Bicknell, J. *Pica: A Childhood Symptom*. London: Butterworth, 1975.
9. Livingstone, S. 'Epilepsy in infancy, childhood and adolescence'. In *Manual of Child Psychopathology*, ed. B. J. Wolman. New York: McGraw-Hill, 1972.
10. Shepherd, M., Oppenhein, B. and Mitchell, S. *Childhood Behaviour and Mental Health*. University of London Press, 1971.

CHAPTER TWELVE

Emotional Disorders in Mentally Handicapped Children

Mental Handicap

Mental handicap, or mental retardation, is usually defined in social terms, as well as according to the subject's level of intellectual function. Thus it is considered to be present when low intelligence is combined with failure to adapt to society. It is therefore a psychosocial concept. Definitions couched in psychosocial terms have been developed mainly to help in deciding which individuals require institutional care or special educational arrangements. For these purposes they have obvious value. But in clinical practice, and for research purposes, they are unsatisfactory in that the individual may cease to be mentally handicapped, according to such psychosocial criteria, once any complicating psychiatric disorder has resolved or been successfully treated.

The division of children, for the purpose of providing them with psychiatric services, into those who are mentally handicapped and those who are not has disadvantages. There is much to be said for considering the psychiatry of all children as a part of the main stream of clinical child psychiatry. In the past the psychiatric care of duller children has tended to be provided largely in hospitals for the mentally handicapped, often far away from the children's homes and families. Moves to reverse this trend are under way, and more community-based sources are being developed[1].

Prevalence of emotional disorders

The Isle of Wight epidemiological study of 10- and 11-year-old children[2] showed that 'intellectually retarded' children (defined as those whose Wechsler Scale IQ – see page 195 – was 2 standard deviations or more below the mean for 'control' children) had psychiatric disorders 3 to 4 times more often than children in the normal control group. Among severely retarded children not attending school, psychiatric disorder was found in 50 per cent of the children compared with 6.6 per cent of the general population. Among these severely disturbed children psychoses and the hyperkinetic syndrome were proportionately more common than in children of higher intelligence[3].

As well as psychiatric disorders as defined in this book, a variety of forms of deviant behaviour are commoner in children of lower IQ than they are in more intellectually able children. Table 2, for example, illustrates this using some findings from the Isle of Wight survey[2].

TABLE 2: SYMPTOMS REPORTED IN 10- AND 11-YEAR-OLD GIRLS
(*Isle of Wight survey*)

	IQ 120 or more	*IQ 79 or less*
Poor concentration		
Parents' report	2·6%	26·4%
Teachers' report	9·1%	62·3%
Fighting		
Parents' report	1·3%	9·9%
Teachers' report	2·6%	11·0%

Causes and Clinical Associations

Some of the causes of mental handicap have been referred to in Chapters 2 and 6. As with other conditions, delayed intellectual development may be due to genetic factors (either specific or polygenic); to brain damage occurring before, during or after birth; and to environmental factors – notably lack of stimulation, emotional and physical depriva- tion, and serious malnutrition which can stunt intellectual as well as physical growth. The causes of intellectual handicap are discussed more fully in books devoted to mental handicap[4,5,6].

The causes of emotional disorder in the mentally handicapped should be considered as described in Chapter 2. In diagnostic formulations, the facts and consequences of the children's intellectual limitations will often be prominent. These limitations tend to make it specially difficult for such children to adapt to various social situations, as well as to cope with school work. Moreover, some mentally handicapped children have associated physical or perceptual problems which cause them further difficulty.

Any of the forms of psychiatric disorder described elsewhere in this book may affect intellectually handicapped children, but there are established associations between low intelligence and infantile autism and other infantile psychoses (see page 85); and between low intelligence and hyperactivity (see page 120). Stereotyped repetitive movements are also commoner in dull children than in bright ones; so too are nail-biting, stuttering and some other behaviours.

The mechanisms responsible for the associations between intellectual handicap and psychiatric disorder are complex. The following points are relevant:

1. There is a relationship between IQ and deviant behaviour in children of normal intelligence as well as in dull children. Thus children who are intellectually above average show less deviant behaviour than those of average intelligence. This could mean that greater intellectual capacity makes social adaption easier, and thus deviant behaviour less likely; indeed this is almost certainly an important factor.

2. There is little evidence that emotional disorders are the cause of a low IQ except in so far as they may impair a child's co-operation in intelligence testing.

3. Organic brain disease is commoner in dull children than in bright ones, and is virtually universal in children with IQs below 50[7]. In such children the organic condition often plays a part in causing the psychiatric disorder. In the Isle of Wight study[2], psychiatric disorder was found to be 3 to 4 times commoner in brain-damaged children than in the general child population. In children with chronic physical disorders which did not involve the brain, such as asthma and diabetes, it was found only slightly more often. Epileptic disturbances (see Chapter 8) are also associated with an increased incidence of psychiatric disorder[8]. Moreover behaviour disturbance often lessens or even disappears following hemispherectomy, an operation sometimes performed to remove half the cerebral cortex when this is badly damaged in children with infantile hemiplegia; similar improvement may also occur following the surgical removal of an epileptogenic focus from the temporal lobe (see page 144). This suggests that the behaviour problems are due to malfunction of the brain in these cases.

4. Social factors may adversely affect both intellectual development and emotional stability. In particular, depriving, hostile and rejecting parental attitudes may have both effects. Studies have also shown that instability is commoner in the families of mentally handicapped children than in those of brighter ones, perhaps in part because there

is a positive correlation between the intelligence levels of parents and those of their children. Retarded children may also be rejected by other children, to the detriment of their emotional development and mental health.

5. The developmental immaturity affecting retarded children means that their language and other social skills are less than those of their peers. These problems, combined with their delay in reaching motor and toilet training milestones, are additional handicaps which may be factors in bringing about the development of psychiatric disorder.

6. Educational failure is strongly associated with psychiatric disorder (another finding of the Isle of Wight study), and dull children inevitably progress more slowly than their brighter peers. In some retarded children, long-standing failure at school seems to be a major factor in causing emotional disorder.

7. Institutionalisation can adversely affect both intellectual development and emotional growth. The unsuitability of many institutions for children was clearly shown in the sociological investigations in the book, *Patterns of Residential Care*[9].

The association between psychiatric disorder and intellectual handicap in children has been discussed helpfully, and more fully, by Rutter in *Mental Retardation*, Volume 3[10].

Treatment

The principles of treatment are the same as those used for other disturbed children, and are discussed in Chapter 14. As in other cases, a comprehensive assessment of the child in the context of his or her family, school and neighbourhood is essential first; the formulation should pay special regard to the clinical associations discussed above. It is often found that social factors such as an unstable or depriving family background and educational failure are militating against the child's healthy emotional development, in addition to the various biological factors which may be operating. Both social and educational stress are in theory susceptible to modification, though the facilities available to achieve this are not always adequate.

In Great Britain there have been developed both paediatric assessment centres which form part of the health services for children, and educational assessment centres which form part of the school system. These centres are designed to help detect developmental problems and delays at an early stage. They can also investigate the nature of developmental problems, learning difficulties, perceptual deficits, emotional disorders and social background problems of children. To do this they have multidisciplinary staffs and can also call on other services, including those of psychiatric units, to assist when necessary.

Many of the problems of mentally handicapped children can be resolved, or better still avoided, by adequate assessment of the children's needs, followed by the provision of the right kind of educational and living environment.

Institutional care is necessary for some children, including most of the very severely retarded. The need is usually determined by the degree of the intellectual retardation, together with the effects of any associated physical handicaps (and these are common in the severely retarded) or emotional disorder. The family is an important factor too, since the capacities of families to cope with handicapped children vary. Institutional care of mentally handicapped children, when it is necessary, should be in small, well-staffed units as near as possible to the children's families. Only a minority of the most severely handicapped require the full facilities of a hospital. In many instances hostels or group homes are better, as well as being less expensive to run and often nearer to the families. Unfortunately many children are still accommodated in large, ill-equipped and frequently understaffed wards of antiquated hospitals. This is not to be recommended.

Psychotherapy with mentally handicapped children presents special problems because of the poor verbal skills and limited concentration of these children. Where emotional problems exist in the child or family, family therapy (see page 222) is often easier to carry out and may be a more hopeful approach.

Behaviour therapy is widely used in treating mentally handicapped children. Forms of psychotherapy that involve verbal language skills are of limited value in these children, but operant conditioning (see page 228) can be very effective. Suitably constructed programmes can promote successful toilet training, the extinction of deviant behaviours like temper tantrums, rocking and head banging, the acquisition of motor and language skills and many other therapeutic aims. As well as the reduction or removal of specific symptoms, successful modification of problem behaviours can have helpful secondary effects on the child's emotional state[11].

Drug treatment has a significant part to play in the treatment of psychiatric disorders in mentally handicapped children. Epilepsy, if present, should be controlled by the use of appropriate anticonvulsant drugs (see page 229). Since motor hyperactivity sometimes responds well to such drugs as haloperidol, phenothiazines and methylphenidate, these substances can be helpful in treating the considerable number of retarded children who show this symptom. The treatment of hyperactive children is discussed on pages 122 and 231, and drug treatment generally on pages 229 to 234.

In conclusion, some general points about helping intellectually handicapped children are worth stating. A middle course has to be steered between asking too much of a handicapped child and asking too little. Facing such a child with tasks in school which are quite beyond him or her can be damaging and lead to anxiety, even despair, and a needlessly poor self-image. On the other hand asking too little, as may for instance happen to the inmate of a large hospital ward, means that the child's potential is not reached. Continuous assessment of these children and their progress, including their reactions to the education, treatment and other help they are getting, is essential. Assessment cannot be a once-for-all process. Continuity of care is important, too. Duller children find change more difficult to deal with. Finally the needs of the family must always be considered. It is possible for the attention given to a handicapped child to affect adversely the care given to other children in the family. The presence of a severely retarded and disturbed child can also affect the parents and the stability of their marriage. All these factors must be taken into account in the management of these difficult problems.

Mental 'handicap' may be regarded as the extent to which intellectual retardation affects an individual's capacity to cope with life in the family and society in which he is living. It is thus as much a function of society as of the individual. Intellectual limitations are a greater problem in a technologically well-developed country than in a less well-developed one where most people are doing unskilled work. The extent to which the handicapped reach a satisfactory adjustment in any society will depend partly on such factors and also upon how society reacts to those who are handicapped.

References

1. Kushlick, A. 'The need for residential care of the mentally handicapped'. *British Journal of Hospital Medicine*, **8**, 161–167, 1972. (Reprinted in *Contemporary Psychiatry*, ed. T. Silverstone and B. Barraclough, Ashford, Kent: Headley Bros, 1975.)
2. Rutter, M., Tizard, J. and Whitmore, K. *Education, Health and Behaviour*. London: Longman, 1970.
3. Rutter, M., Graham, P. and Yule, W. *A Neuropsychiatric Study in Childhood*. London: Heinemann, 1970.
4. Penrose, L. S. *The Biology of Mental Defect*. London: Sidgwick and Jackson, 1972.
5. Iivanainen, M. *A Study on the Origins of Mental Retardation*, London: Heinemann, 1974.
6. Kirman, B. H. and Bicknell, J. *Mental Handicap*. Edinburgh: Churchill-Livingstone, 1975.

7. Crome, L. 'The brain and mental retardation'. *British Medical Journal*, **11**, 897–904, 1960.

8. Eyman, R. K., Moore, B. C., Capes, L. and Zachofsky, T. 'Maladaptive behaviour of institutionalised retardates with seizures'. *American Journal of Mental Deficiency*, **74**, 651–659, 1970.

9. King, R. D., Raynes, N. V. and Tizard, J. *Patterns of Residential Care*. London: Routledge and Kegan Paul, 1971.

10. Rutter, M. 'Psychiatry'. In *Mental Retardation*, Vol. 3, New York: Grune and Stratton, 1971.

11. Watson, L. *How to Use Behaviour Modification with Mentally Retarded and Autistic Children*. Libertyville, Ill: Behaviour Modification Technology, 1972.

CHAPTER THIRTEEN

Disorders in Adolescence

The principles underlying the assessment and treatment of psychiatric disorders in childhood apply also to disorders of adolescence, but there are some practical differences. The pattern of disorders prevalent in adolescence is also somewhat different from that seen in childhood. Adolescence is a time of rapid change, physical, emotional and social. The developmental tasks of this period have been outlined in Chapter 1; the main development is the gradual adoption of the adult role – social, vocational and sexual. During this process doubts, fears and feelings of inadequacy are common. These may cause anxiety which may not be openly expressed. Instead the individual may become aggressive and defiant, or moody and unpredictable. Adolescents often make a show of rejecting adult standards, and of having interests and pursuits other than those which their parents approve. The moods and attitudes of adolescents may vary strikingly over short periods of time.

The prevalence of psychiatric disorders seems somewhat greater during adolescence than in earlier childhood (see page 30).

Adolescent emotional disorders include:

1. Unresolved childhood disorders.
2. Disturbances related to the stresses of puberty and adolescence.
3. Incipient adult-type disorders.

Unresolved Childhood Disorders

Childhood emotional disorders which have neither resolved spontaneously nor been successfully treated will persist into adolescence.

In many instances the symptoms continue with little change at the onset of puberty. This applies to many psychotic disorders and to some conduct, neurotic and mixed disorders.

Sometimes *neurotic disorders* improve at or around puberty. This may be due to the biological drives towards independence which become more active. The peer group, which tends to become a more important influence in adolescence, may also help. The change from primary to secondary school sometimes promotes emotional growth; if the child can face the challenge of an often larger school containing bigger children and requiring more responsibility and independence of decision on the part of its pupils, this can be a useful experience. All these factors may assist the emotionally immature child, who has been overdependent on his parents, to grow up, become more self-reliant and thus come to experience less anxiety in stressful situations. But sometimes they are insufficient. Faced with the challenges of adolescence, some neurotic children cannot cope. Such drives towards independence as exist are not enough and the individuals fall back into the security and comfort of their families. Such children, reaslising unconsciously, if not consciously, their incapacity to fill age-appropriate roles, may become even more anxious, with a worsening of their condition.

School refusal in adolescence may be either a continuation or an exacerbation of a problem which existed before puberty, or a symptom appearing for the first time. Even if onset is during adolescence, however, the origins can usually be traced back to well before puberty. The pattern of school refusal in adolescence tends to be different from that seen in younger children. Adolescents who are anxious about going to school may hide when efforts are made to enforce attendance; others may stay at home and cling to their mothers. In many adolescents with school refusal, difficulties at school are more prominent than is usual in younger children. The 'problems' there, which often concern relationships with peer group or staff, would not be problems to children whose emotional development had been normal and whose family relationships were secure.

The difficulties which the parents of school-refusing children often have in expressing aggression in normal ways, and asserting independence, are usually present in the children too; but in adolescence they frequently become intensified. The adolescent's desire, conscious or unconscious, to be independent, and his awareness of his mother's 'smothering' and protectiveness which prevent this, can cause a build-up of intensely aggressive feelings. This may be expressed through violently aggressive outbursts, expecially under stress, the child behaving at other times in a passive and dependent fashion. In these cases treatment of the whole family group is essential if the underlying problem is to be resolved. Sometimes the members of the family are not willing to enter into such treatment, or the situation proves insufficiently remediable if they do; there is then no alternative, in severe cases, to removing the adolescent from the family for treatment in a residential setting. It seems that school refusal in adolescents tends to be associated with more serious pathology in child and family than is usually the case in younger children[1,2].

Conduct disorders are often exacerbated with the onset of puberty, as the individual's antisocial feelings are reinforced by the normal rebelliousness and rejection of adult standards seen at this age. The adolescent who does not have a secure relationship with his parents, and lacks 'internal' behavioural controls based upon identification with the parents, is very much at risk. He is readily influenced by others of his age, from whom he may well get more acceptance and satisfaction than he receives at home. The nature of the peer group is partly a matter of chance, or at least of what is available in the neighbourhood, but the choosing of friends by adolescents is also influenced by their own attitudes and feelings. If the adolescent becomes part of a delinquent gang the conduct disorder will probably worsen, but some peer groups are beneficial in their effects. One of the aims of youth clubs and other youth organisations is to provide groups which will be constructive and useful to their members.

Psychotic disorders do not themselves usually get either better or worse at adolescence. If they have been improving the improvement often continues, but generally the handicaps of autistic and other psychotic children persist through adolescence[3]. Similarly, if a child has been gradually adapting to a chronic neurological handicap he may continue to do so. There may, however, be secondary emotional disorder due to the child's awareness of the increasing discrepancy between his capabilities and those of his peers. As he gets bigger, and should be getting more independent, his handicaps may show up more strikingly than hitherto. At this stage some psychotic and brain-damaged children who have previously been cared for at home may require admission to residential care or schooling.

Hyperactivity often lessens in adolescence. This applies both to hyperactive psychotic children and to the 'hyperkinetic syndrome' itself. The associated antisocial behaviour and learning problems often continue however[4,5].

A follow-up study of young adults aged 17 to 24 showed that poor socialisation skills and poor sense of well-being were still present significantly more often than in control subjects. This applied also to scholastic skills and restlessness, but not to adjustment in work and living situations, nor to antisocial behaviour, nonmedical use of drugs or serious psychiatric disturbances[6].

Disturbances Related to Stresses of Puberty and Adolescence

An outline of normal development in adolescence has been given in Chapter 1. Sometimes medical or psychiatric help is sought, usually by the parents, because of behaviour which is essentially normal for this age, or is at most an exaggeration of the normal. The parents may complain of the child's rebelliousness, disobedience, staying out late, mode of dress or general rejection of their standards. They may also complain of the shyness, diffidence and lack of self-confidence shown by some adolescents which tends to cover up difficulty in adopting a more independent role. Shyness in some circumstances may be combined with aggressiveness in others. It is often hard to define precisely where normality ends and abnormal behaviour starts, and indeed the division is essentially an arbitrary one; but from the point of view of the advice and help needed by parents and child it is not particularly important. This applies also to the much-discussed question of whether 'adolescent turmoil' is 'normal' or should be regarded as a psychiatric disorder[7]. What *is* important is the assessment of the nature, causes and seriousness of any problems present, leading to help for the family in overcoming them. If a psychiatric label is to be attached, in many instances it will be one of adjustment reaction (see pages 125 to 127).

During adolescence there is need for much give and take between parents and their children. If parents' attitudes are unduly rigid and inflexible, defiance may be provoked in their children. At the same time the adolescent, especially the early adolescent, still very much needs the security of home and family. It can be as unfortunate, even disastrous, for the parents to give too little support to, and take too little interest in, the adolescent, as for them to be excessively strict and rigid.

It is not always the parents who complain or feel worried. The adolescent too often feels anxious, tense or under strain during this period. There are several possible reasons for this.

(a) *The 'dependence–independence' conflict.* The adolescent feels an innate urge to be more independent and to take decisions, and also perceives that this is socially expected of him or her, but may not be able adequately to play such a role. The alternative is to fall back on the family, and others, for support, but reluctantly. Thus help and support given by parents may be accepted in an off-hand and ungracious way.

(b) *Uncertainties about sexual role and sexual adequacy.* The onset of the physical and emotional changes of puberty can vary widely at least between the ages of ten and seventeen. This can cause individuals to feel out of step with their peers, which may lead to considerable anxiety. Fears of sexual inadequacy are common during this period.

During adolescence there is an upsurge of sexual activity, and relationships with the opposite sex become more prominent. During the transition there is often some confusion of feelings and difficulty in dealing with the new situation. The individual may wish to enter into relationships with the opposite sex, but shyness and lack of confidence may make this difficult and embarrassing.

(c) *Peer group influences.* As adolescents draw away from their parents, their peer groups become of greater importance. Adolescent groups are sometimes all of one sex, or they may include both boys and girls. One important purpose they serve is that of providing support for the anxious and insecure individual who feels unable to play an appropriate role unsupported. Members identify with the standards of the group as a whole, and with the support of the group can do things they would feel unable to tackle on their own. Adolescent groups may be as small as two or three but membership may run to ten, twenty or even more. Some are fairly constant, but usually they change as members leave to form or join other groups, and others join. A particular adolescent may belong to several groups of different sizes or types at the same time.

Groups of this sort can be beneficial, helping their members to achieve normal behaviour and adjustment by providing support over a difficult period. The opposite can happen, however, as in the case of delinquent gangs.

Difficulties arising from group membership are mainly concerned with being, or feeling, different from the group. The problem may be one of appearance, race or religion. The groups usually demand a fair amount of conformity to their standards, and inability to meet these may cause the individual anxiety and even lead to rejection by the group.

Adolescent conduct disorders, also known as adolescent behaviour disorders, are characterised by antisocial behaviour, generally similar to that occurring in conduct disorders of younger children. They are often an exaggeration of normal adolescent rebelliousness. The child may stay out later than the parents lay down, play truant from school, be generally disobedient or steal. In more severe cases there may be frank delinquency with conflict with the law. The parents complain of things like the young person's mode of dress or hairstyle, and may consider him generally out of control.

These conditions are manifestations of breakdown in the relationships between young people and the adult world, particularly the parents. During adolescence the parent–child relationship has to undergo much change. Its soundness before puberty is an important factor in determining the extent to which the adolescent will rebel and 'test out' the parents. Another factor is the way the parents react to adolescent behaviour in their son or daughter. Great flexibility, tolerance and understanding, combined with the right amount of firmness and control, are needed. Sometimes abnormal rebelliousness and antisocial behaviour are unconsciously designed to get the parents to control the behaviour of a child who is insecure and afraid of his own aggressiveness. In other instances it is a protest against over-strict demands which the parents make. In yet others it is a reflection of rootlessness and aimlessness in children who have been, in varying degrees, deprived of love and security. Because of the poor quality of their relationships, conscience-formation has been defective and the conflicting pressures and anxieties of adolescence upset the delicate and uncertain balance which has hitherto resulted in reasonably conforming behaviour. In most cases the child's problems are but part of a wider family problem, and are more easily explicable when seen in this context. As well as being a useful treatment, family therapy can be a valuable way of learning how the adolescent's antisocial behaviour fits into the family's structure and functioning.

Many adolescent conduct disorders seem worse than they really are. The reported severity of the behavioural disturbance is on its own an inadequate criterion. Many adolescents emerge as mentally healthy individuals, adjusting satisfactorily to society, after going through a period of difficult behaviour. Factors to be considered in deciding how serious the problem really is include the child's adjustment before puberty, family stability and parental attitudes, and the individual's adjustment in circumstances where the parents are not directly involved. These include school, peer group and the interview situation with physician or other professional.

Running away from home is a common and apparently increasing problem in many societies. The term is applied to leaving or staying away from home, with the intention of staying away at least for some time, in circumstances in which the individual will be missed by those remaining at home. While it occurs at other ages also, it is particularly a problem of adolescents. About 1 in 10 of the youths aged 12 to 13 in the USA have run away from home at least once, which is equivalent to about 2,137,000 young people in the whole country. About 300,000 run away for the first time each year[9]. These figures do not include institutionalised youths. The homes of runaways are characterized by much parent–child conflict and are broken by parental death, divorce or separation more often than in the population generally. Running away can be an escape from such conflicts or a means of avoiding defeat in the battle for independence from the parents.

Adolescent drug taking appears to have increased in the last few decades, although reliable prevalence figures are hard to obtain. Blumberg[10], in an excellent review, quotes reported prevalence rates in American high school students varying from 9 per cent to 42 per cent for marijuana use, 3 to 15 per cent for barbiturates, 2 to 7 per cent for LSD and 1 to 4 per cent for opiates. These figures are for students who had ever used the drug in question, even if only once, and are based on pre-1970 studies. American college students have broadly similar patterns of drug use, and surveys in British universities and colleges have shown prevalences of cannabis use of 10 to 39 per cent.[10] Rates of usage undoubtedly vary greatly from time to time and area to area. Alcohol use and drunkenness among young people have also been reported to have increased in recent years, though a recent review stresses the lack of reliable factual information about the precise extent of these problems[11].

The causes of adolescent drug taking are to be found within the individual and in his or her social group. Most adolescents who take drugs do so as part of a group activity. A prerequisite is availability of the drug, which is probably why the readily available alcohol, tobacco and (in many communities) marijuana are the most widely used drugs.

For many young people the social pressures favouring drug use are strong. If all, or nearly all, of the individual's class or peer group use a drug it can be hard for the person to resist doing do. Drug taking may become part of a social ritual in which all participate.

Factors in the individual also contribute. Drug use is more likely if the parents also use the drug and where one or both parents have been absent during the subject's childhood. Marijuana use is generally commoner in higher socioeconomic groups than in lower ones. Individuals may also have their needs for affiliation, satisfaction of curiosity, altered state of consciousness, recreation, anxiety reduction and general drive reduction met by drug use.[9] It will be seen that these needs include several that may be faced by insecure, uncertain adolescents.

Drug use can also be seen as a learnt habit if the subject finds it rewarding. If some felt need is met, use of the drug is likely to be reinforced. Thus what starts as experimentation as a result of group pressure, may be continued for other reasons.

Among adolescent drug users there is a small proportion who have serious personality problems which usually pre-date the drug use. Drug *abusers* tend to show evidence of psychopathology while the simpler drug *user* appears, from most research studies, to be more like the general run of young people of similar age[12]. The psychopathology may be predominatly depressive, rather than a personality disorder. Some drug abusers have a history of early deprivation.

Some surveys have found alarmingly low ages of onset. A survey of high school students in New York State showed that the median age of first use of marijuana and hard liquor, in children using these drugs, was only thirteen[13]. There is apparently a stepwise progression in drug use [13,14]. This starts with beer or wine, going on to, successively, cigarettes and hard liquor, marijuana and then other illegal drugs such as heroin, cocaine and LSD. Not all adolescents who start on this sequence complete it of course, and indeed the proportion who reach the final stage is quite small.

Social causes of the behaviour include the ready availability of certain drugs. Seeing adults, using alcohol, tobacco and marijuana, young people often wish to imitate them and so appear more grown-up themselves; combined with this is an element of adolescent rebelliousness. The drug use may be infrequent and experimental and may be abandoned after a while. On the other hand, cigarette smoking can be seriously addictive, causing physical and psychological withdrawal symptoms, and in many families and social groups alcohol use is a regular, accepted habit. It too can be addictive.

Progression to 'hard drugs', such as heroin and cocaine is serious, since these often produce major problems of addiction. The taking of drugs by injection, for example, amphetamines drugs ('speed'), barbiturates and heroin is also a bad sign. Complications due to dirty or contaminated injections (infection or hepatitis), and overdosage are ever-present risks.

Drugs used by adolescents include the following:

(a) Alcohol – This is a serious problem in society at large, and its use by adolescents reflects this. It is widely abused by young people. It is a drug of dependence, it causes serious health risks (notably liver damage) and it is an important contributing cause of road traffic accidents.

(b) Tobacco – Cigarette smoking is powerfully addictive and shares with alcohol use the problem of being widely abused by society. Tobacco products, like alcoholic drinks, are widely advertised, often to appeal to young people. Smoking predisposes to lung cancer, heart disease, arterial disease and other health hazards.

(c) Marijuana – (cannabis, hashish, 'pot') is an intoxicant which produces a euphoric state similar to that produced by alcohol. It is illegal in most western countries, though in many, penalties for its use have been lightened in recent years. It does not cause physical dependence, though users may become psychologically dependent on it. Long-term effects of its use are not certainly established, but in the short term it can cause mental confusion and can make a person as dangerous at the wheel of a car as can alcohol.

(d) Amphetamines – are used to produce a state of euphoria; their use can lead to physical dependence and to a psychotic state. Intravenous use can have particularly serious effects.

(e) Hallucinogens – the best known of which is lysergic acid diethylamide ('LSD') – are used often by middle class individuals, to provide an altered state of consciousness and unusual subjective, including hallucinatory, experiences. Currently they seem to be used less than they were a decade or two ago.

(f) Barbiturates are used both orally and intravenously, and can lead to marked states of dependency. There is real danger of overdose, and suicide by barbiturates is quite frequent.

(g) Other tranquillizers and sedatives are frequently used to produce altered states of consciousness by adolescents.

(h) Solvents such as glues used for model-making, nail-polish remover and typewriter correction solutions are quite often used by young people. They are inhaled, often from inside a plastic bag in which the vapour is concentrated. The process is usually know as 'glue-sniffing'. A euphoric state can be produced, leading to mental disorientation and even unconsciousness. The habit seems to be increasing. It carries a significant risk of causing brain damage.

(i) Heroin, cocaine and other major addictive drugs are used relatively infrequently by young people, but their use is serious since dependence readily develops, and the long-term prognosis for those who are addicted is generally poor.

Neurotic disorders may arise *de novo* in adolescents. They are often related to emotional conflict arising out of difficulty in coping with the developmental tasks of adolescence. Most individuals who develop neurotic symptoms have previously shown evidence of emotional immaturity. Clinical pictures similar to those described in Chapter 5 are seen; sometimes these disorders present as school refusal in adolescence for the first time.

Anorexia nervosa, a condition affecting mainly adolescents is discussed in Chapter 10.

Adult-type Mental Disorders Arising in Adolescence

Schizophrenia and affective phychoses become increasingly common once puberty is past. Both are still fairly rare duing the first year of two after puberty, though depressive illness may be difficult to recognise at this time. During middle and late adolescence the frequency of these conditions increases considerably.

The main features of *schizophrenia* have been described in Chapter 6. The diagnosis can be difficult to make in this age period since shyness, diffidence and vagueness of expression are common in anxious adolescents who are feeling unsure of themselves but are not psychotic. It is important not to make a diagnosis of schizophrenia lightly, and without positive evidence of at least some of the main features. Nevertheless, the condition's onset can be insidious and it may be necessary to await developments while bearing the possibility of schizophrenia in mind. Sometimes a period of observation in a hospital psychiatric unit is helpful in making the distinction.

Manic–depressive disorders (page 99) are rare in adolescence, though they do occur. The commonest form of *affective disorder* is depression, which may be atypical in adolescence. Many adolescents with depressed mood are reacting in a way which can be understood in the light of stress which they face. Depression of psychotic intensity (that is with delusions or other disordered contact with reality) also occurs. The onset may be acute, in a boy or girl who has previously been well, and who may or may not be faced with any special family stress or other obvious difficulty; or it may be insidious. The presenting symptoms may not include depression of mood; there may rather be anxiety (perhaps about going to school), panic attacks or somatic symptoms such as headaches or abdominal pain. Slowness of movement or thought may be evident. The presence of depression of mood may only emerge during conversation, in the course of which the adolescent may reveal that he has been or has felt like weeping, has wished he were dead, can get little or no pleasure out of life and may even have contemplated suicide or, perhaps, running away.

There may also be tiredness, irritability, poor concentration, difficulty in coping with school work which the subject could previously manage, sleep disturbance and poor appetite. Some of these symptoms may be confirmed by the parents who may describe the contrast between the patient's present listless, apathetic and unhappy self, and his normal more active, energetic and cheerful personality.

Suicidal behaviour is commoner in adolescents than in younger children. The possibility of suicide should always be borne in mind when an adolescent presents with depressive symptoms. The risk is greater when the situation is the culmination of a period of depression, but it also varies with the severity of the depression. Suicidal behaviour is more likely the less communication there is with others; the isolated depressed child is very much at risk, especially when communication channels have recently broken down. Any previous history of attempted suicide is important in assessing a suicidal adolescent. A long history of self-destructive behaviour is particularly serious; and the more serious any previous attempts have been, the more the subject may now be at risk. Also important is how far an attempt at suicide has been intended as a means of communication and whether the communication has been heeded by those to whom it was directed. If there has been little impact on the environment, the risk of recurrence is greater. Most serious of all are attempts at suicide in isolation, expecially when accompanied by a strong desire to die.

Treatment of Adolescents

Treatment is generally along lines similar to those used at other ages (see Chapter 16), but psychotherapy with adolescents can present special problems. In particular the tendency for adolescents to regard the adult generation in a hostile light, and to resent those in authority, can make establishing a working relationship difficult. It may indeed prevent the adolescent coming for treatment at all.

Treatment can be particularly difficult when the relationship between the adolescent and the parents is disturbed. Adolescents may give a totally different picture of their family situation, and of their relationships with their parents, from that given by the parents. They may deny that any problems exist, while the parents have a long list of complaints about them. In such instances family therapy (see page 222) can be helpful. The point of view of each party in any disagreements can then be stated while all are present, as a first step to examining the problem and trying to resolve it. Family therapy is valuable in a wide range of non-psychotic disorders of adolescence. Its value in psychotic conditions is less clear, despite its having been originally introduced in the USA for this purpose.

Particularly difficult to treat are adolescents who have suffered early deprivation[12]. Many of them have profound difficulty establishing trusting and intimate relationships with people; this limits the effectiveness of psychotherapy, and involvement in a living situation in which the subject can have the opportunity gradually to learn interpersonal skills is probably essential if the problem is to be overcome. This need may be met in a family receiving family therapy, or in a therapeutic group – often the living group in a residential treatment setting. Even then treatment is usually long, difficult and often unsuccessful. Some of these young people abuse drugs and drugs can come to replace human relationships in their lives[15].

Schizophrenia is a serious condition requiring specialist treatment, often initially in hospital. Phenothiazine drugs (page 234) may be of benefit.

Depression also requires energetic and prompt treatment, but not necessarily in hospital unless there appears to be a danger of suicide[16]. Antidepressant drugs are often effective (see page 232). They should be combined with such other measures as the formulation of the case suggests are needed, for example psychotherapeutic support, and alleviation, where possible, of any reality stresses the patient faces, whether at home, school or elsewhere.

Threats and attempts at suicide in adolescents should always be taken seriously. In many cases the suicidal adolescent is found to be isolated and to have problems of communication. The therapist must at once set about establishing communication with the subject (which can be difficult) while showing appropriate interest and concern. This approach should be combined with attempts to open up communication between the adolescent and the family and other significant people, as well as alleviating any other stress which the subject faces.

Outcome

The outlook in adolescent emotional disorders varies with the nature of the disorder present, but prognosis during this age period can be difficult. This is because of the practical difficulties of distinguishing between problems of adjustment to the adolescent role and more serious disorders such as schizophrenia, especially in the early stages. Nevertheless a great deal of disturbed behaviour over the adolescent period does not presage continuing psychiatric disorder or antisocial behaviour. Much can usually be done to help, especially when the family as a whole actively seeks treatment. On the other hand, a disinterested family is a bad prognostic sign.

Helpful sources of further information on adolescents' problems and their treatment are to be found in the books *Psychological Disturbance in Adolescence*[17] and *Youth: Problems and Approaches*[18].

References

1. Coolidge, J. C., Willer, M. L., Tessman, E. and Waldfagel, S. 'School phobia in adolescence: a manifestation of severe character disturbance'. *American Journal of Orthopsychiatry*, **30**, 599–607, 1970.
2. Hersov, L. 'School refusal'. In *Child Psychiatry: Modern Approaches*, ed. M. Rutter and L. Hersov. Oxford: Blackwell, 1976.
3. Rutter, M. 'Autistic children: infancy to adulthood'. *Seminars in Psychiatry*, **2**, 435–450, 1970.
4. Mendelson, W., Johnson, N. and Stewart, M. 'Hyperactive children as teenagers'. *Journal of Nervous and Mental Disease*, **153**, 273–279, 1971.
5. Minde, K., Weiss, G. and Mendelson, N. 'A five-year follow-up study of 91 hyperactive school children'. *Journal of the American Academy of Child Psychiatry*, **11**, 595–610, 1972.
6. Hechtmann, L., Weiss, G., Finklestein, J., Werner, A. and Benn, R. 'Hyperactives as young adults'. *Canadian Medical Association Journal*, **115**, 625–630, 1976.
7. Rutter, M., Graham, P., Chadwick, O. and Yule, W. 'Adolescent turmoil: fact or fiction?' *Journal of Child Psychology and Psychiatry*, **17**, 35–56, 1976.
8. Rutter, M. 'Normal psychosexual development'. *Journal of Child Psychology and Psychiatry*, **11**, 359–383, 1971.
9. Justice, B. and Duncan, D. P. 'Running away: an epidemic problem of adolescence'. *Adolescence*, **11**, 365–371, 1976.
10. Blumberg, H. 'Drug taking'. In *Child Psychiatry: Modern Approaches*, ed. M. Rutter and L. Hersov. Oxford: Blackwell, 1977.
11. O'Connor, J. 'Normal and problem drinking among children'. *Journal of Child Psychology and Psychiatry*, **18**, 279–284, 1977.
12. Amini, F., Salasnek, S. and Burke, E. L. 'Adolescent drug abuse: etiological and treatment considerations'. *Adolescence*, **11**, 281–299, 1976.
13. Hamburg, B. A., Kraemer, H. C. and Jahnke, W. 'A hierarchy of drug use in adolescence; behavioural and attitudinal correlates of substantial drug use.' *American Journal of Psychiatry*, **132**, 1155–1162, 1975.
14. Kandel, D. and Faust, R. 'Sequence and stages in patterns of adolescent drug use'. *Archives of General Psychiatry*, **32**, 923–932, 1975.
15. Wieder, H. and Kaplan, E. H. 'Drug use in adolescence: psychodynamic meaning and pharmacogenic effect'. *Psychoanalytic Study of the Child*, **24**, 399–431, 1969.
16. Toolan, J. M. 'Suicide in children and adolescents'. *American Journal of Psychotherapy*, **29**, 339–344, 1975.
17. Weiner, I. M. *Psychological Disturbance in Adolescence*. New York: Wiley, 1970.
18. Shamsie, S. J. (ed.) *Youth: Problems and Approaches*. Philadelphia: Lea and Febiger, 1972.

CHAPTER FOURTEEN

Psychological Tests

Psychological tests can add to the knowledge obtained at interview about children and their families. The results can help in assessing children's development and evaluating the results of treatment. The administration and interpretation of psychological tests is a part, though a small one, of the work of clinical and educational psychologists; but all who use the information obtained should know something about the tests and what they measure. The tests used with children include:

(a) Intelligence tests.
(b) Tests of educational attainment.
(c) Personality tests.
(d) Tests of specific psychological functions.

Intelligence Tests

Intelligence tests are designed to place children in order according to their ability to perform various tasks. They give an idea of the general ability of each child in relation to the whole population of the same age, and also provide information about how a child functions on particular types of task.

The *Wechsler Intelligence Scale for Children, Revised* (WISC-R) is probably the intelligence test most widely used for children in the clinical setting. It has separate verbal and performance sections, with sub-test scales as follows:

Verbal	*Performance*
General information	Picture completion
General comprehension	Picture arrangement
Arithmetic	Block design
Similarities	Object assembly
Vocabulary	Coding
(Digit span)	(Mazes)

The items in brackets are alternative tests, not usually used and correlating less well with the rest of the scale than the other sub-tests. While the names of the sub-tests give a general idea of the items concerned, the student should examine the actual test materials to discover precisely what their content is.

The test has been standardised on large populations of children so that the mean verbal, performance or full scale IQ at any age is 100. All the ten sub-tests have a mean (scaled) score of 10, though often there is a good deal of 'scatter', a child doing relatively better at one sub-test than another. The standard IQ deviation is 15, which means that about 66 per cent of children will have an IQ between 85 and 115. Two standard deviations (IQ 70–130) will cover about 95 per cent of the population, and three (55–145) will cover over 99 per cent.

The verbal and performance scores give an indication of the child's relative abilites in these two sorts of task and are often clinically more useful than the full scale IQ. The pattern of the sub-test scores can also give useful information, and the WISC-R is nowadays often used more as a diagnostic tool than as just an intelligence test. The child's responses can give the experienced clinician valuable information about thinking disorders, problems with impulsivity and learning difficulties.

The WISC-R is designed for use in the age range six to sixteen. Another scale, the *Wechsler Pre-School and Primary School Intelligence Scale* is used for children in the age range four to six-and-a-half. It is designed on principles similar to those used in the WISC-R.

Another widely used intelligence test is the *Stanford-Binet Intelligence Scale*. The latest (1960) version, known as form L-M, derives ultimately from the test devised by a Frenchman, Binet, in 1905. It covers the age range from two up to adult life. It includes a wide variety of tasks, but these vary at different ages and tend to be verbal rather than non-verbal. The result thus depends largely on the linguistic ability of the child, and for this reason the test is useful in relation to educational achievement and potential. It gives a 'mental age' as well as an IQ, but the test gives less diagnostic information concerning the pattern of the child's abilities than does the WISC, and IQs at different ages are not strictly comparable.

The concept of mental age is used less than it was, but a child's IQ was originally conceived by Binet as the ratio between his mental age and his chronological age, expressed as a percentage. Thus an eight-year-old of exactly average ability would have an IQ of 100. If he functioned like an average seven-year-old, he would have an IQ of $7/8 \times 100$, that is about 88. If he had a mental age of nine-and-a-half his IQ would be $9.5/8 \times 100$, that is 119.

Raven's Progressive Matrices consist of a series of patterns or 'matrices', from each of which a part is missing. This test can be used for the age range six to thirteen. The child being tested is presented with a series of shapes and has to decide which one will complete the matrix. An advantage of this test is that the material is non-verbal; and the task can be demonstrated to deaf or aphasic children, and to non-English speaking children. It is also easily and quickly administered and scored. Although it is quite unlike either the WISC-R or the Stanford-Binet scale, its results correlate reasonably well with the results of these tests. It is a useful non-verbal reasoning test and is thought to reflect innate ability (rather than learned skills) better than most other tests. The test results are expressed as centile scores which can be divided into grades.

The *Peabody Picture Vocabulary Test* is widely used as an easily-administered test of verbal skills.

Several other tests for younger children exist. The *Merrill-Palmer Scale* covers the age range from eighteen months to six years. Allowance can be made, in scoring the test, for items refused or omitted and the test can be scored without the verbal items. The result can be expressed as a mental age, as a centile rank or as a standard score. The test is useful for obtaining a general estimate of a young child's abilities.

The *Griffiths Mental Development Scale* is designed for children in the first two years of life. It has five sections: locomotor, personal-social, hearing and speech, eye and hand, and performance. A mental age can be derived from the five sub-test scores. There is an extension available for use in the age range two to eight.

The *Bayley Infant Scales of Mental and Motor Development* were developed in America, and have also been standardised on British children. The test has separate scales for 'motor' and for 'mental' development, and gives a score for each.

The *Gesell Developmental Schedule* can be used to assess the development of pre-school normal children and of older mentally handicapped children. Four aspects of development are covered: motor, language, adaptive behaviour and personal-social. A developmental age is obtained and a developmental quotient (DQ) can be derived by using the formula:

$$DQ = \frac{\text{developmental age}}{\text{chronological age}} \times 100$$

The DQ is not equivalent to an IQ as obtained on tests like the WISC, since the nature and construction of the test is quite different. These tests are of value in giving a general estimate of the child's level of development, and of areas in which he is lagging or is developing precociously. The precise developmental ages, or DQs, are not of much significance, however, and correlations with IQs on tests for higher ages are low.

THE INTERPRETATION AND VALUE OF INTELLIGENCE TEST RESULTS

The IQ is sometimes misunderstood and over-rated. An IQ may get attached to a child as a sort of permanent label, and is quoted as part of his description. This is an abuse of the whole concept of intelligence testing. One is only entitled to say that on a certain date the child's IQ on a particular test was such and such. The psychologist's comments on the results should also be taken into account. These will usually say whether or not the child was disturbed or co-operative during testing and how reliable the results seem to be. Because of the misuse of IQ figures, psychologists nowadays tend not to quote numerical IQs, but either quote a range or give a verbal description (eg. 'upper end of average range'). The child's approach to cognitive tasks of various kinds is generally considered more important than the test scores.

The question as to what intelligence tests measure is difficult to answer. Strictly speaking, they cannot be said to measure anything other than the ability to do the tasks of which the tests consist. Their practical value results from the correspondence between test ability and performance and the capacity to learn in school and to cope with verbal and manual tasks generally.

Tests of Educational Attainment

While intelligence tests indicate a child's general level of ability and expected achievement at school, they do not measure actual attainments. For this purpose a number of educational tests have been devised. The most important are those which test reading. Tests of arithmetic and spelling also exist.

Attainment tests consist of a series of tasks – word or sentence reading, or arithmetical tasks – of increasing difficulty. The tests are standardised on the general child population, just as are intelligence tests, and the child's performance can be compared with that of an average child of the same age. The results are usually expressed as reading, arithmetic or spelling ages. Quotients can then be obtained, if desired, by comparing, say, the child's reading age with the chronological age, just as an IQ can be obtained from a mental age (see page 197).

It is important to know, in interpreting attainment test results, the population on which the test has been standardised, and how much it differs from the population from which the child tested has come. Levels of attainment vary in different countries, and even in different parts of the same ones. They also differ from decade to decade.

Many different educational tests are available, and only a few examples will be mentioned. In Britain one of the most widely used reading tests is the *Neale Analysis of Reading Ability*. This consists of tests covering word recognition and comprehension, as well as various diagnostic measures, including sound production, auditory discrimination and syllable recognition. In North America the *Wide Range Achievement Test* is much used. As well as testing word recognition, it also assesses achievement in mathematics and spelling. It extends from the 4-year-old level to adult life. Other educational tests are the *Gates-MacGinitie Reading Tests*, which extend from the reading readiness level up to the level expected at about age 14, and the *Canadian Tests of Basic Skills*.

Arithmetic tests are less used nowadays because of the varied and changing methods of teaching arithmetic. Now that schools place less emphasis on mechanical arithmetic and use a more interesting approach to numbers and their relationships, it is usually better to obtain from the teacher a report on the child's progress. There is less emphasis, too, on spelling, and the use of spelling tests has declined accordingly.

Personality Tests

The assessment of personality is more difficult than the estimation of intelligence or educational attainment, and the extent to which tests are used for the purpose varies greatly from clinic to clinic and centre to centre. Many tests have been devised, and undoubtedly a child's response to them is related in some way to his personality characteristics and emotional state. The difficulty lies in interpreting and scoring the results and comparing them with the normal. It is easier to define average reading attainment or average intelligence than to define an average personality. Despite these problems, the results of personality tests can contribute significantly to clinical diagnosis.

Projective tests. The oldest and best known of these is the *Rorschach Test*.

In this test the child (or adult) is asked to look at a number of printed shapes, originally derived from ink blots, and to say what they seem to resemble. The blots in themselves have no designed meaning, so any response the child produces must be a projection. Interpretation is difficult and special training and experience are considered necessary first. In Britain there are relatively few workers who are fully trained in the Rorschach test, and it is used more extensively in North America. The value of the test, even in the hands of those fully trained in its use, is disputed by many psychologists and psychiatrists, but equally its proponents consider it a useful diagnostic tool. The *Children's Apperception Test* (CAT) is probably more commonly used than the Rorschach. It consists of a number of somewhat ambiguous pictures about which the child is asked to tell a story.

The *Thematic Apperception Test* (TAT), although designed for adults, is used instead of, or as well as, the CAT by many clinicians. The TAT has more realistic pictures and also offers a wider variety of pictures and situations.

Two other widely used tests are the *Draw-a-Person Test* and the *House-Tree-Person Test*. In each case the child is asked to draw the items mentioned in the name of the test. The results can be analysed qualitatively and quantitatively to give information about the child's personality and emotional state.

These tests, and similar ones, are not scientific instruments, and do not give scores as valid and reliable as, for example, those of educational attainment. Nevertheless, they can be useful ways of supplementing the clinical interview even if not scored, and may reveal information about the child, and his view of the family and the world generally, which may not emerge during an interview. The Rorschach and CAT, in particular, resemble techniques used by psychiatrists who may ask the child to make up a story, comment on a picture he or she has drawn, give three wishes, make up a dream and so on.

Two tests of 'social adjustment' are quite widely used. The *Vineland Social Maturity Scale* consists of a series of questions which are put to the child's mother, or to someone with a good knowledge of the child. It is concerned with such abilities as dressing, feeding oneself, walking and talking and is a useful and quick way of assessing the level of social development of infants and young children. The various sub-test scores (self-help generally, self-help dressing, self-help eating, self-direction, occupation, communication and locomotion) give a sort of clinical shorthand summary of the child's development. This test can also be used for older children, but for them a combination of clinical interview, IQ and attainment tests is often more useful.

The *Bristol Social Adjustment Guides* consist of questionnaires designed to examine the adjustment of children in school, in residential care and in the family. There are questionnaires for teachers, residential child care staff and social workers, and there are boy and girl versions. Examination of the completed questionnaires often reveals interesting and useful information about the subjects, but the value in clinical practice (as opposed to research, for which the guides have been much used) of the various scores which can be derived from the tests, is uncertain.

The *Bene-Anthony Family Relations Test* consists of a number of figures, representing the various members of the family and one representing 'nobody', each with a little box attached. The child is then asked to 'post' cards with various statements on into whichever box he considers appropriate. If the statement applies to no one in his family it goes into the 'nobody' box. The test is intended to give a picture of the child's view of emotional relationships in the family.

The *Children's Personality Questionnaire of Catell* is an example of a questionnaire-type test. The parent or other adult familiar with the child answers a series of questions. From the responses an estimate of the child's personality and emotional state is made. This test is not widely used.

Tests of Specific Psychological Functions

There are various tests which aim at measuring specific aspects of functioning, other than those which have been mentioned. A few of the more important ones only will be mentioned.

The *Illinois Test of Psycholinguistic Abilities* (ITPA) is a test of various aspects of language development, and it also gives a total language score. It aims to measure 'decoding', the capacity to decipher auditory and visual stimuli (that is, things heard and seen), and 'encoding,' the transfer of ideas into speech and into motor functions. There are also tests of visual and auditory memory, of auditory-vocal and visual-motor association, and of auditory and visual closure. The 'closure' tests are designed to investigate the child's capacity to identify and select different auditory and visual stimuli as appropriate.

This test is a useful clinical and research tool for the investigation of disorders of language development. In cases of delayed development it gives an indication of the nature of the defect, and thus of the sort of treatment needed. It gives a test age for each of the sub-tests, as well as a total language age. The results can be expressed on the test form as a graph or profile which gives a pictorial impression of the child's language capacities and of how much variation there is among them. The test covers the range 2 years 4 months to 10 years 3 months.

The *Reynell Developmental Language Scales* comprise two scales measuring verbal comprehension and one measuring expressive language. The verbal comprehension test 'B' is intended to be parallel to test 'A' but requires minimal responses from the child and so is useful for cerebral palsied or very shy children. The test has been standardised on a large population of English children. There are separate norms for each sex, and an incidental point is that girls develop language (as assessed by this test) more quickly than boys. These scales are valuable clinical tools in the assessment of children with delayed language development.

The *Lincoln-Oseretsky Motor Development Scale* is a test of the motor ability of children. Some of the items involve hand and arm movements and others large body movements, for example jumping and balancing tasks. Norms are available and the test enables motor development to be assessed in relation to age and compared with intellectual development. The test is useful in investigating 'clumsy' children (see Chapter 7), and some children with brain disorder.

The *Bender Visual Motor Gestalt Test* involves the copying of a series of designs. The child's copies are then scored in a particular way. It has been suggested that the test can help establish a diagnosis of brain damage, but its practical value for this purpose is very limited. It merely provides a brief sample of the child's visual-motor abilities.

The *Berry Visual Motor Test* also involves copying figures, but has been better standarised on normal populations than the Bender Test, in place of which it is often used.

The *Frostig Test of Developmental Perception* is designed for use with children aged about four to ten years. It is a useful screening test for children suspected of needing special perceptual training. It deals with five important areas, namely eye–hand coordination, figure–ground perception, the ability to perceive 'constancy in shape' and 'position in space', and spatial relationships; it is linked to a series of training programmes. Both the tests and the training programmes can be administered individually or in a group setting.

General Points

This survey is far from complete but gives an idea of the range of behaviour which psychological tests try to measure. Tests should always be administered and interpreted by someone trained and experienced in their use, normally a clinical or educational psychologist, and their limitations, as well as their considerable usefulness, must always be borne in mind. This applies, perhaps with even greater force, to 'group tests'. These are often used in schools to measure educational attainment and 'intelligence'. A group of children, large or small, write answers to various questions and/or instructions on a form. The tests are often constructed on multiple choice lines, the subject being given a number of answers from which to choose. While these tests have obvious practical value, the results are less reliable than those of individual tests, and it is harder to detect the child who for one reason or another (perhaps illness, fatigue or hostility) is not co-operating. The results of group 'intelligence tests' sometimes differ greatly from those of individual tests; they also tend to be predominantly verbal tests, and so reflect the child's level of academic attainment. They are considered to have practical value in schools, however.

For further information on tests, various reference books are available[1,2] and the test materials themselves may be examined.

References

1. Johnson, O. G. and Bommarito, J. W. *Tests and Measurement in Child Development: Handbook I.* San Francisco: Jossey-Bass, 1971.
2. Anastasi, A. *Psychological Testing*, fourth edition. New York: Macmillan, 1976.

CHAPTER FIFTEEN

Legal Aspects of Child Psychiatry and Problems of Child Abuse

All developed countries have found it necessary to have a framework of law to deal with children who offend against society in various ways, or who are neglected, inadequately cared for or physically abused by their parents or others. Psychiatrists and other professionals working in the mental health field are sometimes asked for help in such cases by courts and other statutory bodies, for example the 'children's hearings' established in Scotland; and also by social agencies concerned with child welfare. In Great Britain these include the social services departments of local authorities and various voluntary agencies. In North America this function is often carried out by state-funded child welfare agencies called Children's Aid Societies, Family Service Agencies and such like. Many children and adolescents referred for psychiatric assessment or treatment are already in the care of statutory agencies either because they have committed offences or because they have been inadequately cared for or have been abused.

It is necessary for professionals working in this field to have a sound knowledge of the relevant legislation. This varies according to the country, state or province concerned and there are so many differences that it is impossible even to summarise them in an introductory book such as this. Moreover, changes are quite often made in child welfare legislation. As an example of the areas to be covered, and of certain legal frameworks which can be used to deal with them, the current situation in Great Britain is summarised in Appendix A (page 254). Those working elsewhere should review the legislation that applies in their jurisdiction.

Two important aspects of the practice of child psychiatry and related disciplines are the writing of reports for use by courts and the assessment and treatment of families in which there has been, or may have been, abuse of a child by the parents or others. Expert advice and help is also sometimes sought in cases where there are disputes between separated or divorced parents about custody of or access to the children of the marriage. Referrals of this nature appear to be getting more frequent, probably because of rising divorce and family breakdown rates.

Writing Reports for Courts

While the form and content of court reports will differ according to local practice, the type of court concerned and the circumstances of the case, certain general principles are widely applicable. The assessment of these children and their families should be done in the same way as in other cases (see Chapter 3). It is important that the parents as well as the child are seen; this can present difficulties if the child is in custody, but it is important to insist on seeing all the relevant family members. Sometimes an interview with the whole family group is helpful (see page 41). While there are often social workers' and other reports available, it is important to have at least one face-to-face interview with everyone concerned. However good a report is, it can never be a substitute for an in-person meeting.

A school report is often available; if not, one should be obtained. It may be important to interview, either in person or by telephone, the child's teacher, or one of them. Reports should also be obtained from any other agencies that have been involved.

In writing the report the following general points are important.

1. Write in plain, readily-understood English, without the use of jargon. Always remember that judges, magistrates and lawyers may not understand medical or psychological terms.
2. Bear in mind that your report may be read out in court or shown to the defence, so that the subject or the family may learn of its contents. If the report includes essential information which must not be disclosed in court (which is not, for example, the best place for a child to learn that he was born illegitimately or was adopted), this should be plainly marked 'confidential'.
3. Avoid referring to questions of guilt or innocence. These are for the court to decide.
4. Do not quote information given by the child, the family or others as if it were fact. It is better to use phrases like 'He said that ...' or 'They described ...'

5. Do not repeat information given in other reports, unless you have a special reason for doing so.
6. Make sure that your meaning is expressed plainly and un-ambiguously, avoiding vague terms and phrases like 'immature' or 'borderline intelligence', both of which, if used at all, would require further definition. Rather than saying, 'He is immature', say 'In his relationships with his parents and other family members he behaves more like a child five years younger'. Do not quote IQ figures; instead explain your view of the child's level of intellectual function and its significance in the particular case.

The precise form of the report is less important than ensuring that all the relevant information is included. A useful way of setting out reports is as in the following numbered paragraphs, each of which can be the subject of a paragraph or, in a long report, a section with its own sub-heading.

1. State the sources of information which you have used, including any reports (from school, social worker, etc.) you have read, as well as when, where and whom you interviewed.
2. Draw the court's attention to what you consider are the important points of the history you obtained and that presented in other reports.
3. Outline the results of your examination of the child, avoiding technical terms, but explaining in language a lay person will under-stand the nature and consequences of any psychiatric disorder which you found to be present.
4. Formulate the case in lay terms, so as to explain how, in your opinion, the behaviour or circumstances leading to the child's appearance in court have arisen. The formulation should take into account all relevant emotional, biological, social, educational and other factors.
5. Conclude with any recommendations for treatment, or other suggestions which you think may be helpful to the court in taking the best course of action.

Word the report in moderate terms. Avoid apportioning blame. Remember you are giving guidance to the court, not telling it what to do. Use short sentences and words as far as possible.

Most children seen for juvenile or family courts prove not to have any major psychiatric condition such as a psychotic illness. The psychiatrist's report, while useful to the court in ruling out such a condition, may mainly be of value in the understanding which it gives of the case as a whole.

The following specimen report illustrates one form which a report to a court may take.

Child Psychiatry Clinic
Endhampton District Hospital
Farr Road
Endhampton

Special Psychiatric Report on Andrew Barry Charles, born 1.1.66 [Address].
Charged with theft of bicycles, house-breaking.

I saw this boy on 31 December 1978. He was accompanied to the clinic by his parents and by Miss Harris, the social worker concerned with his case. I interviewed Andrew first, then saw his parents, following which I saw all three together for a short time; I then had a discussion with Miss Harris. In addition, I have read Miss Harris's social report dated 29 December 1978, the report prepared by Mr James, Andrew's school principal dated 20 December 1978, and that of the educational psychologist, Mr Keen, also dated 20 December.

HISTORY

Miss Harris's report covers the main points about Andrew's development and the family situation. I think the following matters are specially relevant.

1. Andrew was born with a harelip and cleft palate, which caused feeding difficulties and repeated admissions to hospital during his first two years of life. Although these deformities were in due course surgically repaired, the Court will notice that there is still some slight disfigurement.
2. Andrew's relationship to his mother seems never to have been a close one. The parents told me they feel this was due to his frequent admissions to hospital early in life, and they say he was never a 'cuddly' baby like their older son, Luke.
3. There were difficulties of adjustment when Andrew first went to school, and he was late learning to read. His educational progress has always been poor and I note that the psychologist finds Andrew's reading to be about two-and-a-half years retarded, despite average intelligence.
4. Adjustment in the secondary school at which Andrew started at the beginning of last term has been particularly poor. Andrew is said to have truanted repeatedly and the offences for which he is appearing in court were committed while truanting and in company with another child who was also truanting.
5. Andrew has been a life-long bedwetter.
6. There have been difficulties in the relationship between the parents. Mr Charles left Mrs Charles 18 months ago to live with another woman, but returned 6 months later. Although Mr and Mrs Charles were able to tell me about this, and say that the relationship between them has now improved, they also indicated that considerable tensions persist. Mrs Charles seems bitter about having been 'deserted for 6 months', as she puts it.

7. Miss Harris reports that the neighbourhood in which Andrew lives is one in which there is a high level of delinquency.

EXAMINATION

I found Andrew to be a friendly, co-operative, pleasant boy. He was well dressed and seemed well cared for. I noted the scar and slight facial deformity mentioned above. He spoke freely and answered questions readily. Once he had settled down in the interview he gave a full and apparently frank acount of his life, including his situation at school and at home. I detected no abnormality of his thought processes, nor was there any evidence of any abnormal mental processes (such as delusions or hallucinations). His mood was appropriate to the situation.

Andrew told me that he has never liked school, and in particular dislikes his present school which is 'too big' and where he feels he has been bullied and teased a lot. He denies, however, that he is teased about his facial appearance. He said he finds most subjects difficult, but enjoys woodwork and games. According to Andrew another boy he met on the way to school suggested that they stay off school, and it was also this boy's idea that they should steal the bicycles, which are the subject of one of the charges against Andrew. He was prepared to talk freely about the incidents which led to his appearance in court.

Andrew was also able to talk about the tensions in the home. He told me that he feels his parents favour his brother who has been more successful at school and has never got into any trouble with the police. Andrew is also sensitive about his bedwetting, a problem his brother does not have. He spoke about the period when his parents were separated and I got the impression that he would like to think of that as in the past, but is not completely confident that he can.

I found no abnormality on physical examination, except for the facial deformity I have mentioned.

OPINION

In my opinion Andrew is not suffering from any serious psychiatric disorder, but there are psychological factors which may have contributed to his recent delinquent acts. He appears to be a boy with a poor self-image, not adequately secure in his family relationships and not getting much satisfaction from school. Family relationships generally do not seem to be warm, and Andrew appears to be the less favoured of the two children. He is seen by his parents as a less attractive child, and his congenital deformity, the subsequent periods in hospital, the difficulty in feeding him (his mother says he was always a sickly child) and his bedwetting have all probably militated against the development of a warm relationship between Andrew and his parents, expecially his mother. In addition, there are tensions in the marital relationship, and the parents were separated for a time. A further problem is that Andrew has never settled well into school, nor obtained much personal satisfaction from it. Lacking fulfilment both at home and at school, it is not surprising that he has drifted into delinquent activities with other children with whom, perhaps, he can achieve more status.

RECOMMENDATIONS

The family as a whole need continuing help of the type Miss Harris has recently started to provide. Andrew's problems should be dealt with in the context of his home and family. I do not believe he would benefit from removal from the family at present, but I think a supervision order would be helpful. Miss Harris could then continue working with the family, as she tells me she would like to do. She could also, in consultation with the psychologist and school staff, look into how Andrew might be helped at school. If he can achieve greater success there it is likely to help his self-image.

I do not think that Andrew requires psychiatric treatment, but the family might benefit from family therapy. This would involve a series of treatment sessions involving the whole family. Miss Harris might like to consider this and discuss it with the family. If, in due course, the family wish to participate in a series of such interviews I should be glad to co-operate with the social worker in trying to arrange the treatment at this clinic. In any event Andrew will inevitably remain 'at risk' of getting into further trouble for some months after treatment starts.

A report should be no longer than is necessary to convey the information the court needs, but opinions and conclusions unsupported by an indication of the information on which they are based carry less weight than those which are so supported. The report should help the court to a better understanding of child and family as well as, if possible, offering advice on treatment or placement. It should be interesting and readable. An over-long report may be skimmed through, not read. Sometimes it is helpful, in discussing recommendations, to list various possible courses of action and then discuss the relative merits and disadvantages of each, perhaps without coming down firmly in favour of any particular one.

Further guidance on preparing reports for courts is to be found in a paper by Gibbens[1].

Child Abuse

Child abuse is being recognised with increasing frequency, and this is reflected in the more frequent referral of children, parents and families in which abuse is suspected to psychiatrists and their colleagues. Historical accounts suggest that child abuse has occurred for as long as records exist, and it seems to have increased in frequency and severity with the onset of the industrial revolution. It is only fairly recently, however, that the frequency of violence towards children within families became appreciated. In 1946 Caffey[2], a radiologist, described cases of multiple fractures of the long bones in association with subdural haematoma in children. He suggested that the fractures were due to trauma, and it has subsequently become established that physically abused children often show X-ray evidence of old fractures.

In 1962 the term 'battered child syndrome' was coined[3]. Other present-day terms used include 'child abuse' and 'non-accidental injury in children'[4]. In 1968 the book *The Battered Child*[5] appeared; this reviewed various aspects of child abuse, including its history.

The *incidence* of child abuse is hard to assess. Many cases are concealed and definitions vary. There may be anything from 1 to 12 ascertained new causes per 1000 children of serious physical non-accidental injury to young children annually[4]. Kempe[6] has suggested that in the USA 6 children per 1000 suffer non-accidental injury annually, a total of 40,000 known cases. Rates certainly vary in different places.

Probably the best epidemiological study is that of Baldwin and Oliver[7]. These authors investigated the extent of severe child abuse involving children aged under 5 in north-east Wiltshire during a seven-year period. The last 1½ years of the period was studied prospectively, the remainder retrospectively. Strict criteria for 'severe abuse' were used. A much higher rate of abuse – nearly 1 per thousand in the first three years of life – was found in the prospective study. This was 2.6 times the rate in the retrospective study. There were four deaths in the retrospective study and two in the prospective. Both studies probably underestimated the true incidence, and aimed only to cover severe cases. Overall, 225 separate incidents of abuse were recorded in 38 children, a mean of 5·9 per child, with a range of 1 to 23. Many injuries would of course have healed and so must have gone undetected. This valuable paper contains much other useful information on these children and their families.

The *causation* of child abuse is complex. Factors in the parents, factors in the child and social factors all play their parts. Many abusing parents are judged to have personality disorders; they often appear immature and many have been abused themselves in childhood. They frequently seem to have a poor 'internal model' of how to rear children and make quite excessive demands on their children in terms of the behaviour they expect at any particular age. Some abusing parents are depressed or otherwise mentally ill.

Factors in the child undoubtedly contribute too. Children's temperamental differences have been mentioned (page 21). A child who cries a lot, is very active and has low biological rhythmicity and negative mood quality is likely to be more at risk for abuse than a child with easier temperamental attributes.

The quality of the parents' marriage, if there is one, is likely to be important. The more satisfactory the relationship is between husband and wife the less likely is the occurrence of child abuse. The wider social context is important too. Young inexperienced mothers are sometimes left to bring up children in states of social isolation, often in multi-storey buildings with difficult or no access to play facilities, and cut off from the extended family. It is also usually possible to see these as dysfunctional families and to make a diagnosis in family system terms (see page 23).

Gil[8] suggests that there are three levels at which child abuse occurs. The first is the home, where the abusers are usually parents or permanent or temporary parent substitutes. The second is that of the institutional level: day care centres, schools, courts, child care agencies, welfare departments and correctional and other residential settings may abuse children by failing to provide them with the circumstances needed for their healthy development. The third level is that of society at large, which allows 'millions of children in our society' to live in poverty and to be denied adequate nutrition, health care, education, housing and neighbourhood conditions generally. This, however, is to take a wider view of child abuse than simply the physical injury of children.

Clinical features. Cases of child abuse present in many ways, but seldom do families come asking for help with the problem. Physically abused children are often brought to hospital emergency departments with a story that they have fallen downstairs or out of bed or against an item of furniture or household appliance. The tales told by parents can be detailed and imaginative, but they are usually inconsistent and nearly always incompatible with the child's injuries. Moreover, a full and careful examination of the child usually reveals evidence of previous injury and X-rays of the long bones and skull may show evidence of old fractures in various stages of healing. Cases of child abuse are sometimes reported to child welfare agencies by neighbours or relatives, who perhaps hear the child screaming or observe the injuries. Other cases come to notice at school, in day care centres or during routine physical examinations. The injuries may consist of bruising of any degree of severity, fractures, injury to internal organs perhaps with internal bleeding, intracranial haemorrhage with consequent damage to the brain or loss of vision due to ocular injuries. Death occurs in from about 1 to 23 per cent of cases in various surveys reported[4].

In addition to the physical injuries, many abused children show evidence of being under-fed and otherwise neglected and ill-cared for. Medical attention may not be sought when needed. These factors can adversely affect development (see page 26). On the other hand some children who have been physically injured appear in other ways well cared for. It seems that in these cases satisfactory general physical care is interrupted by episodes of rage on the part of parent or other adult, during which injury is inflicted on the child.

Sometimes an off-hand, uncaring parental attitude, a failure to relate normally to the child and a lack of concern about the child's condition on the part of the parent are present. The parents may be reluctant to have the child admitted or investigated and may have been to many hospitals on different occasions. There are often other family and marital problems, alcohol or drug use and the parents may give a history of abuse or neglect when they were children.

Abused children tend to show difficulty in enjoying themselves, behavioural problems, low self-esteem, withdrawal, oppositional behaviour, hypervigilance, compulsive behaviour (see page 69), a pseudo-adult manner and learning problems at school[9]. They may appear fearful towards their parents, for example getting upset when father is heard returning home, and they may show 'reversed caring', by anxiously looking out for the parent's needs, offering mother one of her cigarettes and so on[4]. In severe cases of neglect the child may be obviously ill cared for, dirty, under-nourished or dehydrated. Child abuse occurs in all socio-economic groups.

Assessment and *treatment* present great difficulties and require mature clinical judgement, extensive experience and a patient, painstaking and empathic approach to the families concerned. Thorough clinical and X-ray examination of the child is essential in any suspected case. Sexual molestation sometimes occurs as a feature of child abuse and the examination should include inspection of the genitals and anus[10].

Treatment is inevitably a multi-disciplinary process, once child abuse is established. The relevant child welfare agency is responsible for the immediate welfare of the child and must decide whether to remove the child from the care of parents or guardians. Admission to hospital may be necessary, and paediatric or surgical treatment may be needed. Meanwhile investigation of the family is carried out, usually by a social worker from the child welfare agency. Psychiatric help is often sought at this stage, either for parents, for the child or for the whole family group. These families must be approached in a sympathetic, non-punitive way. It is best to tell the parent(s) about the child's injuries, making it clear that they are not compatible with the story given, but not demanding an admission or confession. The interview can then often proceed on the basis of an unspoken understanding of the parents' part in the problem. It is unhelpful to get angry with people who abuse children; this militates against forming a therapeutic relationship and the therapist must control the feelings of outrage which most of us sometimes feel when dealing with these cases. It is also important not to get over-involved. Many children abusers are plausible, attractive, even charming people; or the therapist may come to feel sorry for them because of their hard or deprived lives. They may be expert at manipulating social agencies and authority figures, for example by suggesting that their behaviour and attitudes are changing, and so flattering the therapist, when there has been no real change in the situation. The naïve therapist can easily be deceived.

Long and difficult treatment is usually necessary. The treatment and management of the child must be integrated with help for the family. The return of the child to the family requires careful consideration, full assessment of the current situation, close supervision and detailed follow-up.

Some abused children have to be removed permanently from their families, others require prolonged treatment or substitute care to repair the emotional damage done prior to treatment.

The *outcome* of child abuse is grim. Scott's review[4] indicated that permanent mental handicap, blindness and cerebral palsy may occur in surviving seriously injured children. Between 2 and 4 per cent of children in hospitals for the subnormal in Britain are said to be brain-damaged through assaults by parents. It is certain that in very many other cases there are less obvious defects and the burden of emotional disturbance consequent upon child abuse can only be surmised. Milder forms of abuse such as malnutrition can also probably have significant adverse effects on children's development[11].

Prevention of child abuse is obviously to be much preferred to treatment. There is reason to believe that a preventive health service for young children and their families, with more frequent visits of nurse or other workers to such families is helpful[12]. Vigilance by all professionals concerned with families containing children is essential. In all jurisdictions there are provisions for the compulsory reporting of suspected child abuse to the relevant authorities, and those with such suspicions should not hesitate to report them. In addition, the wider social problems of which gross child abuse is but an extreme example need to be tackled. Approaches to this are discussed in Chapter 17.

Many areas maintain a register of cases, or suspected cases, of child abuse. This can be helpful as these families often move frequently and consult a succession of hospitals, agencies and doctors.

Custody and Access Disputes

Psychiatrists and other mental health workers are sometimes asked for help in cases in which parents are in dispute about who should have custody of children, or about access to children in the custody of, usually, the other parent[13]. This situation may arise in relation to divorce proceedings, or simply when there is a separation, legal or otherwise. Sometimes disputes of this sort continue long after a divorce and seem to be a vicarious way the parents continue their relationship.

The assessment of these children and their families follows the same principles as apply in other cases (see Chapter 3), and reports can be written along the same general lines as described earlier (page 205). There are, however, some special problems. The psychiatrist or other professional is often retained and paid by one or other side and this can lead to a situation in which two psychiatrists, each having access to only one side of the story, make conflicting recommendations. This is not usually in the best interests of the children.

A better plan is for the psychiatrist to be retained by both parties, each of which contributes to the fee. It is then possible for the person making the assessment to see and assess all concerned and, in many cases, to see everyone together on at least one occasion. This process sometimes leads to negotiation between the parties in the psychiatrist's presence, and following this some cases are settled without a battle in court. Even if this does not occur, the person making the assessment ends up with a more comprehensive view of the situation and is better able to present to the court a balanced view which aims to serve the best interest of the child or children concerned. This approach has been used in various places with considerable success.

References

1. Gibbens, T. C. N. 'Preparing psychiatric court reports'. *British Journal of Hospital Medicine*, **12**, 278–284, 1974.
2. Caffey, J. 'Multiple fractures in the long bones of infants suffering from chronic subdural haematoma'. *American Journal of Roentgenology*, **56**, 163–173, 1946.
3. Kempe, C. H., Silverman, F. N., Swede, R. F., Droegemuller, W. and Silver, H. K. 'The battered child syndrome'. *Journal of the American Medical Association*, **191**, 17–23, 1962.

4. Scott, P. D. 'Non-accidental injury in children'. *British Journal of Psychiatry*, **131**, 366–380, 1977.
5. Helfer, R. E. and Kempe, C. H. *The Battered Child*. Chicago: University of Chicago Press, 1968.
6. Kempe, C. H. 'Pediatric implications of the battered baby syndrome'. *Archives of Disease in Childhood*, **46**, 28–37, 1971.
7. Baldwin, J. A. and Oliver, J. E. 'Epidemiology and family characteristics of severely-abused children'. *British Journal of Prevention and Social Medicine*, **29**, 205–221, 1975.
8. Gil, D. G. 'Unravelling child abuse'. *American Journal of Orthopsychiatry*, **45**, 346–356, 1975.
9. Martin, H. P. and Beezley, P. 'The emotional development of abused children'. *Developmental Medicine and Child Neurology*, **19**, 373–387, 1977.
10. Sgroi, S. M. 'Sexual molestation of children'. *Children Today*, **4**, 18–21, May/June, 1975. (Reprinted in *Annual Progress in Child Psychiatry and Child Development*, 1976, ed. S. Chess and A. Thomas, New York: Brunner/Mazel, 1977).
11. Tizard, J. 'Nutrition, growth and development'. *Psychological Medicine*, **6**, 1–5, 1976.
12. Wynn, A. 'Health care systems for pre-school children'. *Proceedings of the Royal Society of Medicine*, **67**, 340–343, 1974.
13. Chamberlain, C. and Awad, G. 'Clinical consultation in custody and access disputes'. In *New Directions in Children's Mental Health*, ed. S. J. Shamsie. New York: Spectrum, 1979.

CHAPTER SIXTEEN

Treatment of Child Psychiatric Disorders

Since child psychiatric disorders are multifactorial in origin, a variety of treatment approaches may need to be used. These include:

Psychotherapy with the child.
Casework help for the family.
Family therapy.
Group therapy for children or parents.
Behaviour therapy.
Drug treatment.
Inpatient treatment.
Daypatient treatment.
Alternative families.
Educational measures.
Speech therapy.
Other measures, including removal from parental care.

Psychotherapy with the Child

Psychotherapy is treatment which is mediated through a relationship between patient (or client) and therapist. There are several different schools of psychotherapy and many techniques. Every contact between child and therapist is of emotional significance, and may be either of psychotherapeutic value or, if it is an unsatisfactory contact, anti-therapeutic. Certain principles, therefore, need to be borne in mind when dealing with any emotionally disturbed child, whether or not psychotherapy is the specific treatment which is being employed.

1. Never criticise the child. Children must be accepted as they are. If a child's symptoms are the expression of repressed anxiety or hostility, disapproving attitudes in the therapist are likely to make the anxiety or hostility, and thus the symptoms, worse. Acceptance of children, however, does not imply approval of all they do. Indeed it will often be common ground between disturbed children and their therapists that there are aspects of their behaviour, perhaps many of them, that require to be changed.

2. Bear in mind that most children do not come for treatment of their own accord. They are brought by others, usually their parents, who are worried about them or angry with them. They may thus come for treatment with the expectation that they will meet someone who is also going to be anxious about or angry with them. Indeed some parents have, before coming for help, told the child to expect 'a good talking to'. In such cases the therapist often has to work hard to gain the child's confidence and it may take several interviews to do so.

3. Do not plunge straight into a discussion of the symptoms, unless these are raised by the child.

4. Instead, try to understand the child's feelings and view of the world. It is only when there is this sort of understanding between children and their therapist that free communication, such as is essential to successful treatment, becomes possible. The child should come to see the therapist as someone who is concerned to help. This will not prevent the expression of angry feelings towards the therapist; in fact when the child has strong aggressive feelings which need expression it will help this process.

5. Remember that limits have to be set, in a psychotherapeutic interview as in other situations. While the free expression of feelings is to be encouraged, there are naturally things the child cannot be permitted to do. These will include physically hurting the therapist and dangerous activities like playing in a hazardous way with live electrical fittings. There are also limits which must be set to the damage permitted to the fabric of the building, or its equipment. Limits should be imposed on the basis of 'I can't allow you to do that', but with an understanding of the child's desire to do it and explanation of the dangers of what is desired or the reasons why it cannot be allowed.

The techniques and application of psychotherapy can be learned only by working with disturbed children, and carrying out treatment, under supervision. This account will aim only to give a general illustration of the process.

Before embarking on psychotherapy it is necessary to have a clear aim, and to know what the treatment is intended to achieve. This aim should have been stated in the initial diagnostic formulation. *Supportive therapy* is aimed at helping the child to cope more easily with any current stress. The stress may be an acute one likely to subside in course of time, for example the illness or admission to hospital of a parent, or the grief reaction following a bereavement. Alternatively the stress may be a continuing one which cannot easily be removed. The child may thus need long-term help in dealing with a difficult reality situation, for example a family disturbed in one way or another. At the other extreme there is *psychoanalysis*, which aims at achieving a radical change in the child's emotional state and reactions. Between supportive therapy and full psychoanalysis there is a range of intermediate possibilities, designed to achieve more limited goals than analysis, or to deal with particular facets of the child's emotional life.

Psychoanalysis is a highly specialised treatment for which long and expert training is needed. In Britain most child psychiatry departments and clinics have no trained analyst on their staff, so this treatment is not widely used. In North America psychoanalysts are commoner especially in certain centres. Psychoanalysis usually involves hour-long treatment sessions up to five days a week over a period of months or even years, so that even in clinics where trained psychoanalysts are available the number of children they can treat is strictly limited. The object of the treatment is to explore fully the child's unconscious life and fantasies, and deal with any problems found, in the context of the relationship between child and therapist. Anna Freud[1,2] and Melanie Klein[3] were pioneers in the field of child analysis.

Psychotherapy with children usually has more limited aims than those of psychoanalysis, which is perhaps more a research tool, and a means of developing theoretical understanding of emotional disorders, than a widely applicable treatment. Psychoanalysis has, however, contributed greatly to the practice of psychotherapy generally.

There are wide variations in technique, depending on the theoretical orientation of the therapist, the treatment goals and the patient's age. Some therapists make extensive use of verbal interpretation of the child's statements and play; others make little or even no use of interpretation. Some therapists take a more active and directive role than others.

As a rule, the younger the child, the more contact has to be made through the medium of play, but some children even as young as three or four do talk freely. How freely they communicate verbally depends on their intelligence, language development and emotional state. Common to all psychotherapy are, first, the development of a working relationship with the child; secondly, an appraisal of the feelings and ideas the child expresses in the context of the relationship; and thirdly the use of the relationship to help resolve the child's problems.

How does the treatment help the child? At the first level there is the simple process of acceptance of the child's feelings. We all know that we often feel better after we have spoken to an accepting and understanding person about things that are worrying us or which we are angry over or ashamed of. This applies also to the feelings of disturbed children. It accounts for the considerable improvement which sometimes follows a single interview, even one intended primarily as diagnostic. For some children it is a new experience to be listened to and given the full attention of an accepting adult; and when such children find that their revelations do not shock, worry or cause the therapist to feel outraged, this may reduce the intensity of their emotions.

Very often it is not sufficient for children simply to express their feelings and have them accepted by an adult with interest in and concern for their point of view. There also has to be emotional interchange with the child over a period of time. In these emotional transactions children often manifest behaviour and attitudes similar to those they manifest towards their parents, or other key figures. They can thus play or talk about their difficulties with the therapist, rather as young children work out things in fantasy play. This too may sometimes be sufficient to enable them to overcome their problems.

At the next level 'interpretation' is added to the emotional interchange with the child. This aims to put the problems or conflicts, into words and thus help the children to understand them. Interpretations are generally withheld until the meaning of a child's play or talk is clear. Speculative interpretations which are incorrect may be harmful, though they are often ignored or rejected by the child.

Alan was an eight-year-old boy, very tense and anxious and sleeping badly, who was brought by his mother because of his stealing. He was the second of three sons.

The symptoms were seen as a reaction to the strict, rigid and emotionally cold attitudes of his mother. The marriage was mother's second, the first never having been consummated. Throughout her first marriage mother had worked in a factory and had saved up a considerable sum of money. She appeared an obsessionally rigid person. She did not believe in buying toys or books for children, saying they were a waste of money as the boys just destroyed them. The house was thus bereft of play materials; instead it was piled high with cartons of groceries and other products bought in bulk to save money. Mother dominated the family and father was allowed to do little except earn a wage and bring it home. As well as complaining of Alan's stealing, mother complained bitterly of his coming into the house without taking his boots off, untidying his bedroom, and other items of behaviour which in many families would probably not have been considered as particularly abnormal.

Alan had repeatedly stolen money both at home and at school, where he had taken it from other children's pockets and from his teacher's handbag. He came into the consulting room neatly dressed and cleanly turned out. At first he was obviously apprehensive and guarded in what he said. He called the psychiatrist 'sir'. He looked longingly at the toys in the room, and smiled and relaxed visibly when invited to play with them, which he did. By the third interview he had become less tense, and more prepared to relax and to play and talk freely. He spoke, without being specifically asked, of some of the things about which he had been in trouble at home, for example losing his new diary down a gap between the skirting board and the wall in his bedroom.

Alan enjoyed play and spent much of his time playing in the sand tray. There were available a variety of toy figures including soldiers, cowboys, Indians and others, and they included sets of different sizes. In the session he arranged a battle, the big figures being ranged against the little ones. The therapist did not comment on this. In the fifth session Alan elaborated on it. A similar scene was again arranged and he explained that the people at one end (who were the small ones) wanted some water but the people at the other end (the large ones) wouldn't let them have it. A bloody battle was then enacted, all the large figures and all but two of the small ones getting killed. The two survivors then went and got their water. The therapist commented that the small ones had won but nearly all of them had been killed, at which Alan said, 'They're not dead really, they're just pretending' and picked them all up. The therapist then said that perhaps Alan sometimes felt like the small people who couldn't get the water they wanted. At this Alan said, 'Yes, and the small ones don't always win', whereupon the therapist said that perhaps Alan wished they did. This led on to a short discussion of the relationship between parents and their children.

COMMENT

This vignette is intended only to illustrate the course of therapy with children. Alan had great difficulties in his relationship with his mother. He was not able to talk about these at first but he soon began to play them out. He appeared to identify himself (and perhaps his brothers) with the small figures and his mother (and probably by extension other adults) with the big ones. The apparent meaning of his play was interpreted to him, and he accepted the interpretations offered. Subsequently his feelings were explored further though in the sixth interview he completely changed his activities to doing sums which he himself had written on the blackboard.

While treatment was proceeding with Alan, his mother was being seen weekly by a social worker who was helping her to understand her feelings towards Alan and her family generally, as well as the children's needs. It is of interest that following the fifth treatment session with Alan she reported a marked improvement in his behaviour at home, and his stealing stopped. The latter was of the 'comforting' variety (see page 54) and it ceased to be necessary once Alan's feelings were being understood, accepted and explored at the clinic. The aim of treatment, eventually achieved, was to enable mother to meet Alan's needs as far as she was able, and for Alan to be able to cope with what remaining problems he faced without resorting to stealing or developing other symptoms.

While psychotherapy must be learnt primarily through supervised experience, there is also an extensive literature on it[4,5].

Casework Help for the Family

Psychotherapy with the child is usually combined with help for the family, often given by a social worker. The process is usually called 'casework'. It is usually the parents who most need help, but there may be other family members, grandparents, uncles, aunts or siblings, who also require to be involved. Sometimes it is satisfactory for the same person to see both the parents (or other family members) and the child, but there can be advantages in having two different therapists involved. Each party can then feel they have someone who is concerned with their particular point of view and problems. This may be especially helpful when the relationship between parents and child is characterised by mutual suspicion, hostility or distrust. In many milder cases, separate and intensive work by two professional people is not, of course, required.

Sussenwein[6] has reviewed the methods used by social workers. She has identified the following ways in which they intervene in families: by the provision of advice and material aid, by using the interview interaction, by techniques designed to modify behaviour and by promoting environmental changes.

These four methods of intervention cover the main needs which the parents of disturbed children may have. Some parents lack factual information about how to handle or bring up their children, and benefit from direct advice. Some also lack the knowledge, means or initiative to obtain material things required and can be helped to do this.

Interviews provide opportunities for the release of feelings, for the clarification of issues in the client's mind, for encouragement and for promotion of increased understanding of the self. The relationship which develops between social worker and client can also provide a secure base in the client's emotional life and it can be a social and emotional learning experience.

Sometimes social workers use techniques based on learning theory. The essence of this approach is to identify circumstances which precede or follow behaviour which is to be modified. Once this has been analysed the behaviour may be modified by altering these circumstances (see pages 227 to 229).

The environmental changes social workers may promote to help their clients include mobilising community resources (play groups, day-care centres, youth groups and the like) and community workers (youth leaders, school counsellors, credit counsellors and so forth) to help the family as appropriate. Sometimes the environmental change may involve the family's relationship with neighbours or the extended family. Isolation of the nuclear family can be a very real problem.

These measures are not necessarily combined with the provision of psychotherapy for the child. They may be used along with any other form of treatment given to the identified disturbed child, or they may be the main or the only intervention in a particular case.

Family Therapy

The family therapist looks at the symptoms reported in the 'identified patient' as but one aspect of the functioning of the family as a whole. This is not to deny that individual children have their own special problems for which they may require special help, but it aims to provide this help in the context of the family as a whole. (Of course if the sole problem is, for example, a child's reading difficulty, and in other respects the family is functioning well, no question arises of psycho-therapy of any sort). It is uncertain how often family therapy is the best approach, but some centres nowadays use it as almost their only treatment method. It may be that these centres differentially attract referrals suitable for family therapy, other children being sent elsewhere. It is also the case that many children have no functional families and are in the care of child welfare agencies; but even in such instances a 'family' approach to problems may be possible, the child's substitute parents or family being involved in place of the natural family. Indeed a better name for family therapy is probably 'systems therapy', since the treatment may be applied to systems other than families. This point is made by Walrond-Skinner[7], who also provides an excellent outline of general systems theory and its application to families. A brief account of systems theory also appears in Chapter 2 (page 23); and an outline of how to assess family groups is to be found in Chapter 3 (pages 41 to 44).

Family therapy must start with an assessment of the family. What the therapist needs to know is what Minuchin[8] calls its 'structure'. The basic idea is that within a family unit members relate according to certain arrangements, which govern the transactions between them. These arrangements, which are not usually explicitly stated or even recognised, form a whole – the structure of the family. The family structure cannot be immediately assessed by the therapist, who can only discover it by joining the family.

'Joining' the family implies participating in its conversation and in its non-verbal communications. At first what Minuchin[8] calls 'accommodation' is necessary. Accommodation consists of the adjustments the therapist must make in order to join the family. Initially the therapist accepts the family's organisation and way of doing things. Processes used in accommodation include 'maintenance', the deliberate supporting of the family's structure as when the dominant mother is treated as the leader or the subsystem pattern is accepted or even encouraged; 'tracking', the following by the therapist of the family's communications and behaviour which are encouraged to continue; and 'mimesis', the adoption by the therapist of some aspects of the family members' behaviour, for example their speed or style of speaking, or the sharing with them of some common experience.

Having joined the family the therapist becomes a participant-observer and can form a working hypothesis, or family diagnosis, as outlined on pages 43 to 44. This leads to a plan of intervention which tests the hypothesis. If the hypothesis is correct, and the interventions are well planned, change comes about. If not then it probably doesn't, and another hypothesis or intervention must be formulated. Change occurs as a result of the therapist's behaviour, including the directives and tasks given the family. The process can only be learnt on the job. It is best taught using one-way observation screens, closed circuit television and videotape. The learner can thus observe other therapists at work, as well as participating in and carrying out treatment himself under the supervision of a more experienced therapist. Particularly valuable are the opportunities videotapes provide for therapists to examine and discuss with others their recorded treatment sessions.

The following case history is quoted to illustrate, not teach, the process. Fuller descriptions of family therapy are to be found in the many books and papers on the subject. Valuable books are those by Minuchin[8]; Haley[9]; Glick and Kessler[10]; Minuchin, Rosman and Baker[11]; and also *Family Therapy: Full Length Case Studies*[12], in which the work of 13 family therapists is illustrated. Perusal of this and other literature will make it clear that family therapy depends very much on the therapist's use of his or her own personality in a creative, empathic way. Many different ways of changing families obviously exist.

These all involve altering the family's 'homeostasis', or fixed patterns of functioning, preferably in a way that will promote growth.

The Y family consisted of Mr Y, aged 49, Mrs Y, aged 44 and three children, Karen (15), Bruce (12) and Pamela (6). Pamela was referred because she was very 'insecure' (as her mother put it) and afraid of being alone and of the dark. She would not go to bed, or to the toilet, on her own. She was sleeping with her parents and she was a 'whining' child who, when she wanted something, usually persisted till she got it. Karen was reported by the parents to be rebellious and difficult, and to communicate little with her parents, while Bruce was well behaved and presented no problems. Mr Y was much preoccupied with the 'illness' for which he had been treated by two psychiatrists, and had had a period of inpatient care. His symptoms consisted of depression, feelings of inadequacy and severe obsessive-compulsive symptoms of three years' duration. He had trouble-some checking rituals which made it difficult for him to carry out his job as a bank clerk.

At the first family interview Mr Y spoke of how depressed and useless he felt. He said he had lost interest in life and was no longer part of the family. Mrs Y agreed and said she felt like a widow, depending for what support she got upon the two older children. She spoke in a calm, smiling, condescending way. Karen complained that she and Bruce were not allowed to settle their differences and have a relationship between themselves, because of interference by the parents. Mrs Y said she felt she had to inter-vene because otherwise Karen would 'kill' Bruce. Bruce, a big boy for his age, said he thought Karen and he could settle their differences on their own, but he didn't seem too concerned about the matter. Karen went on to complain of many restrictions the parents placed on her activities and of the way the family is 'ruled by the clock'. She said she was very unhappy, wanted to leave the family to live on her own as soon as she could and felt Bruce was favoured at her expense. Bruce agreed about the latter point. Pamela said little, and soon left the family circle to play on her own else-where in the room.

All members of the family saw Mr Y as useless and of no value to them, but Mrs Y and Karen were particularly forthright in saying this, and Karen asked why her father couldn't 'make an effort' as she had done recently when she returned to school after having influenza.

At the second session Karen complained bitterly of feeling left out of things in the family. She resented the fact that Bruce, as she saw it, was treated as more grown up than she was and she described Pamela as a 'menace' who always got her way either by making a nuisance of herself or by 'sucking up' to mother.

At this time the family structure seemed to be as follows:

Mr Y was on his own, far apart from the rest of the family.

Mrs Y was close to, and related warmly with, Bruce and Pamela (though she was irritated by Pamela's behaviour).

Karen was closer to her mother than to her father, but all her relationships in the family were characterised by much hostility.

Mr and Mrs Y did not operate as a parental couple, each independently stating his or her opinion on whatever was discussed, but never talking to each other or coming to a mutual agreement.

The aim of treatment at this stage was to establish the parents as an effective couple caring for the children in a united and appropriate fashion.

The closeness of Mrs Y and Bruce became increasingly obvious and it soon transpired that Mrs Y washed the hair and cleaned the shoes of this pubertal 12-year-old. She also turned to him for help in the house, for example to do odd jobs. Mr Y was considered by all to be 'too ill' to do these, and there had accumulated a long list of tasks too big for Bruce which, to Mrs Y's ire, had simply not been done. The therapist initiated a discussion of these jobs, asking Mr Y what they consisted of, how long each would take and which were the most urgent. With Mrs Y participating, an agreement was reached that Mr Y would carry out one of them (the repair of a kitchen shelf) by the next session. At the same session the question of whether Bruce could wash his own hair and brush his own shoes was discussed. Both parents, and indeed the whole family including Bruce, agreed that he could and should. Thus both parents had tasks to perform by the time of the next session, father to do a minor household repair, mother to allow her 12-year-old to do more for himself.

Having joined the family group and formed an opinion about the family structure, the therapist was trying to restructure the family through his interventions. He did not accept the father's uselessness. He looked for the positive aspects in all members' roles in the family, reinforcing and supportin them. Through his interventions he was able to help the family demonstrate, for example, that Mr Y could still repair shelves; Mrs Y did not have to wash Bruce's hair since Bruce was well able to do this himself; Karen was capable of going to watch an evening football match involving the team she supported without any harm coming to her (which the parents had not believed); and Pamela (who had been subjected to little discipline and much indulgence) could do as she was told. Moreover, as such demands were made on Pamela it became easier to get her to bed at night.

Throughout the twelve sessions of treatment with this family, the therapist tried to treat Mr and Mrs Y *as a parental couple* when discussing any matters concerning the children. If one expressed a view about any of the children (and initially it was usually the mother), the opinion of the other was sought. On many occasions the parents were encouraged to discuss matters together there and then, or occasionally between interviews, so that they could bring their joint decision to the next session, and an agreement was reached. The children too were encouraged to discuss things together, and by this means the many differences between Karen and Bruce were reduced. In fact Karen and Bruce proved to have a warmer relationship than had at first been apparent, and the ease with which many of their differences were settled surprised everyone.

As is almost invariable in such treatment, the family tended to resist change. In the early stages Mr Y complained of the 'tension' he felt and at the end of most sessions he asked for tranquillisers. During one two-week break in sessions he even consulted another psychiatrist (who agreed, in discussion with the therapist, not to offer treatment). Thus many of the changes in the family were followed by a tendency to resort to former transactional patterns. The therapist's response was to emphasise the positive aspects of the family's functioning and to maintain an optimistic, good-humoured attitude. It even became clear that Mr Y's role in the family had never been quite as negative as the whole family had indicated: for example, he had always helped Pamela with her schoolwork when she needed this.

COMMENT

The above is but an outline of the sort of thing that may happen in family therapy. The main point is that it was the family that was taken as the unit for treatment, which was concerned with the 'here-and-now' functioning of the family. Therapy aimed to alter the family functioning rather than to look at, or treat, any member of the family as an individual. Although the family came with Pamela as the presenting problem, they were quickly able to see that her symptoms were but part of a wider family problem. (Not every family is able to see this so readily, even when it is clear to the therapist). In the course of twelve family therapy sessions, considerable changes in family functioning occurred, with a more equal relationship developing between husband and wife, and a happier one between the parental couple on the one hand, and the children on the other. There were still stresses in the marital relationship, however, and Mr Y's obsessive-compulsive disorder, while less troublesome, was still evident. The children's symptoms had lessened considerably and all three seemed a good deal more content than they had been before.

Group Therapy

Children, adolescents or parents may be treated in groups[13,14]. As with individual therapy, there are a variety of approaches to group therapy, but the basic idea is that members of the group help each other through their interaction and the modelling they can provide for each other. Thus the active, outgoing child can act as a model for the quiet, inhibited one, and vice versa. Group therapy may be particularly valuable for children who have difficulty with peer relationships.

Group therapy with younger children usually involves primarily the use of play, while with adolescents discussion is more usual, with the problems of the individual group members often being dealt with directly. In all forms of group therapy the therapist leading the group has an important role in facilitating constructive and helpful interchange between group members.

Parent groups can sometimes achieve many of the aims of individual casework with parents, both more effectively and more economically. The focus of the group is usually on matters concerned with problem children and their management. Variable amounts of instruction may be given by the leader, but an important part of the process is the interaction between the parents, and their group problem-solving. It can also be helpful to a parent to know that he or she is not the only one with a difficult child or with problems in child management. Philipp[15] has provided an excellent account of the conduct of parent training groups. The emphasis is on finding solutions, rather than apportioning blame or elucidating causes, and social learning theory principles and behaviour modification techniques can be useful in this (see below).

Behaviour Therapy

Behaviour therapy seeks to use learning theory as the basis for altering children's behaviour and modifying or removing symptoms. It aims to achieve precise therapeutic goals, either the elimination of symptoms (for instance bedwetting or temper tantrums) or the development of behaviour regarded as desirable (such as attendance at school in the child who has difficulty in going, or various social skills). Behaviour therapists do not seek to interpret the behaviour they modify, nor to promote insight into the dynamics of the problem. Indeed, many behaviour therapists question both the value of interpretation, and the psychodynamic view of children's disorders. They take the view that problem behaviours are learned and can be eliminated and replaced by other behaviours through the provision of new learning experiences. Regardless of what theories are accepted, however, it is clear that behaviour modification is of value in certain conditions. It is perhaps not surprising that more models than one are applicable to the understanding and treatment of the wide range of psychiatric disorders of children.

Behaviour therapy can either alter the circumstances leading up to a behaviour or the circumstances following it. The first approach is known as 'respondent conditioning'. The second as 'operant conditioning'. In either case individual or group treatment may be used. An example of *respondent conditioning* is 'systematic desensitisation'.

> Quentin was seen at the age of twelve. When he was seven he had seen the film *Born Free* and became frightened, and nearly fainted, when a snake was shown on the screen. But the fear of snakes seemed to have developed slowly before that, and had been evident during earlier visits to a zoo.
>
> When seen, Quentin was handicapped in that he could not go to a zoo, into a pet shop (in case there was a snake there) or a toy shop (where there might be a rubber snake), watch animal programmes on television (lest a snake was shown) or go near the biology laboratory at school (in case there was a snake in it). All pictures of snakes had had to be removed from his biology books. There was also some fear of large worms, eels, frogs and lizards, probably generalised from his fear of snakes. Otherwise Quentin and his family appeared emotionally stable and there were no other problems.
>
> Quentin was treated by systematic desensitisation. After training in relaxation he was asked to imagine snakes, then later shown black-and-white pictures, all in a controlled, graded fashion, in the context of relaxation exercises. Eventually he progressed to a large model of a snake and finally a visit to a zoo where he was able to enter the reptile house and view each snake for a satisfactory period of time. By the end of treatment he had become an expert on snakes, and showed eagerness to read magazine articles on them. At follow-up $2\frac{1}{2}$ years after the end of treatment Quentin remained symptom-free.

In this treatment the child is first taught to relax muscle tension, prior to presentation of the phobic stimulus. After relaxation has been achieved the phobic object is presented in mild form, perhaps as a small, uncoloured picture, or even by asking the child to imagine it. There is then a gradual, planned increase in the intensity of the stimulus, the rate of increase being such as to enable the child to maintain his relaxed state. This treatment is usually successful for specific phobias, but results are less good when there is generalised anxiety.

Operant conditioning is the planned modification of behaviour through manipulation of the consequences which are seen to control the behaviour. If every time a boy touches something hot he receives a painful burn he will soon stop that behaviour; and if every time he has a temper tantrum he is given what he wants by his parents he will soon be using tantrums as a means of getting things. The behaviour of all of us is affected in this way; if every time we pass a door we try it and find it locked, we will soon stop trying the door. In behaviour therapists' terms the behaviour has been 'extinguished' by 'non-reinforcement'.

Operant methods include the planned positive reinforcement of desired behaviour, negative reinforcement of undesired behaviour and extinction of behaviour by providing no response to it. Positive reinforcers may be small and immediate (e.g. candies), or they may be social (words of praise and a smile). In some settings token economy systems have been found useful. The children acquire tokens for certain behaviour, and in some systems lose them for others, and the tokens are later redeemable for material rewards such as money, or for privileges or status. This sort of programme is often used in residential and day treatment centres, and has also been used successfully in schools, group homes and other settings. This method, like many of the forms of behaviour therapy, lends itself very well to the treatment of groups of children[16,17].

Behaviour therapy, usually using operant methods, has been used for obsessive-compulsive behaviour, anorexia nervosa, temper tantrums, aggressive behaviour, delinquent behaviour, language disorders, enuresis and many other problems. The use of the pad and buzzer in enuresis is described on pages 110 to 113. Behaviour therapy techniques now have an assured place in child psychiatry. They continue to be developed and there appears to be a trend towards locating treatment in the child's environment (home, school, hospital ward, treatment centre), rather than in the therapist's office. Many more detailed accounts of this treatment approach are available[18,19,20].

Drug Treatment

Drugs have only limited usefulness in child psychiatry. The main indications for their use are in the control of epilepsy, and in the treatment of hyperactive children, certain depressed children and, possibly, some neurotically anxious children and children with particular behaviour problems.

Anticonvulsant drugs should always be prescribed for children having epileptic fits, and they are normally continued at least until the child has been free of fits for two years. While phenobarbitone is often effective in controlling fits, expecially major ones, it can make behaviour disorders worse, or may even create them (in the form of aggressiveness, overactivity, poor concentration and generally difficult behaviour) where they did not previously exist. It is therefore best avoided where there is any question of associated psychiatric or behaviour disorder. Other useful anticonvulsants are phenytoin, primidone, carbamazepine, pheneturide and sulthiame. Two or more of these may need to be used in combination in difficult cases. Sulthiame

TABLE 3: ANTICONVULSANTS: DOSAGE, BLOOD LEVELS AND SIDE-EFFECTS

Drug	Dose	Effective blood level	Adverse effects
Carbamazepine	10–30 mg/kg/24 hr	8–18 mcg/ml	Double or blurred vision Drowsiness Ataxia Nausea, vomiting, abdominal discomfort
Ethosuximide	15–50 mg/kg/23 hr	20–40 mcg/ml	Drowsiness Nausea, vomiting or diarrhoea Depression
Nitrazepam	0·3–3·0 mg/kg/24 hr		Drowsiness Weakness Ataxia (usually transient)
Phenobarbitone	5–10 mg/kg/24 hr	10–20 mcg/ml	Drowsiness Ataxia Nystagmus Depression (see also text, p. 229)
Phenytoin	3–8 mg/kg/24 hr	10–20 mcg/ml	Headache Acne Hypertrophy of gums Blood disorders
Primidone	5–25 mg/kg/24 hr	5–15 mcg/ml	Drowsiness Nausea Vomiting Fatigue Irritability
Pheneturide	100–200 mg/24 hr (2–5 years) 600 mg/24 hr (6–12 years)	3–15 mcg/ml	Drowsiness
Sulthiame	3–15 mg/kg/24 hr	10–50 mcg/ml	Headache Tingling in limbs Nausea, vomiting or diarrhoea Drowsiness Ataxia

and carbamazepine are particularly useful in temporal lobe epilepsy. For *petit mal* the most useful drug is ethosuximide.

Table 3 indicates the dose ranges usually effective in the age range

4 to 12. Younger children require weight-related doses 1·25 to 1·5 times as great, the latter figure applying to infants. Monitoring of anti-convulsant therapy by obtaining measures of the blood levels of the drugs used is possible today, and this gives a more accurate indication of the doses required. Expert interpretation of the results is necessary, however. For example primidone is converted in the body to pheno-barbitone and phenylethylmalondiamide (PEMA), both compounds also having anticonvulsant properties, and the rate of conversation varies from one individual to another. The use of drugs in combination also presents special problems: for example sulthiame blocks the break-down of phenytoin, and these two drugs should not be used together without regular estimates of the blood phenytoin level. The table simply gives the usually required dose range and a rough idea of the effective blood levels and commoner adverse effects.

In the treatment of hyperkinetic children, epilepsy, if present should first be controlled. This may be followed by a reduction of the hyper-activity. In most cases there is no evidence of epilepsy and the choice of drugs lies between a stimulant drug, a phenothiazine tranquilliser such as chlorpromazine, and haloperidol. There is evidence that all these drugs are effective in reducing hyperactivity[21]. The stimulant mainly used at present is melthylphenidate, but the chemically related amphetamine drugs are also effective. Although these drugs are stimulants in adults, they have a paradoxical effect in children. Many phenothiazine tranquillisers have been used, particularly chlorpro-mazine and thioridazine, but it is generally agreed that major tranquil-lisers adversely affect learning and cognitive functioning[21]. Haloperidol is of value particularly with certain target symptoms – excess motor activity, restlessness and aggressive and impulsive behaviour[22]. These drugs may be given along with anticonvulsants in epileptic children whose behaviour remains hyperactive even after control of the epilepsy is achieved.

In other behaviour disorders, including some of those associated with brain damage, drug treatment may help, but only as part of a wider treatment programme which takes into account the child's motor, perceptual, social and educational status. Phenothiazine tranquillisers such as chlorpromazine, fluphenazine, perphenazine or thioridazine may help reduce symptoms, especially on a short-term basis; so also may haloperidol (see Table 4).

Drugs are of limited value in neurotic disorders, but temporary relief from acute and severe anxiety may be provided by such tranquillisers as diazepam, chlordiazepoxide and perphenazine. Drugs should not be a substitute for a psychotherapeutic approach designed to help children in the context of their families and wider life situations. They

TABLE 4: TRANQUILLISERS: DOSES AND SIDE-EFFECTS

Drug	Dose	Adverse effects
Phenothiazine drugs		
chlorpromazine	1–3 mg/kg/24 hr	Drowsiness
thioridazine	(night sedative dose up	Muscular rigidity
	to 3 mg/kg/24 hr)	Tremor
fluphenazine	0·05–0·25 mg/kg/24 hr	Jaundice
perphenazine	0·15–0·30 mg/kg/24 hr	Precipitation of epilepsy
		Skin rashes (Chlorpromazine may cause photosensitive skin rash)
Haloperidol	0·025–0·5 mg/kg/24 hr	Painful muscle spasms
		Muscular rigidity and tremor
		Drowsiness
		Depression

Other drugs for hyperkinetic children

dexamphetamine	0·25–0·5 mg/kg/24 hr	Excitement
methylphenidate	0·2–0·7 mg/kg/24 hr	Sleeplessness
		Loss of appetite
		Failure to gain weight and height
		Palpitations
		Headache
		Abdominal cramps
		Drug dependence (not usually a problem in hyperactive children)

Benzodiazepine compounds (dosage for over-fives)

chlordiazepoxide	5–10 mg two or three times daily	Drowsiness
		Skin rashes
diazepam	2–5 mg two or three times daily	Muscle tenderness or weakness

Note:The muscle spasms and tremor which may be caused by phenothiazines and haloperidol can be prevented by simultaneous administration of an anti-Parkinsonian drug, e.g. benzhexol 1–5 mg twice daily.

may, however, occasionally help by controlling anxiety in the short term while other measures are being instituted. The antidepressant imipramine has been reported to be of use as an adjunct in the treatment of school refusal[23].

Table 4 shows the doses and main side-effects of the various tranquillising drugs which have been mentioned. In all cases dosage should be adjusted individually with the aim of obtaining the response sought without serious side-effects.

The value of antidepressant drugs in children is uncertain. Since depression in children is often reactive to severe environmental stress, a main therapeutic aim should be to reduce the stress, or to support the child in coping with it. There have been few satisfactory clinical trials of antidepressants in children, but it is probably reasonable to try their effect in obviously depressed children, especially those who do not respond to other treatment. Drug treatment is usually indicated in adolescents with depressive illnesses of the types seen in adults. The drugs mainly used in children and adolescents are the tricyclic anti-depressants such as imipramine, amitriptyline and dothiepin. Imipramine has also been reported to be of value in hyperactive children and in some behaviour disorders.

Table 5 indicates the doses of antidepressants which may be useful in the age range five to twelve. Over about twelve, adult doses may be given. No information is available on weight-related doses needed in children. Doses at the lower end of the ranges mentioned should be given at first, with subsequent gradual increase over a few weeks until a satisfactory response is obtained, adverse effects appear or the maximum recommended dose is reached. The doses at the higher ends of the ranges mentioned are probably higher than are usually needed in children as young as five to eight.

TABLE 5: ANTIDEPRESSANT DRUGS IN OLDER CHILDREN $(5+)$: DOSES AND SIDE-EFFECTS

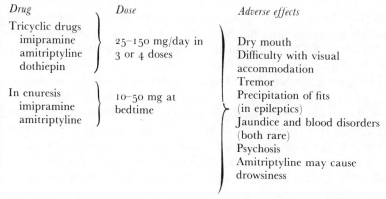

Drug	*Dose*	*Adverse effects*

Tricyclic drugs
  imipramine
  amitriptyline
  dothiepin
	25–150 mg/day in
	3 or 4 doses
		Dry mouth
		Difficulty with visual
		accommodation
		Tremor

In enuresis
  imipramine
  amitriptyline
	10–50 mg at
	bedtime
		Precipitation of fits
		(in epileptics)
		Jaundice and blood disorders
		(both rare)
		Psychosis
		Amitriptyline may cause
		drowsiness

Despite the side-effects mentioned in the table, these drugs can be safely used in children if administered cautiously and without sudden increases of dose and if once a satisfactory response is obtained, the dose is reduced to a smaller maintenance one.

In nocturnal enuresis the administration of imipramine or amitriptyline at bedtime has been shown in controlled trials to reduce the frequency of wetting, but the effect tends to be short-lived, subsequent relapse being common.

Drugs do not appear to alter the course of infantile psychosis, but are sometimes useful in dealing with specific symptoms like hyperkinetic behaviour or sleeplessness. Older children with psychotic conditions resembling adult-type schizophrenia may be helped by phenothiazine drugs such as those listed in Table 4. Long-term maintenance therapy may lead to prolonged remission of symptoms, but on the whole children with late-onset psychosis of childhood seem to respond less well than adults with schizophrenia. Here again, however, there is a lack of satisfactory evidence from properly controlled trials.

TABLE 6: HYPNOTIC DRUGS: DOSES AND SIDE-EFFECTS

Drug	*Dose*	*Adverse effects*
Chloral	20–50 mg/kg/24 hr	Nausea
Dichloralphenazone	Maximum dose 1 g	Vomiting
Triclofos		
Promethazine	15–30 mg (in age range five–twelve)	Dizziness
		Lack of co-ordination
		Blurred vision
		Excitement
		Blood disorders (rare)

Sleeplessness may occasionally merit treatment with drugs, though toddlers who do not sleep can be difficult to sedate effectively. Table 6 shows the dose ranges for some hypnotics which may be used to induce sleep in children. Chloral and the following two compounds are closely related substances with very similar effects. If they are proved ineffective, chlorpromazine or thioridazine (see Table 3) can be useful, especially in young children, or promethazine may be tried.

Recent years have seen the development of a large, and sometimes confusing, literature on drug treatment in child psychiatry. Excellent recent reviews are those of Shaffer[24] and Wiener[25]. The tables above are designed simply to give a general idea of dosage and adverse effects. For full information pharmacological texts and the manufacturers' literature should be consulted.

Inpatient Treatment

Children are admitted for residential treatment either because of behaviour so severely disturbed as to make treatment or even care elsewhere difficult or impossible, or because it is thought that removal of the child for a limited period from the home environment to one designed to provide a more helpful living and treatment situation will be beneficial.

As a rule inpatient treatment is but an episode, albeit sometimes quite a prolonged one, in the course of treatment.

Examples of severe disturbance necessitating admission are extremely aggressive or hyperactive behaviour, serious depression with perhaps suicidal ideas, very bizarre and withdrawn psychotic behaviour and severe anorexia nervosa. Admission can also be of benefit in some neurotic disorders, for example severe school refusal.

Adverse environmental circumstances which may make it desirable to admit children for treatment include unstable homes with much marital disharmony, severe parental rejection of the child, gross over-protection and certain conditions of emotional deprivation. (These circumstances are often faced also by children admitted because of the severity of their disturbance). Admission is indicated where it seems likely, or at least possible, that more can be done to alter the adverse environment while the child is having treatment in hospital, than would be the case if he stayed at home for treatment. It is sometimes easier to help the family, and change the parents' attitudes for the better, while they are relieved of the constant irritant of the child's disturbed behaviour. If at the same time the child is receiving treatment in the unit, it may in due course be possible to reintroduce him in a less disturbed state into a less disturbed family, and then continue treatment as a daypatient or outpatient.

Admission must always be considered in the light of the family situation or, if the child is not living with his family, the situation in the group home, foster home or wherever he is living. Requests for admission are sometimes disguised attempts by parents or others to get rid of an unwanted child. Sometimes the request is a symptom of the 'scapegoating' of a child, and the right course is to treat the family as a group, to try and understand why this is and help the family to change. In such circumstances it may strengthen the family's disturbed way of functioning to collude with it by admitting the child.

An essential feature of the treatment provided for children in psychiatric inpatient units is the general emotional environment in which the children live. This may be supplemented by, and indeed is in part made up of, such other treatments as recreational and occupational therapy, educational help, administration of drugs and behaviour therapy. While all these things can be provided on an outpatient basis, inpatient care also provides for the child a living environment which can be altered to suit his particular psychological needs.

In most British inpatient units the nurses play the central role in the care and treatment of the children. In North America this role is often carried out by child care workers. These workers are usually part of a larger treatment team which will include other professions

– psychiatrists, psychologists, social workers, perhaps non-medical psychotherapists. An emotionally warm, relaxed atmosphere is needed; however disturbed and difficult the child's behaviour it should not be met by angry or rejecting attitudes on the part of the staff. Yet, as in individual psychotherapy, limits have to be set. The point is that the child's present clinical state and behaviour are accepted. The implicit assumption is that the child's behaviour is a consequence of an underlying disturbance, which needs to be understood. The required changes in behaviour will follow the resolution of the underlying problems. It is to help achieve this that the staff are working with the child – not against him.

A recent innovation, apparently useful in residential treatment as well as in other therapeutic situations, is 'positive peer culture'[26]. This seeks to help individuals by creating a culture in which they help others. The emphasis is thus not on what is being done to the subject, but on what members of the group, or the group as a whole, can do for others.

The treatment needs of the different children in a hospital unit vary. The psychotic child who tends to withdraw must be brought into contact with people by any means available. Immature, overdependent neurotic children must be given progressively more scope and encouragement to stand on their own emotionally, and cope with relationships with others without constantly requiring support from parents or the staff. Such children will need a steadily decreasing amount of non-anxious support as they improve. Children with severe conduct disorders require calm, consistent, accepting limit-setting. Such children often behave conformingly for the first few days, or even weeks. Once they begin to feel more sure of themselves in their new situation their aggressiveness, destructiveness and negativism emerge. Unconsciously they expect this to be met by hostility and rejection such as they have probably experienced at home and elsewhere. Indeed, their admission may be seen by them as a manifestation of rejection. Such children benefit from firm limit-setting (which may involve physically restraining them from damaging other people or property), while they themselves are nevertheless subject to warm attitudes of acceptance.

Inpatient treatment can also be useful in some developmental disorders, for example soiling, and in certain psychosomatic disorders.

Inpatient units have a useful diagnostic function. In cases of particular difficulty, a period of observation while the child is resident may clarify the diagnosis. The assessment of psychotic children is sometimes made easier by inpatient observation; so also is the estimation of the relative importance of an adverse home environment in psychosomatic disorders and in some developmental disorders and neurotic conditions.

Admission to a psychiatric unit is usually best avoided in the case of the child who has no home or a home so grossly disturbed or unsatisfactory as to be quite unsuitable. Such children, if admitted, tend to become overdependent upon, and attached to, the unit with consequent emotional trauma and feelings of rejection when they are discharged. Children without homes in which they can live should first be found substitute homes, usually in conjunction with the appropriate child welfare agency. In such cases close co-operation with the child welfare agency is necessary, and some treatment centres have set up arrangements whereby specially selected, trained and supported foster parents provide homes for children during, and often following, inpatient treatment[27].

Residential treatment is a specialised subject applicable only to a small proportion of disturbed children. It is discussed more fully in the book *The Residential Psychiatric Treatment of Children*[28].

Day Treatment

Day treatment[29,30,31] can provide many of the benefits of inpatient treatment without totally removing the child from home, and at less expense. Children can spend a substantial part of their waking hours in a therapeutic milieu, yet continue to live with their families, who are, however, relieved of much of the stress of coping with their disturbed behaviour. Day treatment does not carry the risk, ever present in inpatient care, of child and parents losing contact with each other and of the problem coming to be denied on one or both sides. It can often be helpfully combined with family therapy or casework.

Day treatment can also be useful when the child's behavioural problem is selectively manifest at school, the child's adjustment at home being satisfactory. Since most day treatment units have teachers on their staff, the educational needs of these children can often be met during a period of attendance at such a unit.

Day treatment usually involves attendance from about 9 a.m. until 4 or 5 p.m., 5 days a week, but hours may vary and attendance may be for fewer than 5 days weekly or may be confined to mornings, afternoons or evenings.

Alternative Families

In recent years use has been made, in some centres, of families in the community as places where children can receive 'residential' treatment.

Examples are the 'parent–therapist' programme in Hamilton, Ontario[32], the Alberta Parent Counsellors[33], and the Kent Family Placement Project in England[34]. In these programmes families are specially selected, trained and paid, and then take into their homes disturbed children needing treatment away from their own homes. The alternative families receive continuing help in this work, a main feature of this being regular group meetings under the leadership of a professional worker. Meanwhile work is done as indicated with the natural families, as it would be during inpatient treatment. These schemes appear to be of real value and can provide a good alternative to inpatient treatment. They are also less costly.

A somewhat similar scheme, the 'family care programme' in Toronto, provides alternative families for children receiving inpatient treatment, in cases where the child has no family that can provide a suitable home[27]. As well as visiting their child in the treatment centre, the 'foster care workers' provide, as necessary, a weekend home and, often, later a home for the child to live in upon discharge. In the rather frequent cases where the child's family has broken up or rejected the child, this appears greatly to facilitate and shorten residential treatment and prevent subsequent relapse.

Educational Measures

Where educational problems are present, as they often are in disturbed children, treatment must include appropriate educational measures. These may include remedial teaching for the child, a change of educational methods of transfer to a different class or school. Advice from educational psychologists is helpful on these matters.

In many countries special schools and classes exist for disturbed children, either as part of the general school system or as private establishments. In Great Britain local education authorities have a statutory duty to provide special education for 'maladjusted' children requiring it, and for this reason many local authorities run special schools for maladjusted children. There are also a number of privately run schools. There are both day and residential schools for maladjusted children; some take day pupils and residential pupils. In North America the arrangements for the education of disturbed children are more varied. Many of the schools that specialise in this area are privately run, but many boards of education run special classes. There are also a number of special schools attached to residential and day treatment centres. Children who are facing chronically unstable, adverse family environments and whose behaviour is disturbed or development adversely affected, can often benefit greatly from suitable residential schooling. Skilled, accepting care in these schools is combined with special educational help in small classes. The schools are often small (up to about 80 pupils, but normally nearer 40) and have a higher staff:pupil ratio than ordinary schools. While at school the children are often able to develop relationships with the staff which are more satisfying and constructive than those they have with their parents. Yet they have not been removed from the care of their parents, with whom they live during school holidays, half-term breaks and perhaps weekends. Very often their adjustment at home improves as their educational problems begin to resolve as a result of their treatment in school. Many of these schools also have social workers on their staffs who can help families with their problems while the child is away at the school. The development of schools for maladjusted children has been well described by Bridgland[35].

While special schools and classes are valuable for some children, most disturbed children are educated in ordinary schools and classes. Many more minor educational problems can be dealt with in such settings, often with some additional help from educational psychologists or remedial teachers. A helpful recent review of the education of disturbed children is that of Laslett[36].

Speech and Language Therapy

Most centres treating disturbed children have one or more speech therapists on their staff. Since speech and language disorders are often associated with emotional disturbance, it is important that expert assessment and treatment by a speech therapist should be available. Speech therapists have an important role in the assessment and treatment of children with developmental language disorders (see pages 150 to 153).

Removal from Parental Care

Some children do not have families with which they can live. This may be because of the death or desertion of one or both parents, but provision is also needed for the care of children who do not receive an adequate standard of care within their families. In all developed countries there are child welfare agencies, often run by the state but sometimes by private organisations, to deal with these children (see pages 204 to 205).

Where a child has a family with which it would be possible to live if the care available in it was adequate, efforts should naturally first be made to improve the standard of care the family gives. This is one important function of the social workers who staff child welfare agencies. If these efforts fail, or when there is no family with which the child can live, alternative care is necessary. This can often be done with the consent of the parents, or next of kin, but it is sometimes necessary for the child to be taken into care against the wishes of the next of kin (see Chapter 15).

Many children who have had to be removed from their families have experienced unstable, rejecting and perhaps depriving conditions prior to being taken into care, so that their emotional development has been retarded and abnormal. They may show severe behavioural abnormalities and commonly have conduct disorders, developmental disorders, educational problems or other difficulties, often in various combinations. The child welfare agencies concerned have the often very difficult task of meeting these children's needs, and psychiatric help is often sought.

The substitute environment provided for these children usually consists of either a group home or a foster home. The large and often rather impersonal children's homes, or 'orphanages', of the past have now been mostly replaced by much smaller homes, often consisting of ordinary houses in which the children are cared for in the same way as in an ordinary family. Unfortunately, however, many mentally handicapped children are still cared for in large, impersonal and under-staffed institutions, the drawbacks of which are well described by King and colleagues[37]. Happily there is a trend towards caring for these children in smaller units, such as hostels or group homes.

Today homes do not usually contain more than about ten to fifteen children, and ideally should probably have rather fewer. An increasing number take the form of family group homes in which a married couple, perhaps assisted by one or two other staff, look after the children, the husband going out to work at a job as would the father in an ordinary family. Foster care consists of placing the child in an ordinary family, the foster parents being selected from people who have volunteered for the work. They are paid a sum for the child's keep but care for him in their own home.

Substitute care of this type is the main need of some emotionally disturbed children. After removal from the disturbed family, their disorders often gradually settle in the more stable environment in which they are placed. As well as requiring skilled and patient management, however, they may also require other treatment measures such as have been outlined above. It is for this reason that child welfare agencies often seek help from psychiatrists and psychologists, as well as employing social workers. Inter-disciplinary assessment is often helpful in deciding the nature of a deprived child's problems and his placement and management.

Many western countries also have 'training' or 'correctional' schools for delinquent children, and especially adolescents. Their value has been questioned, and the environment and help they offer their clients varies greatly. In some, however, progressive and humane therapeutic programmes exist, whereas others are primarily custodial and/or punitive. In some jurisdictions these establishments have been abolished, and at the time of writing they are being greatly reduced in numbers in Ontario. In Great Britain they were formerly called 'approved schools' and were under the jurisdiction of the Home Office, which also runs prisons for adults. They are now renamed 'community homes' and are run by social services departments, which are also responsible for other child welfare services. An interesting study of a number of former approved schools is that of Millham and colleagues[38].

References

1. Freud, A. *Normality and Pathology in Childhood*. London: Hogarth Press, 1966.
2. Freud, A. *A Short History of Child Analysis*. London: Hogarth Press, 1972.
3. Klein, M. *The Psychoanalysis of Children*. London: Hogarth Press, 1932.
4. Allen, F. H. *Psychotherapy with Children*. New York: Norton, 1942.
5. Adams, P. L. *A Primer of Child Psychotherapy*. Boston: Little Brown, 1974.
6. Sussenwein, F. 'Psychiatric social work'. In *Child Psychiatry: Modern Approaches*, ed. M. Rutter and L. Hersov. Oxford: Blackwell, 1976.
7. Walrond-Skinner, S. *Family Therapy: The Treatment of Natural Systems*. London: Routledge and Kegan Paul, 1976.
8. Minuchin, S. *Families and Family Therapy*. Cambridge, Mass.: Harvard University Press, 1974.
9. Haley, J. *Problem-Solving Therapy*. San Francisco: Jossey-Bros, 1976.
10. Glick, I. D. and Kessler, D. R. *Marital and Family Therapy*. New York: Grune and Stratton, 1974.
11. Minuchin, S., Rosman, B. L. and Baker, L. *Psychosomatic Families: Anorexia Nervosa in Context*. New York: Harvard University Press, 1978.
12. Papp, P. (Editor) *Family Therapy: Full Length Case Studies*. New York: Gardner Press, 1977.
13. Ginott, H. G. *Group Psychotherapy with Children*. New York: McGraw-Hill, 1961.
14. Yalom, I. *The Theory and Practice of Group Psychotherapy*, second edition. New York: Basic Books, 1975.
15. Philipp, R. 'Conducting Parent Training Groups: Approaches and Strategies'. In *New Directions in Children's Mental Health*. ed. S. J. Shamsie. New York: Spectrum, 1979.
16. Wagner, B. R. and Breitmeyer, R. G. 'PACE: a residential, community oriented behaviour modification programme for adolescents'. *Adolescence*, **10**, 277–286, 1975.
17. Hoefler, S. A. and Bornstein, P. H. 'Achievement Place: an evaluative review'. *Criminal Justice and Behaviour*, **2**, 146–168, 1975.
18. Patterson, G. R. *Families: Application of Social Learning to Family Life*. Research Press, Champaign, Ill., 1975.

19. O'Leary, K. D. and O'Leary, S. G. *Classroom Management: The Successful Use of Behaviour Modification.* Elmsford, N.Y.: Pergamon, 1977.
20. Bergin, A. and Garfield, S. (eds). *Psychotherapy and Behaviour Change.* New York: Wiley, 1971.
21. Cantwell, D. 'Psychopharmacologic treatment of the minimal brain dysfunction syndrome'. In *Psychopharmacology in Childhood and Adolescence*, ed. J. M. Wiener. New York: Basic Books, 1977.
22. Barker, P. 'Haloperidol'. *Journal of Child Psychology and Psychiatry*, **16**, 169–172, 1975.
23. Greenberg, L. M. and Stephans, J. H. 'Use of drugs in special syndromes'. In *Psychopharmacology in Childhood and Adolescence*, ed. J. M. Wiener. New York: Basic Books, 1977.
24. Shaffer, D. 'Drug Treatment'. In *Child Psychiatry: Modern Approaches*, ed. M. Rutter and L. Hersov. Oxford: Blackwell, 1976.
25. Wiener, J. M. (ed.). *Psychopharmacology in Childhood and Adolescence.* New York: Basic Books, 1977.
26. Vorrath, H. H. and Brendthro, L. K. *Positive Peer Culture.* Chicago: Aldine, 1976.
27. Barker, P., Buffe, C. and Zaretsky, R. 'The disturbed child: providing a family alternative'. *Child Welfare*, **57**, 373–379, 1978.
28. Barker, P. (ed.). *The Residential Psychiatric Treatment of Children.* London: Crosby Lockwood Staples, 1974; New York, Halsted Press, 1975.
29. Chazen, R. 'Day treatment of emotionally disturbed children'. *Child Welfare*, **48**, 212–218, 1969.
30. Gold, J. and Reisman, J. 'An outcome study of a day treatment unit school in a community mental health centre'. *American Journal of Orthopsychiatry*, **40**, 286–287, 1970.
31. Linnihan, P. C. 'Adolescent day treatment'. *American Journal of Orthopsychiatry*, **47**, 679–688, 1977.
32. Levin, S., Rubenstein, J. S. and Streiner, D. C. 'The parent-therapist programme: an innovative approach to treating emotionally disturbed children'. *Hospital and Community Psychiatry*, **27**, 407–410, 1976.
33. Larson, G., Allison, J. and Johnston, E. 'Alberta Parent Counsellors: a community treatment programme for disturbed youths'. *Child Welfare*, **57**, 47–52, 1978.
34. Hazel, N. 'How family placements can combat delinquency'. *Social Work Today*, **8**, 6–7, 1977.
35. Bridgland, M. *Pioneer Work with Maladjusted Children.* London: Crosby Lockwood Staples, 1971.
36. Laslett, R. *Educating Maladjusted Children.* London: Crosby Lockwood Staples, 1977.
37. King, R. D., Raynes, N. V. and Tizard, J. *Patterns of Residential Care.* London: Routledge and Kegan Paul, 1971.
38. Millham, S., Bullock, R. and Cherrett, P. *After Grace-Teeth.* London: Human Context Books, 1975.

CHAPTER SEVENTEEN

Prevention of Child Psychiatric Disorders

It is obviously better to prevent child psychiatric disorders than to treat them once they are established. Less attention has, nevertheless, in the past been given to prevention than to treatment services. It is important, however, since treatment methods are by no means uniformly effective and in any case are unavailable to many children and families who need them.

Types of Prevention

Prevention has been divided into primary, secondary and tertiary types[1].

Primary prevention in the field of child mental health consists of planned programmes designed to reduce the incidence of specific pathological conditions, whether psychiatric illness or mental handicap in a population of children not currently suffering from such conditions.

Secondary prevention aims at early diagnosis and case finding, followed by intervention to bring the disorder rapidly under control, so that there is minimal impact on the subject.

Tertiary prevention consists of measures taken once a disorder is established. It aims to limit the effects of the disorder, to prevent it getting worse and to give support to the afflicted individual or family.

This chapter will deal principally with primary prevention.

The *prevalence* of a disorder is the number of cases at a given time in a specified population. It is a function of two independent variables

– *incidence* and *duration*. Incidence is a measure of the number of new cases occurring during a specified time period; duration is the length of time a disorder persists, that is, the time from onset until either recovery or death. An increase in either incidence or duration will thus cause a greater prevalence. It will be clear from the definitions of the different types of prevention mentioned above that primary prevention aims to reduce prevalence by lowering the incidence of disorders, while secondary prevention aims to do it by shortening the duration of disorders.

The Development of Concepts of Primary Prevention

There has been a great increase in interest and activity in primary prevention since the publication in 1964 of Caplan's book *Principles of Preventive Psychiatry*[1]. It has become clear that there are things which can be done to the environments in which people live which will reduce the incidence of psychiatric disorders and mental handicap. Albee has been a leading research worker in the field and played a leading part in organising the first Vermont Conference on the Primary Prevention of Psychopathology, held in 1975[2]. Since then conferences have been held annually. The second one dealt with 'environmental issues'[3] and the third, the proceedings of which were not yet published as this book was written, with 'promoting social competence and coping in children'. The published proceedings of these conferences are a valuable source of information on primary prevention.

Approaches to Primary Prevention

Epidemiology is a basic tool without which programmes of primary prevention are not possible. It is concerned with the incidence, prevalence and distribution of disorders in communities. By means of epidemiological studies it is possible both to determine a baseline so that the effectiveness of a preventive programme can be judged, and also to identify *risk factors* which make the development of particular disorders more likely. Primary prevention is then based on this information and also on knowledge about *intervening variables*, those factors which determine whether individuals at risk do or do not develop the disorders in question. No risk factor is 100 per cent effective, and in any epidemic some individuals will escape. Primary prevention aims to alter the environment so that more escape.

Risk Factors Relevant in Primary Prevention

The following factors are known to be of significance for primary prevention.

(a) Genetic factors. Reference has been made elsewhere to genetic factors in the causation of child psychiatric disorder (page 17). It has proved possible, for example, to reduce the incidence of mental handicap due to phenylketonuria by the routine testing of the urine of newborn infants and the provision of an appropriate diet to those who show evidence of the condition. The provision of genetic counselling services can also reduce the incidence of certain genetic disorders. It is often combined with amniocentesis, in genetically 'at risk' pregnant mothers. Amniocentesis is the prenatal examination of the amniotic fluid, which enables a number of foetal abnormalities to be detected early in pregnancy. Pregnancy can then be terminated.

(b) Pregnancy risk factors. These include toxemia of pregnancy, various infections of the mother (rubella, syphilis, toxoplasmosis) and other factors such as smoking and, probably, severe alcoholism. Programmes designed to reduce these risk factors have met with great success. Congenital syphilis and the mental retardation and other results of maternal rubella in early pregnancy are now very rare where good antenatal care is practised.

(c) Birth trauma. It has long been known that birth trauma can cause damage to the brain, as well as to other parts of the foetus. Good obstetric care reduces this and is thus an important element in primary prevention.

(d) Prematurity and neonatal medical disorders. Apart from their direct effects, these may have indirect ones as a result of prolonged separation of infant and mother. Treatment in a special care unit may disrupt mother–infant bonding (see page 49).

(e) Accidents in and outside the home. These are common causes of neurological and other injuries, which may lead to psychiatric disorder or mental handicap.

(f) Poisons. The most important is lead (see page 93).

(g) Physical illnesses, especially of the central nervous system. The risks are particularly great when illnesses are prolonged and lead to repeated admissions to hospital.

(h) Cultural deprivation. Many studies have shown higher prevalence rates of psychiatric disorders, as well as of mental handicap and learning failure at school, in culturally deprived homes than in other homes.

(i)   Family disharmony and disruption. Children from such families generally have higher rates of emotional and behavioural disorders.

(j)   Parental mental illness. This is a particularly serious risk factor when both parents suffer mental illness, and also when the disorder is severe and prolonged.

(k)   Early school failure. This is often associated with specific learning disorders, hyperkinesis and neurological problems.

(l)   Experience of being in the care of a child welfare agency. This is discussed further below.

(m)   Large family size. This has been shown to be associated with an increased incidence of juvenile delinquency.

   The above list of risk factors is not exhaustive, but in the case of all those mentioned there is some evidence to support the listing. Many other risk factors certainly exist. In some cases there is suspicion of their role but no proof; others are no doubt as yet unsuspected.

   Protective factors may be contrasted with risk factors. They are factors which make the development of a disorder less likely. The World Health Organisation publication *Child Mental Health and Psychosocial Development*[4] lists the following possible protective factors.

(a)   Sex. For little understood reasons girls seem to be less susceptible to psychosocial stress in childhood.

(b)   Temperament. An adaptable temperament seems to protect against the effects of deprivation and disadvantage.

(c)   Isolated nature of stress. Even chronic stresses, if isolated, tend to cause little damage, but multiple stresses interact to potentiate the adverse results.

(d)   Coping skills. There is evidence that children can acquire the skills to cope with various stresses. For example it has been shown that children who are used to brief, happy separation experiences, such as short stays with friends or relatives, cope better with the stress of hospital admission.

(e)   A good relationship with one parent. Such a relationship helps protect against the adverse effects which result when a child is brought up in a discordant, unhappy home.

(f)   Success or good experiences outside the home. Good schooling can apparently help mitigate the effects of a bad home environment.

(g)   Improved family circumstances. Later years spent in a harmonious family setting seem to lessen the effects of earlier adverse family circumstances.

Rutter[5] has provided a valuable review of factors relating to 'in-vulnerability' – the ability of some children to survive gross deprivation and psychosocial stress without developing psychiatric disorders. While affirming that genetic factors are important causes contributing to children's psychiatric problems, he also cites evidence that one way in which genetic factors operate is through their influence on the responsiveness of individuals to environmental stresses. This suggests that if the latter are reduced, the genetic predisposition may be countered.

Preventive Measures

Epidemiological data, combined with evidence concerning risk factors, intervening variables and protective factors, enable rational plans to be made for programmes of primary prevention. It has already been pointed out that the provision of genetic counselling services and of facilities for amniocentesis can reduce the incidence of cases of some forms of mental handicap. Our knowledge of risk factors also suggests that the provision of good antenatal and obstetric services will be of value.

Accident prevention, which can be achieved by making roads, vehicles and homes safer, is likely to have some primary preventive value. The removal of lead from paint and the safe disposal of lead-containing waste can be expected to reduce the incidence of cases of lead poisoning. Measures which control infectious diseases, especially those affecting the central nervous system are relevant.

Factors such as cultural deprivation, family disharmony and parental mental illness present difficult challenges. It has been established, however, that social change which can lead to lessening of the psychiatric morbidity in communities can be brought about by specific interventions. A classical study is that of Leighton[6], who described changes in a rural community over a 10-year period. At the start of the period the community was impoverished materially, culturally, educationally and socially, with a high prevalence of broken marriages, interparental strife and child neglect. As a result of a number of changes in the community, notably group action and the emergence of local leadership, there were great improvements in all these areas over a 10-year period. Factors that contributed to the change were the activities of the official responsible for adult education in the area and those of the local teacher. Some external factors, such as electrification of the village, helped but for the most part the changes in the community came from within. Outside people and agencies did, however, act as catalysts. The role of the 'consolidated school', in a town several miles away, appeared to be important. The village children started going to this school during the course of the study. The influence of this school, through the ideas, concepts, values and standards of behaviour brought home by the children, seemed important and helpful. (More recent research has confirmed that the influence of the school, as a social institution, on the psychosocial development of its students is of great significance[5]). The changes described by Leighton are reported to have been accompanied by a great lowering of the prevalence of psychiatric disorder over the 10-year period of the study. This contrasted with other communities that in 1952, when the study started, were equally disintegrated but remained so in 1962. These communities showed no comparable decline in the prevalence of psychiatric disorder.

In most western societies rural poverty and disintegration is today less prominent as a problem than are various urban problems. A similar model for change can, however, be used. It is set out in a paper by Cordoza and colleagues on 'improving mental health through community action'[7], though the example they use concerns not children, but the elderly. The essence of the approach is that 'conditions stressful to individuals frequently derive from the social characteristics of communities'. Communities may be regarded as systems containing various subsystems (see page 23 for a further discussion of systems theory). These systems have two dimensions. One is the 'structure' of the community – its social stratification, kinship networks and leadership hierarchy. The other dimension consists of 'shared feelings, attitudes, values and opinions', which make up the structures and can be called shared sentiments. Structure and sentiment interact to make up the community's functioning, which may or may not promote good mental health in particular families and individuals. Cordoza and his colleagues describe the 'Sommerville' project, which seemed to show that the intervention of a 'catalyst', in this case a member of a mental health team, could change the structure of the community. The worker operated by 'weaving networks of communication between resources and people who knew about them'. The authors acknowledge that the study, like other similar ones, lacked a 'control' group. That is to say it is impossible to be absolutely sure that the beneficial changes did not come about by chance. Nevertheless, evidence that these measures are effective is increasing.

In Britain the term 'intermediate treatment' has been used for interventions of a similar kind. This approach involves the use of various social work techniques, but especially 'community work'; this seeks to involve 'the participation of the parents and adults of the neighbourhood in the planning of services to children and youth, while fostering the involvement of the youngsters in the life of their community'. In other words, the idea is to enable communities to function better as communities. The book *Intermediate Treatment*[8], from which the above quotation is taken, describes pilot schemes in seven 'areas of deprivation' in England. While results are difficult to evaluate, schemes of this sort seem to offer real hope of being of value in both primary and secondary prevention.

An important 'high risk' group of children consists of those who have been in the care of child welfare agencies at some time in their life. Such children show psychiatric disorder later in childhood much more often than children who have not experienced a period of agency care[9]. While the reasons for this are complex, and are probably related more to the instability of these families and their relative lack of supporting social networks than to the fact of the children having been in care, it is clear that this is a vulnerable group. The provision of excellent alternative care for children deprived of normal, stable, secure family life is likely to be of great preventive value. The question of the provision of services to such children, and how their results might be evaluated, is discussed further in the book *Care Can Prevent*[10].

The known association between large family size and juvenile delinquency[11] suggests that measures which make birth control more readily available may be of value.

Secondary Prevention

This involves early diagnosis and case finding, followed by intervention to bring the disorder under control as rapidly as possible. The screening of populations to detect disorders at an early stage is of value here. In most school systems children are tested and assessed regularly to detect early evidence of both emotional disorders and learning disabilities. Many children in whom evidence of disorder is detected in this way come from troubled families. In these cases treatment often involves the whole family group, and what is secondary prevention for one child may be primary prevention for other, as yet undisturbed, children.

Many screening devices are available for detecting early signs of disorder in children. These include Rutter's scales for use by teachers[12] and by parents[13] and the Bristol Social Adjustment Guide[14].

The treatment methods required in dealing with early cases detected by secondary prevention programmes are similar to those required for established disorders, as described in the earlier chapters of this book.

Many schools have special psychological and remedial services for children with learning problems.

Most communities have services which both provide support and help for families raising young children and are available to detect early signs of problems in the children. In Britain the principal service is that provided by *health visitors*, specialised nurses who have the statutory duty to visit the families of all children soon after birth and at intervals thereafter. In North America similar functions are performed by *public health nurses*.

Tertiary Prevention

This consists of measures taken once a disorder is established. It aims to limit the effect of the disorder, to prevent its getting worse and to give support to the affected individual or family. It requires active involvement and usually a lot of work by those doing the prevention but it may be essential, for example with families in which there has been serious abuse or neglect of children. Generally, however, primary and secondary prevention are preferable and more economic uses of scarce professional time. Various agencies and services run intensive programmes for families containing children at high risk. *Family service units*, for example, aim to give intensive help, if necessary over a long period of time, to families which are functioning especially badly. The staff are prepared if need be to spend substantial periods of time in the home, supporting the family; helping them with their emotional and social handicaps; demonstrating, if necessary, basic techniques of home management and the care of children; and gradually enabling the family to function better on its own. Despite their great value, such units are few in relation to the number of families they could help, and economic factors are likely to prevent much expansion of such services.

Other Points Concerning Prevention

One of the problems in discussing primary prevention is that, as Kessler and Albee have pointed out[15], 'practically every effort aimed at improved child rearing, increasing effective communication, building inner control and self-esteem, reducing stress and pollution, and such like – in short everything aimed at improving the human condition – may be considered to be part of primary prevention of mental or emotional disturbance'. It is, therefore, important that professionals in the field, when they recommend preventive programmes, do so on the basis of data which at least suggest that the programme will be effective – and also cost-effective. If data are lacking, means of evaluating new programmes should be built into the plans.

This sort of approach is important because whether preventive measures are taken to deal with particular problems often depends on community attitudes, and especially those of community leaders. Wild claims, programme failures and extravagantly expensive schemes do not endear professionals to the communities they serve. Moreover, in many instances it is the collective motivation of communities that determines whether or not preventive programmes are implemented. For example finances allocated to education authorities and child welfare agencies usually depend on delicate political considerations.

The widespread dissemination of information on the stresses which society places on its members, and on how such stresses may be alleviated is very important. In this connection the National Children's Bureau has published a series of brief reviews or 'highlights'. These summarise current knowledge about various groups of children that are at risk. They quote relevant references and are a useful guide to the literature[16].

At the level of society as a whole, the view is expressed by many people that modern, western society fails to provide an appropriate environment for the raising of emotionally healthy children. These people point to the rising crime, delinquency, family break-up and divorce rates as evidence of this. Writing from an ecological point of view Goldsmith[17] sees modern urban society as undermining the essential functions of the family, which in turn is undermined as the basis of our social system. He believes that the educative, economic, welfare and social control functions of the family have all largely been taken away by the modern industrial state. At the same time increasing numbers of poor, dispossessed, alienated people struggle to bring up children in deteriorating inner city areas. Economic and social problems make this increasingly difficult. Goldsmith's solution is 'de-urbanisation' – the settlement of people in smaller, ecologically balanced societies. But Goldsmith and others like him believe that even more radical changes in society, such as those suggested in the 'Blueprint for Survival'[18], are required if modern civilisation is to be set on the right tracks.

Writing from a mental health point of view Bronfenbrenner[19] also points out that, 'in recent decades the American family has been falling apart'. He believes that children's needs are being met less and less effectively and he too sees this as due to changing social standards. How is it, he asks, that we can deliver men and survival systems to the moon, but not health care to the neighbourhood? Bronfenbrenner believes that it is the self-centredness of members of today's society, and the failure of people to contribute adequately to the community in which they live, which is at the root of the problem. His solutions are seemingly less radical than Goldsmith's, but nevertheless require drastic changes in society.

The decline in religion is probably related to the other changes in society. The great religions of the world offer sound codes by which human beings may live together. Many western nations have largely abandoned their former Christian heritage, with its obligation to love and help others, and to put God and other people before self. Instead a self-seeking materialism seems to be preferred in which, as Bonfenbrenner[19] puts it, 'doing your own thing (is) our undoing'. Material possessions are the main aim of many in today's society. These have their limitations as a background for family life and the rearing of children.

These matters are of course political, social, and moral issues rather than clinical ones. They concern all of society, not just mental health professionals. Nevertheless, those involved in the mental health field should be especially aware of such issues and bring them constantly to the notice of the wider society of which they are part.

References

1. Caplan, G. *Principles of Preventive Psychiatry*. New York: Basic Books, 1964.
2. Albee, G. W. and Joffe, J. M. (eds). *Primary Prevention of Psychopathology. Volume I: The Issues*. Hanover, New Hampshire: University Press of New England, 1977.
3. Forgays, D. G. (ed.). *Primary Prevention of Psychopathology. Volume II: Environmental Issues*. Hanover, New Hampshire: University Press of New England, 1978.
4. World Health Organisation. *Child Mental Health and Psychosocial Development*. Geneva: WHO, 1977.
5. Rutter, M. 'Invulnerability or why some children are not damaged by stress'. In *New Directions in Children's Mental Health*, ed. S. J. Shamsie, New York: Spectrum, 1979.
6. Leighton, A. 'Poverty and social change'. *Scientific American*, **212**, No. 5, 21–27, 1965.
7. Cordoza, V. G., Ackerly, W. C. and Leighton, A. H. 'Improving mental health through community action'. *Community Mental Health Journal*, **11**, 215–227, 1975.
8. Leissner, A., Powley, T. and Evans, D. *Intermediate Treatment*. London: National Children's Bureau (8 Wakley Street, London, EC1V 7QE), 1977.
9. Wolkind, S. and Rutter, M. 'Children who have been "in care" – an epidemiological study'. *Journal of Child Psychology and Psychiatry*, **14**, 97–105, 1973.
10. Barker, P. *Care Can Prevent: Child Care or Child Psychiatry?* London: National Children's Home, 1973.

11. West, D. J. and Farrington, D. P. *Who Becomes Delinquent?* London: Heinemann, 1973.
12. Rutter, M. 'A children's behaviour questionnaire for completion by teachers: preliminary findings'. *Journal of Child Psychology and Psychiatry*, **8**, 1–11, 1967.
13. Rutter, M. 'A children's behaviour questionnaire for completion by parents'. Appendix 6. In *Education Health and Behaviour*, ed. M. Rutter, J. Tizard and M. Whitmore. London: Longman, 1970.
14. Stott, D. H. 'The prediction of delinquency from non-delinquent behaviour'. *The British Journal of Delinquency*, **10**, 195–210, 1960.
15. Kessler, M. and Albee, G. W. 'An overview of the literature of primary prevention'. In *Primary Prevention of Psychopathology, Volume 1*, ed. W. Albee and J. M. Joffe. Hanover, New Hampshire: University Press of New England, 1977.
16. National Children's Bureau 'Highlights' (obtainable from the Bureau at 8 Wakley Street, Islington, London EC1V 7QE). At the time of writing 33 of these highlights have been published.
17. Goldsmith, E. 'The future of an affluent society: the case of Canada'. *Ecologist*, **7**, 160–194, 1977.
18. Goldsmith, E., Allen, R., Allaby, M., Dovoll, J. and Lawrence, S. 'A blueprint for survival'. *Ecologist*, **2**, 1–43, 1972.
19. Bronfenbrenner, V. 'Doing your own thing – our undoing'. *Child Psychiatry and Human Development*, **8**, 3–10, 1977.

Child Welfare Legislation in Britain

The Children's Act, 1948

This Act applies to England, Wales and Scotland. It provides for local authorities to assume care of children in circumstances which are defined in Section 1 of the Act as follows:

(a) The child has no parents or guardian, or has been abandoned by them; or
(b) the parents or guardian are unable for health reasons or because of 'other incapacity or any other circumstances' to care properly for the child.

In either case the intervention must be necessary in the interests of the child's welfare. This section of the Act does not allow the local authority to keep a child in their care against the wishes of parent or guardian, and the parents or guardian have to contribute financially towards the child's maintenance by the local authority. Having taken the child into care the local authority may place him with relatives, in a foster home, in a children's home or wherever seems most appropriate.

Section 2 of the 1948 Act enables the local authority to assume parental rights if:

(a) the parents are dead and there is no guardian; or
(b) parent or guardian has abandoned the child, is prevented by permanent disability from caring adequately for the child, or 'is of such habits or mode of life as to be unfit to have care of the child'.

The parents or guardian must be notified if this action is taken and can appeal to the juvenile court (in Scotland the sheriff), to have parental rights returned to them. The resolution assuming parental rights can also be rescinded by the local authority at any time if this appears to be in the interests of the child.

The Children and Young Persons Act, 1963

The main importance of this Act is that it made it the duty of every local authority in England, Wales and Scotland to 'make available such advice, guidance and assistance as may promote the welfare of children by diminishing the need to receive children into or keep them in care ... or to bring (them) before a juvenile court'. It thus gave local authorities wide powers to do preventive work with children and their families. It also allowed them to make arrangements with 'voluntary organisations or other persons' to do such work on their behalf. Unfortunately subsequent legislation has imposed so many other duties upon local authority social services departments that the amount of preventive work they are able to do with resources available to them is limited.

The Children and Young Persons Act, 1969

This Act provides for care proceedings to be taken by juvenile courts (in England and Wales) if any of the following circumstances apply:

1. The child's 'proper development' or health is being prevented or impaired, or there is reason to believe that this probably will happen because it has happened to another child in the same household.
2. The child is exposed to 'moral danger'.
3. The child is beyond the control of parent or guardian.
4. The child is of compulsory school-age but is not receiving appropriate full-time education.
5. The child is guilty of an offence, other than homicide.

In addition the child must need care and control which he is unlikely to get at home. In such cases the court may make one of the following types of order:

1. An order requiring parent or guardian to 'enter into a recognisance' to take proper care and exercise control over the child.

2. A supervision order.
3. A care order.
4. A hospital order or a guardianship order, under Part V of the Mental Health Act, 1959. This only applies when certain offences have been committed.

A care order under the above provisions can only be made if the subject is under 16, but it is possible for such an order to be made between the ages of 16 and 17, following conviction for certain offences.

Action under the Mental Health Act is rarely taken in children, but supervision orders and care orders are frequently made in the cases of delinquent children, and children being inadequately cared for by their parents. A supervision order places the child under the supervision of, usually, a social worker on the staff of the social services department, or a probation officer. The court can also make it a condition of the supervision order that the child receives psychiatric treatment. A care order means that the local authority takes over the care of the child, usually with a view to placing him in a more suitable environment such as a foster home or children's home. In many cases delinquent children, once they are admitted to care, go initially to special assessment centres. An assessment is made, usually over a period of a few weeks, of each child, his family and his needs, with a view to providing a suitable long-term placement for him, as well as establishing as far as possible what are the underlying problems contributing to his delinquency (see Chapter 4).

The 1969 Act abolished the former approved schools, which became community homes under the control of the local authority social services departments. (The approved schools were the responsibility of the Home Office, and were run by a variety of bodies.) Nowadays the court can no longer, for example, commit a child to 'approved school training'; it simply makes a care order whereupon the responsibility for deciding what should be done for the child falls to the professional social workers of the appropriate local authority. After the child and his family have been assessed, and any necessary expert (for example psychiatric) help has been obtained, any of the placements mentioned above may be arranged. The child may, if it seems best, be allowed to return home under supervision. Casework help for the family, or psychiatric, educational or other help for the child may be arranged.

When the local authority staff consider that a care order should be discharged, they apply to the juvenile court which can either discharge the order completely or replace it by a supervision order. Otherwise care orders cease to have effect when the subject reaches the age of 18, unless the order was made after the age of 16, when it lasts to age

19. A local authority can, in other cases, apply to the court for the order to be extended to the age of 19.

The 1969 Act also provides for the making of a place of safety order by a magistrate under certain circumstances, principally those which could also lead to a care order. This can be done when action is urgently needed. The child or young person can then be detained in a place of safety (for example, children's home, foster home or assessment centre) for up to 28 days. The police can also detain children and young persons for short periods under conditions laid down by this Act.

Under the 1969 Act 'young persons' between the ages of 10 and 14 need not be prosecuted for crimes, but instead can be subject to the 'social proceedings' which have been outlined. Below 10 they are not considered criminally responsible for their behaviour. From the age of 14 prosecution for certain crimes is possible, but 'social proceedings' can be used in other circumstances up to age 17. None of these statements applies to homicide for which special arrangements apply; a child of any age may be charged with homicide, following which the trial must take place in a higher court. Even in such cases, however, Section 39 of the Children and Young Persons Act, 1933, empowers the court to forbid the publication in newspapers of the child's name, address or school or of other information which might identify him, as is always the case in juvenile courts.

The Social Work (Scotland) Act, 1968

In Scotland, a new procedure was introduced in 1970 following the Social Work (Scotland) Act, 1968. It provides for children under 16 who are either receiving inadequate family care or have committed an offence to be brought before a *children's hearing*. This consists of three people from a selected panel for each local authority area. An official known as the reporter decides which children should appear before the hearings; cases are brought to his attention by policemen, teachers or indeed any members of the public. The reporter co-operates with the local social work department, the staff of which make any necessary investigation of the child's family circumstances. It is only those cases in which compulsory measures may be necessary that are brought before the hearings. Other cases are dealt with informally by social workers, but some are found not to need any help.

The function of the hearing is to decide what measures are most likely to help the child and the family overcome their problems. It can only proceed if the family accept the allegations, for example, that an offence has been committed or the care the child is receiving is inadequate.

If these facts are disputed the matter is taken to the sheriff who decides on the facts. If he accepts that the facts are as alleged, the child's case goes back to the hearing so that the most appropriate treatment measures can be decided. There is also provision for appeal against treatment measures decided on by the hearing.

The hearing has a wide range of powers. There is first full consideration of the case, including any psychiatric report that may be available, and discussion with the child and family. The hearing may decide that social work help is needed, that compulsory supervision by a social worker is necessary or that the child should be placed away from home for a time (for example, in a children's home or residential school); or it may take no action. Progress is reviewed periodically and children can, if necessary, remain under the jurisdiction of the hearings until aged 18.

The Social Work (Scotland) Act, 1968, largely repeals and replaces the sections of the Children and Young Persons (Scotland) Act, 1937, which dealt with bringing children before the courts.

Glossary

This glossary is intended primarily for readers who may not have a medical or psychological background. Certain terms which are adequately explained where they occur in the text have been omitted.

Affect Mood. Thus an *affective psychosis* is one in which the primary feature is deviation from normal of the mood (e.g. towards depression).

Agenesis Failure to grow normally.

Amino acid An organic nitrogen-containing compound made up of amino and acidic groups. Proteins are more complex compounds composed of amino acids arranged in various patterns.

Anal fissure A longitudinal ulcer in the wall of the anal canal. Often causes severe pain on defaecation.

Anorexia Loss of appetite.

Antibiotic A drug which controls infections by acting against the causative organisms. An example is penicillin.

Anticonvulsant Acting against or preventing fits, that is any of the varieties of epilepsy.

Anti-Parkinsonian drug A drug which controls the symptoms of Parkinsonism (see below).

Aphonia Inability to phonate normally despite normal articulation, with the result that subject talks in a whisper. Often a hysterical symptom (see Chapter 5).

Apraxia The inability to carry out a purposeful action despite possession of the ability to perform all the individual movements required for the action. The subject cannot synthesise movements to produce the desired result.

Autistic Behaviour controlled by factors within the individual, rather than by the reality situation in which he is living.

Autonomic nervous system A system of nerves supplying heart muscle, blood vessels and certain glands. Affects heart rate, blood pressure and action of glands.

Autosomal To do with those chromosomes not involved in sex determination. An autosomal gene is one carried on any chromosome but a sex chromosome.

Barium enema A special type of X-ray in which a barium compound is given as an enema to show up the rectum (the terminal part of the intestinal canal) and the colon (the part above it) radiographically.

Basophilic stippling Stippling of the basophils, one group of the white blood cells. This is shown up on microscopic examination of the cells, suitably stained.

Benzodiazepine The chemical name of a group of substances some of which (e.g. chlordiazepoxide) are thought to have a tranquillising, anxiety-reducing action.

Body-image The view which an individual has of the size, shape and nature of his body. In part this is made up of feelings and ideas of which the subject is not fully consciously aware.

Carbohydrate A group of organic chemical compounds made up of carbon hydrogen and oxygen atoms arranged in a particular way. An example is glucose. Carbohydrates are very important constituents of the body and of the diet.

Centile Centile ranking puts a series of scores or values in order according to the percentage which occurs at or below each figure. Thus if the heights of a group of children of a certain age are so arranged, the 50th centile will be that height at or below which half of the children's heights fall. Similarly one in ten will fall at or below the 10th centile, and 97 in 100 will be at or below the 97th centile.

Cerebral cortex The outer, surface, layer of the brain. Also known as the grey matter, it is infolded to increase its area. It is vital for many associative mental processes notably those concerned with thought. Incoming neurological messages are also received in the cortex, and outgoing ones (for example those leading to voluntary movements of limbs) originate in it.

Cerebral dominance One or other lateral half of the higher part of the brain (the cerebral cortex) is normally dominant. In right-handed individuals the left cerebral hemisphere (which controls the right side) is thus the dominant one.

Cerebral palsy Weakness of various muscle groups, sometimes widespread and usually present from early in life, due to damage or maldevelopment of the brain. Many forms exist. The muscles are often abnormally stiff and rigid (or 'spastic'), though this is not so in all forms. Cerebral palsied patients are often referred to as *spastics*.

Chelating agent A chemical substance which combines with, and thus inactivates, metallic ions. Such agents are therefore useful in treatment of lead poisoning and also in removing excess copper from the body in hepato-lenticular degeneration.

Chorea A group of conditions in which there are involuntary movements (of face, tongue, limbs, etc.) which consist of parts of normal organised movements. They are not under voluntary control however, and are fragmented, irregular and purposeless. The movements themselves are called *choreiform* movements.

Chromosomes Very small bodies contained in the nuclei of cells. The normal human complement is twenty-three pairs of chromosomes. The chromosomes carry the genetic material responsible for controlling the development of cells and thus of the whole organism.

Cluster analysis A statistical technique which groups together variables which have more in common with each other than with variables in other groups.

Colon The part of the intestine immediately before the rectum. Shorter and of larger diameter than the small intestine which precedes it.

Conditioning A term derived from learning theory. It describes various ways in which human beings and animals can be systematically taught to respond in particular ways to stimuli of one sort or another. In Pavlov's classical experiment a dog was conditioned to salivate by giving food at the same time as a bell was rung; then when the bell only was rung it still salivated – a *conditioned response*. In *operant conditioning* the dog might be put in a position in which it could obtain food by pressing a lever. Doing this at first by chance (or by coaxing) it would learn how the action was rewarded and would thus be conditioned to perform it repeatedly.

Conflict A clash between the demands of reality and those of unconscious drives and feelings. This can lead to anxiety and other forms of emotional disorder, the cause not being consciously understood by the subject.

Contingency This refers to the consequences which follow particular behaviours. In behaviour therapy these are planned so as to bring about changes in behaviour.

Convulsions An alternative term for major epileptic fits, and often used to describe such fits when they occur in babies and young children.

Coproporphyrin A breakdown product of haemoglobin, the red oxygen-carrying substance in the red blood cells.

Cystic fibrosis A disorder affecting various glands in the body. It causes the mucus secreted by the glands to be abnormally thick so that, for example, the secretions of the pancreas are abnormal, causing intestinal symptoms and sometimes death, especially in babies. Also affects the lungs and other parts of the body.

Defence The process of dealing with feelings such as anxiety or guilt by means of mental mechanisms such as those described in Chapter 1.

Delirium A state of clouded consciousness with confusion and disorientation, often due to an acute febrile illness or to excessive doses of drugs acting on the brain. Can also occur in various forms of acute brain disease.

Dementia The deterioration of intellectual function, usually due to degeneration of or damage to areas of the brain.

Depression A state of morbid sadness or lowering of mood.

Desensitisation Treating undue sensitivity to a stimulus by carefully graduated, controlled and increasing exposure to the stimulus. The latter may be a physical allergen (like pollen in hay fever or asthma) or an object or situation which causes fear or anxiety (as in phobic states, see page 68).

Developmental Used in a special sense to describe certain disorders which are considered to be primarily anomalies of the development of normal function, e.g. speech.

Diabetes In the commonest of this group of diseases, diabetes mellitus, the blood sugar level is raised and there are thirst, production of excess amount of urine and other serious symptoms. Can be fatal, but responds to insulin, other drugs and diet.

Dominant In genetics, a dominant trait is one which is manifested when the factor (or *gene*) concerned is carried on only one of a pair of chromosomes.

By comparison a *recessive* trait is only manifested when the trait is carried on both members of a pair of chromosomes.

Echolalia The repetition, inappropriately, of words or phrases spoken to the subject. In *delayed echolalia*, the repetition occurs later, perhaps by hours or even days.

Electroencephalograph Often known as an EEG, this is a record of the variations in electrical potential between different parts of the brain. Normally a number of channels are recorded simultaneously using electrodes placed at different points on the skull.

Encephalitis Inflammation of the brain, having a variety of causes.

Encephalopathy Disease of, or affecting, the brain.

Endocrine Endocrine glands are those which produce hormones which circulate in the blood stream to produce various general effects on the function of the body. Endocrine disorders are those in which the functioning of these glands, or of the hormones they produce, is abnormal.

Enema The introduction of a liquid into the rectum, usually to promote the evacuation of faeces.

Enzyme Enzymes are complex chemical substances with the role of enabling particular chemical reactions to take place in the body. Numerous enzymes are known to exist, facilitating a vast number of chemical processes needed for the normal functioning of the body.

Fantasy The production of mental images to provide gratification or satisfaction often not obtainable in reality. The term *fantasy* is also often used for the images themselves.

Gene penetrance Refers to the proportion of individuals in whom a gene has an effect. If a dominant gene has an effect in every individual carrying it, penetrance is 100 per cent. If only a proportion of the individuals are affected the penetrance is less and is expressed as the percentage of individuals who are affected.

Hallucination The subjective experience of a sensory perception not arising in the external world. Thus auditory hallucinations may take the form of hearing voices when no one is actually speaking; and visual hallucinations of seeing things which in reality are not there.

Hemiplegia Paralysis, often with stiffness and increased tone, of the muscles, affecting one half (left or right) of the body. Due to a neurological disorder involving the opposite side of the brain, or spinal cord.

Hormone Substance produced by an endocrine gland (see above), to circulate in the blood stream and carry out its particular function.

Hyperkinesis Excessive motor activity, with little apparent purpose.

Hypochondriasis Excessive preoccupation with physical symptoms, often seen in unduly anxious individuals.

Hypomania A milder form of mania (see below).

Identification The acquisition of the views and attitudes of another person as a result of a close, usually loving or admiring, relationship with that person.

Infection A disease caused by the establishment and multiplication in the body of organisms such as bacteria or viruses.

Institutionalisation The effects upon individuals of a prolonged period of living in the impersonal atmosphere of an institution. Characterised by overdependence on the staff, loss of initiative and a progressive inability to cope with life in the outside world.

IQ Intelligence quotient. See page 195–197.

Maladjusted Primarily an administrative, educational term used to describe a group of children requiring a certain special type of educational provision. Also sometimes used, loosely, to describe any child who is emotionally disturbed in one way or another.

Malocclusion The condition that exists when the teeth do not meet in the most efficient way.

Mania A state of excitement, euphoria, excessive activity and impaired judgement. The opposite of depression.

Marijuana A substance produced from the leaves of the plants *cannabis indica* or *cannabis sativa*. Often smoked as cigarettes to produce a pleasurable, euphoric state. Its possession and use are illegal in Britain and many other countries.

Meningitis Inflammation of the meninges, the membranes covering the brain and spinal cord.

Metabolic Metabolism is the process whereby substances entering the body are processed, used in various ways, and their breakdown products excreted from the body. Metabolic processes are those concerned with this, and metabolic disorders are those in which some of the processes are not functioning normally.

Micturition The passage of urine.

Mutism Emotionally determined refusal to speak despite the physical capacity to do so.

Myelin A substance forming the sheaths of nerves. Loss of their myelin sheaths causes failure of the function of nerves, as in *demyelinating diseases*.

Neurological To do with the nervous system, that is the brain and spinal cord, and the nerves connected with them.

Nystagmus Repeated, quick to-and-fro movements of the eyes.

Organic To do with the physical structures of the body. Thus an *organic disease* is one in which there is demonstrable physical abnormality of the parts or organs involved.

Otologist A specialist in disorders of the ear and of hearing.

Palpitation The sensation of rapid beating of the heart.

Parkinsonism A condition in which there is muscular rigidity, tremor which is worse on voluntary movement and weakness of voluntary movements. The muscles of the face and also those responsible for speech may be affected as well as the limb muscles. Usually due to damage to or disease of certain structures in the base of the brain. Can also be caused as a side-effect of various drugs used in psychiatry.

Peptic ulcer A form of ulceration of the inside of the wall of the stomach or the duodenum (the part of the alimentary tract into which the stomach leads).

Phenothiazine The generic name of a group of drugs used to control some forms of psychotic behaviour (notably schizophrenia). They are also used as tranquillisers for other conditions, and have other medical uses. The first one brought into clinical use was chlorpromazine, but many others are now available.

Phobia An irrational fear.

Photophobia A dislike, and often active avoidance, of light. Occurs in certain brain diseases, e.g. encephalitis and meningitis.

Projection A term used in psychology for ideas arising from within an individual which are attributed to some other person or object. (See also Chapter 2.)

Psychiatrist A medically qualified practitioner who has specialised in the study and treatment of patients with disorders affecting the mind.

Psychologist A person with training and expertise in the scientific study of behaviour. Psychologist are non-medical graduates who, after their university course, often do further training in their special branch of psychology. Clinical and educational psychologists are those mainly concerned in child psychiatry.

Psychopathology The abnormalities of the mind, often mainly unconscious, responsible for or associated with mental and emotional disorders.

Pyloric stenosis Obstruction at the lower end of the stomach, where it joins the duodenum. Can be a congenital disorder requiring operative treatment in the early days or weeks of life.

Recessive See under *Dominant*.

Regression The reversion to a mode of behaviour and/or an emotional state appropriate to a younger age.

Rubella German measles.

Spastic Showing increased muscle tone. People suffering from cerebral palsy are sometimes referred to as 'spastics' because of the increased tone which is a feature of many forms of the condition.

Spina bifida In this condition there is a defect in the vertebral column, and often also in the underlying spinal cord. May be symptomless in mild cases, or may cause mild or severe neurological disorders.

Standard deviation A measure of the scatter of a series of values round the mean. The amounts by which each of the values differs from mean are taken and each is squared. The square root of the mean of these squares is the standard deviation. In practice the following formula is used.

$$SD = \sqrt{\frac{\Sigma(Y - \bar{Y})^2}{n - 1}}$$

where n is the number of values of the measurement, Y; $\bar{Y}$ is the mean of all the values of Y and Σ signifies 'the sum of'.

Subarachnoid haemorrhage Bleeding from one of the arteries lying beneath the arachnoid membrane, which covers the surface of the brain. Is often due to a congenital aneuyson (or saccular swelling) on the artery.

Subdural haematoma An accumulation of blood resulting from bleeding underneath the dura, a membrane covering the brain, superficial to the arachnoid. Subdural haemorrhage often develops slowly following a head injury.

Sublimation The expression through socially acceptable behaviour of drives, where the direct expression would be unacceptable.

Suppository A solid preparation of a drug for rectal administration.

Syphilis A venereal disease due to an organism, *Treponema pallidum*. In its later stages it can affect the central nervous system and cause dementia and other abnormalities.

Systemic infection An infection affecting the body as a whole.

Temporal lobe One of the areas of the cortex of the brain. The temporal lobes are situated in the lower, lateral parts of each cerebral hemisphere.

Tics Involuntary spasmodic contractions of muscles, often repetitive and sometimes worse under stress. The movements are more stereotyped and repetitive than choreiform movements.

Toxaemia The presence in the circulating blood, and thus in the body tissues generally, of harmful substances (toxins) formed by infective agents like bacteria or viruses, or produced in the body cells as a result of a disease, injury or other disorder.

Toxoplasmosis A disease due to protozoal organisms (*Toxoplasma*) affecting muscle fibres and other cells.

Tranquilliser A drug with the primary action of reducing anxiety and tension or quietening disturbed, restless, aggressive or psychotic behaviour.

Tricyclic Tricyclic antidepressants are so called because of their chemical structure. The first of the modern antidepressant drugs to be brought into use was a tricyclic compound, imipramine, and several other related drugs are now also in use.

Truancy The wilful avoidance of school.

Urethra The passage leading from the bladder to the exterior, for the passage of urine and also, in the male, seminal fluid.

Index